"Bob Kellemen has made a significant contribution ┊ centered family counseling in his latest book. Readers will encounter a work that is both thorough and comprehensive, biblical and user-friendly. Bob possesses an inimitable ability to take big concepts and principles and organize them in memorable ways, and *Gospel-Centered Family Counseling* embodies this well. I have no doubt that this work will become a go-to reference for ministry leaders and counselors for years to come."

> **Jonathan D. Holmes**, executive director, Fieldstone Counseling;
> author of *Counsel for Couples: A Biblical and Practical Guide*
> *for Marriage Counseling*

"As I read *Gospel-Centered Family Counseling*, I was struck yet again by the thoroughness of Scripture for approaching counseling issues in wise and winsome ways, especially the crucial topic of the Christian family. Bob has put together a thorough, well-organized, biblical counseling strategy for equipping us to help families live God-honoring lives. This realistic yet hopeful approach also oozes with the compassion of Christ as counselors learn to minister to saints, sufferers, and sinners whose family relationships have been impacted by the fall. I will use it in our ministries at our church and recommend it at the schools where I teach. Thank you, Bob!"

> **Dr. Ernie Baker**, pastor of counseling, First Baptist Church, Jacksonville;
> chair of the online BA in biblical counseling at The Master's University;
> author of *Marry Wisely, Marry Well*

"Having spent over twenty years as a biblical counselor, I've often wondered why our movement has written so little on the subject of family counseling. My experience is that most biblical counselors are just not well trained in navigating the complexities of whole-family counsel. Having been trained in family therapy, I have a deep appreciation for Bob Kellemen's inclusion of both parents and their children in the family counseling process. *Gospel-Centered Family Counseling* is theologically robust, philosophically refreshing, and methodologically rich. I highly recommend it to those counseling families and those training caregivers to work with parents and families."

> **Dr. Garrett Higbee**, director of pastoral care for the Great Commission
> Collective; founding board member for the Biblical Counseling Coalition

"In this training manual for pastors and counselors, Dr. Bob Kellemen draws on his many years of family counseling to provide us with a sharpening tool. The counseling questions in this book are as good as the sage wisdom provided! I served on a church staff with Bob and have observed his counseling care and insight firsthand. There are few more qualified to train us, and this book will equip both new and veteran caregivers in the care of souls, families, and the church."

Steve DeWitt, senior pastor of Bethel Church;
author of *Eyes Wide Open: Enjoying God in Everything*

"In *Gospel-Centered Family Counseling*, Dr. Bob Kellemen provides outstanding help for biblical counselors, pastors, lay leaders, and students working with and ministering to families. This is a biblical and extremely practical equipping resource I will refer to regularly as I seek to become a better and better family counselor."

Dr. Amy Baker, editor of *Caring for the Souls
of Children: A Biblical Counselor's Manual*

"I was taught throughout *Gospel-Centered Family Counseling*, and it gave me scriptural insights and biblical wisdom for family and marriage mission statements. Bob is a wise mentor in this book and in life. As he sits next to you, he will not expect counseling perfection. He will gently equip you to help families and guide you in humility, prayer, and confidence in the Lord and his Word."

Dr. Ed Welch, counselor and faculty, CCEF;
author of *Side by Side: Walking with Others in Wisdom and Love*

GOSPEL-CENTERED
Family Counseling

An Equipping Guide
for Pastors and Counselors

ROBERT W. KELLEMEN, PhD

BakerBooks

a division of Baker Publishing Group
Grand Rapids, Michigan

© 2020 by Robert W. Kellemen

Published by Baker Books
a division of Baker Publishing Group
PO Box 6287, Grand Rapids, MI 49516-6287
www.bakerbooks.com

Printed in the United States of America

Library of Congress Cataloging-in-Publication Data
Names: Kellemen, Robert W., author.
Title: Gospel-centered family counseling : an equipping guide for pastors and counselors / Robert W. Kellemen, PhD.
Description: Grand Rapids, Michigan : Baker Books, a division of Baker Publishing Group, 2020. | Series: The equipping marriage and family counselors series
Identifiers: LCCN 2020003084 | ISBN 9780801094354 (paperback)
Subjects: LCSH: Family counseling—Religious aspects—Christianity—Handbooks, manuals, etc. | Pastoral counseling—Handbooks, manuals, etc. | Bible—Psychology—Handbooks, manuals, etc.
Classification: LCC BV4438 .K45 2020 | DDC 259/.12—dc23
LC record available at https://lccn.loc.gov/2020003084

In keeping with biblical principles of creation stewardship, Baker Publishing Group advocates the responsible use of our natural resources. As a member of the Green Press Initiative, our company uses recycled paper when possible. The text paper of this book is composed in part of post-consumer waste.

green press INITIATIVE

20 21 22 23 24 25 26   7 6 5 4 3 2 1

Contents

Acknowledgments

My motivation for writing *Gospel-Centered Family Counseling* began while I was serving as counseling pastor at Bethel Church in northwest Indiana. Many pastors, ministry leaders, and lay leaders from Bethel journeyed with me as we counseled, discipled, and shepherded many families. I want to thank each of them for their co-ministry, encouragement, and friendship: Pastor Steve DeWitt, Pastor Brad Lagos, Pastor Mark Culton, Pastor Dexter Harris, Pastor Dan Jacobsen, Pastor Jared Bryant, Pastor Chris Whetstone, Pastor Gary Butler, Pastor Dustin Rouse, and ministry leaders/lay leaders Ken Barry, Lauri Mollema, Gail Morris, Skye Bryant, Jennifer Culton, Laura Sauerman, Caitlin Marsee, Joy Katts, Amanda Wilson, and Melissa Anderson.

Before, during, and after I wrote *Gospel-Centered Family Counseling*, I've been serving alongside the ministry team at Faith Bible Seminary in Lafayette, Indiana. Thank you for your ministry in my life: Pastor Steve Viars, Pastor Brent Aucoin, Pastor Rob Green, and Kirk Fatool.

Foreword

Imagine a family comes to you for help and says, "We're a mess."

Maybe it's two frustrated parents with an angry teenager, and there's a lot of conflict, name-calling, and bitterness in the home. Maybe it's a mom and dad with three preschool-age children, and the children rule the home. Or it could even be a family where multiple kids are struggling—one is severely depressed, another is hooked on porn—and the parents are at a complete loss for what to do.

What do you do? How do you help? What do you say? Where do you go in Scripture? How do you pray? What counseling skills do you employ? How do you help them out of the mess?

Here's why my dear friend Bob Kellemen is an *invaluable* guide for you. He's written a book that's worthy of your attention . . . a book unlike anything else I've read.

Bob has helped tons of struggling families. And his approach is different than what you get out of generic counseling books. As you engage this material, you will find that . . .

Bob loves God's Word. What's clear from the very beginning is that Bob Kellemen's counseling philosophy and methodology are rooted in the Word of God. *Gospel-Centered Family Counseling* is biblically rich and faithful to teach God's perspective on these matters.

Bob understands that theology matters. Our theology—what we believe about God, humanity, Christ, sin, and faith—has bearing on our life. What we believe transforms how we live. Bob gets this, so *Gospel-Centered Family Counseling* is structured first as a theological primer on the family. We come to understand, for example, how a parent's holy love provides children with a taste of God's holy love while also creating a home that is safe, stable, and secure.

Bob's book is practical, equipping you with hands-on relational/counseling competencies. A rich and gospel-centered theology does you no good if you don't know what to do in the counseling room. What do you do when the teenager gets angry or the father begins to pout or the mother starts crying? How do you help families be honest about their hurts and pains without just unloading all their pent-up anger? Bob understands that the counselor needs help to grow in their practical skills, so he loads up the book with twenty-two relational competencies.

For example, in chapters 6 and 7, you'll grow in your ability to facilitate empathy within the family. You've heard how the counselor should empathize with the counselee. That's Counseling 101. And you can understand how a counselor could show empathy for a family unit. That's Counseling 201. But what about assisting a family to build empathy *between one another*? That's Advanced Family Counseling 301.

Bob has the whole family in view. Frustrated and concerned parents who send a troubled teenager to a therapist are not normally included in the counseling sessions. The counselor works with the teenager, but the often busy and overworked parents are usually on the sidelines, with only some consultation. The counselor keeps the parents informed but mainly works to help the troubled teen work on heart issues, acting out, and anger.

But what if we put *every* family member in the room? Bob teaches you to interact with family dynamics in real time. You coach the parents and the teenager *together*. You help them to share and work through issues *together*. You help them to build bridges and take steps toward one another *together*. You're interacting with the family as a unit, not just as individuals. You don't get reports from parents about how the teenager treats them with disrespect; rather, you see it happen in person. You don't get secondhand accounts from the teen about how the parents are angry or belittling; instead, you see it play out right in front of you. This kind of work is not for the fainthearted counselor. It requires a level of competence and hopefulness that goes beyond typical individual counseling.

Bob has parents primarily in view. Bob gets that loving, patient, self-sacrificial, grace-centered, Christ-honoring parents are the key to the health of the family. If you shepherd the parents well, they in turn will shepherd their children. We don't just fix the kids in therapy. Our goal is much grander—to change a family culture. To do that, we've got to start with the shepherds— the parents whom God has entrusted with children.

I love this book. I promise that if you read *Gospel-Centered Family Counseling*, it will strengthen your faith and you'll become a more skilled and godly family counselor. It might even revolutionize your approach and care of families.

That's enough from me. Now it's time for you to hear from the author himself. Let's begin.

Deepak Reju, PhD, pastor of biblical counseling and families,
Capitol Hill Baptist Church, Washington, DC; author of
Preparing for Fatherhood and *The Pastor and Counseling*

Series Introduction

As an equipper of pastors and counselors, I hear all the time how intimidating marriage and family counseling is. Recently, an experienced pastor shared with me:

> Marriage counseling? I'm clueless. I feel like I'm standing in traffic on an expressway with cars going both ways, half of them the wrong way, most of them swerving out of control. I have no idea how to move from my good theology of marriage, to actually helping the troubled couple sitting in front of me.
>
> Family counseling? Don't even get me started on that. By the time family members get to me, they're so angry that they aren't listening to each other. And half the time, they don't even want to listen to me!

The Purpose of This Two-Book Series: Filling the Gap

The contemporary Christian world churns out books—great books—on marriage and the family. Theory of marriage and family? Tons of books. Books for couples? Scores of books. Books on the family and parenting? Boatloads.

However, even in the biblical counseling world, we have next to nothing available about *procedures*—the how-to of counseling hurting couples and families. *Pastors and counselors desperately need help in relating their theology to marital messes and family chaos.* They need training manuals on the nuts and bolts of the procedures and processes of helping the couple or family sitting in front of them.

Gospel-Centered Marriage Counseling and *Gospel-Centered Family Counseling* step into this void. This two-book series of equipping guides provides practical, user-friendly training for pastors, counselors, lay leaders, educators, and students.

Not Your Parents' Counseling Books

These two books walk you as the reader through step-by-step training to develop your *skills and competencies* in marriage and family counseling. In fact, "reader" is the wrong word. "Participant" is better.

Gospel-Centered Marriage Counseling and *Gospel-Centered Family Counseling* are workbooks—think of them as working books or even workout books. Thus the subtitle *An Equipping Guide for Pastors and Counselors*. Chapter by chapter, skill by skill, as a participant you will use the questions, exercises, role-play directions, sample dialogues, and much more to develop your competency and increase your confidence as a biblical marriage and family counselor.

Introduction

I *enjoy* individual counseling. While it can be messy and complex, listening to, engaging with, and entering into a person's soul struggle is an honor. While it's exhausting and demanding, journeying together with another person to Christ's healing hope is a joy.

However, like some of you, for many years I *endured* counseling couples and families. Counseling individuals is complex enough. Where do you start? What do you listen for? How do you compassionately speak truth in love? How do you relate God's eternal story to a person's earthly story?

Marriage counseling is even more complex than individual counseling. Now you have three sinners, saints, and sufferers in the same room—the wife, the husband, and the counselor! Where in the world do you start?

But family counseling? Now you have a whole group of struggling folks gathered together in the same room. What is family counseling even supposed to look like? Do you only counsel the parents? Only the children? Everyone together? What's the goal? What does success look like?

In the biblical counseling world, we talk about counseling the *hard cases*. The idea is that some counseling situations simply require a bit of encouragement and direction, while other cases require an extra measure of wisdom, patience, grace, discernment, expertise, and time. But as society breaks down more and more, I experience just about every family counseling situation as a hard case. I used to teach a lot about Romans 15:14 and God's people becoming competent to counsel. Now, when it comes to counseling families, I increasingly experience myself as *incompetent* to counsel. That sense of incompetency *in myself* is exactly what has motivated me to write this book—I am writing it first for me. I long to grow more competent *in Christ* and his Word as I counsel the hard cases—and all cases—of families in turmoil.

I can relate to those of you who see family counseling as intimidating. So, for me and for you, I've searched Scripture, asking:

> *What would a model of family counseling look like that*
> *was built solely on Christ's gospel of grace?*

Thus the title of this book: *Gospel-Centered Family Counseling*. This is *not* a secular family systems therapy manual. This book seeks to equip God's people to competently relate Christ's gospel to family suffering and sin.

Learning How to Relate Truth to Family Life

The answer to feeling intimidated and incompetent is not to ignore the issue—because that's impossible. Family issues are increasingly flooding the church. When I first began counseling three decades ago, individual counseling made up over 75 percent of my counseling load. Now, in my role as the pastor of counseling ministries for a multisite church with thirty-five hundred members and eighteen pastors and ministry leaders, 75 percent of our counseling load is marriage and family related. The tide has turned. Marriages are a mess. Families are in disarray. *The pastors and counselors I know are frantically searching for practical, biblical help.*

The answer to feeling intimidated by family counseling is learning how to lovingly help families—especially parents—apply biblical truth to their family life. We need equipping in the nuts and bolts of the truth-in-love process of helping the distressed family sitting in front of us.

Biblical: A GRACE Foundation

I have written *Gospel-Centered Family Counseling* to provide that needed hands-on training in *biblical* family counseling. Think first about that word "biblical." Part 1 of this book offers a theological primer for biblical family counseling. Theology matters. Christ's gospel of grace makes a daily difference in our families. Christ's eternal story invades and impacts our daily story. So in the first three chapters I will introduce you to a GRACE model of family counseling, family life, and parenting (fig. I.1).

Figure I.1

Five Marks of GRACE-Focused Family Living and Counseling

G God-Dependent Families—Parental Dedication (The Workout Room)

R Revelation-Based Family Wisdom—Parental Discernment (The Study)

A Accepting and Affirming Grace Relationships—Parental Devotion (The Playroom)

C Care-Fronting the Heart—Parental Discipline (The Family Room)

E Equipping for Life—Parental Discipleship (The Living Room)[1]

Hands-On: An Equipping Guide

But how? How do we take theology, the gospel, grace, and Christ's story and relate them to the troubled family sitting in front of us? Let's turn now to the phrase "hands-on." Consider the subtitle of this book: *An Equipping Guide for Pastors and Counselors.* This is not just a book *to read.* It is a training manual *to use.* After every section of every chapter you will find training exercises under the heading "Maturing as a Biblical Family Counselor." Overall you will have the opportunity to engage in hundreds of such equipping exercises.

This is why part 2 of this book provides practical training for biblical family counselors. Figure I.2 lists twenty-two biblical family counseling relational competencies that we will develop in chapters 4–13. Figure I.3 offers a snapshot of the model of biblical family counseling that will be introduced in chapter 4, which will be the foundation for your equipping in this training manual.

I have never been wild about words like "skills" and "techniques" when used with biblical counseling. A central verse that shepherds my counseling ministry is 1 Thessalonians 2:8: "Because we loved you so much, we were delighted to share with you not only the gospel of God but our lives as well." Paul shares the gospel of God—he models gospel-centered ministry. He also is delighted to share his own soul because he loves people so much and because they are so dear to him. Paul models truth and love, gospel and relationship. While "relational competency" is still not the greatest phrase, I have chosen it to try to capture the gospel/relationship combination central to biblical family counseling.

Throughout *Gospel-Centered Family Counseling* you will learn a step-by-step process for developing twenty-two family counseling relational competencies. You will learn how to relate Christ's eternal truth to messy, complex families today. For that to happen, please prioritize time for responding to the Maturing as a Biblical Family Counselor training exercises. You can use these individually. They are also ideal for small group lab usage, where you receive counseling training in a group setting. You will notice that many of the interactive questions relate to your own life. Maturing as a biblical counselor is never just about developing counseling competencies. It is also about growing in Christlike character.

Family: Equipping and Empowering Parents as Family Shepherds

Consider a third word: "family." Here is the premise central to this book:

> *Children need good, godly parenting more than*
> *they need good, godly counseling.*

Or to say this another way:

> *The biblical family counselor must never replace the parents as the primary shepherds in the home.*

In *Gospel-Centered Family Counseling*, we want to equip parents in twenty-two family shepherding relational competencies. While we may counsel children without their parents in some sessions—depending on age and family situation—it is my conviction that:

> *Biblical family counselors are counseling parents to be their children's best biblical counselors and parental shepherds.*

This is *not* a book on counseling children or counseling teens—although we need books on those topics for sure. This *is* a book on counseling the entire family where the primary focus is on empowering parents to shepherd their family. Parents, teens, and younger children are counseled in the context of counseling the entire family. We can picture the process like this:

> Counsel the family → Counsel the parents → The parents shepherd their children → Counsel individual family members primarily within the context of counseling the family

You might wonder why I didn't just title this book *Gospel-Centered Parental Counseling*. I intentionally chose the word "family" for a vital reason that is based on another key premise:

> *Biblical family counseling is not individual counseling with an audience.*

The power of family counseling is the ability to observe how the family interacts and how the parents parent—right in front of you. Rather than just hearing secondhand reports that "Jimmy is disobedient" or "Mom and Dad are unfair," you watch a family's dance unfold before your eyes.

Additionally, the power of family counseling resides in the ability to do homework during each session. Rather than you just assigning homework between sessions, the parents and children *work on their home* in front of you so that you can coach the family and equip the parents to shepherd their children. This "in front of you" aspect is central to the approach you will learn in *Gospel-Centered Family Counseling*.

Some Caveats

Life in a fallen world is really messed up! Sometimes those family messes reside in the heart of an abusive mother or father (or both). When you become aware of an abusive parent, you do not start with family counseling. You start with family intervention. The church gets involved—church discipline, church discipleship, church restoration, church care. The community gets involved—authorities are contacted, children are protected, resources are collected and used.

Sometimes those family messes reside in the heart of a teen. It could be depression. It could be addiction. While the family surely needs and can benefit from counseling, the teen also needs individual counseling and can benefit from a host of other resources.

How You Can Use This Book

While you can certainly benefit from this book individually, I have also designed it with a view for use in a group training setting. When using *Gospel-Centered Family Counseling* in a small group lab, read the assigned chapter *before* the lab meets. Do not use lab time for lecturing on the content. Interact briefly about how the content relates to the practice of family counseling, but reserve most of the lab time for the following suggested activities.

- Respond in writing to the Maturing as a Biblical Family Counselor questions *before* your small group meets.
- During your small group meeting, interact about the questions.
- The questions related to your life provide opportunities to counsel one another during your small group meeting. A premise of this book is that *we become effective biblical counselors by giving and receiving biblical counseling in community*.
- The questions related to family counseling situations provide opportunities for role-playing family counseling. They also provide opportunity for real-life family counseling if family members are invited into parts of the group time.
- After role-playing or real-life family counseling, offer feedback to one another so you can grow together as biblical family counselors.

Figure I.2

Overview of Gospel-Centered Family Counseling
22 Biblical Family Counseling Relational Competencies

Infusing Hope

  H Having Hope as a Family Counselor (chap. 5)

  O Offering Hope to Hurting Families (chap. 5)

  P Prompting Parents to Tap into God-Given Resources (chap. 5)

  E Encouraging the Family to See Signs of Christ on the Move (chap. 5)

Parakaletic Biblical Family Counseling for Suffering Families

- **Sustaining**: Like Christ, we care about each other's hurts.

    L Looking at Families through the Lens of Suffering (chap. 6)

    O Observing, Openly Joining, and Orchestrating the Family Dance and the Family Dirge (chap. 6)

    V Venturing Together across the Family Chasm (chap. 7)

    E Equipping the Family to Comfort Each Other with Christ's Comfort (chap. 7)

- **Healing**: Through Christ, it's possible for us to hope in God together.

    F Framing Family Healing Narratives (chap. 8)

    A Applying Our Identity in Christ (chap. 8)

    I Integrating in Our Victory through Christ (chap. 9)

    T Training in Teamwork on the Family Quest (chap. 9)

    H Honing Homework That Works (chap. 9)

Nouthetic Biblical Family Counseling for Sinning Families

- **Reconciling**: It's horrible to sin against Christ and each other, but through Christ it's wonderful to be forgiven and to forgive.

    R Recognizing Destructive Family Relationships (chap. 10)

    E Enlightening Family Members to Destructive Family Relationships (chap. 10)

    S Soothing the Family's Soul in Their Savior (chap. 11)

    T Trust-Making (chap. 11)

- **Guiding**: It's supernatural to love each other like Christ, through Christ, for Christ.

    P Putting On Christ's Wisdom Perspective (chap. 12)

    E Empowering Families to Live in Light of Their Victory in Christ (chap. 12)

    A Activating Application (chap. 13)

    C Coaching Families (chap. 13)

    E Emboldening Families (chap. 13)

Figure I.3

Comprehensive and Compassionate Biblical Family Counseling

Parakaletic Biblical Family Counseling for Suffering Family Members

- **Sustaining**: Like Christ, we care about each other's hurts.
- **Healing**: Through Christ, it's possible for us to hope in God together.

Nouthetic Biblical Family Counseling for Sinning Family Members

- **Reconciling**: It's horrible to sin against Christ and each other, but through Christ it's wonderful to be forgiven and to forgive.
- **Guiding**: It's supernatural to love each other like Christ, through Christ, for Christ.

Maturing as a Biblical Family Counselor

1. Regarding the theory and theology of family life:

   a. What reading have you done about family life—biblical teaching about roles of parents, responsibilities of children, parental discipline and discipleship, understanding children, etc.?

   b. How easy or hard has it been for you to translate those teachings into practical, relational ways to help the family sitting in front of you?

2. Regarding the practice and methodology of family counseling:

   a. What reading have you done in family counseling practices and methods? To what extent have you been able to find biblical resources on the how-to of counseling families?

   b. On a scale of 1 to 10 (1 = Not prepared to do family counseling and 10 = I could teach family counseling), currently how prepared are you to do family counseling?

3. I admit to being intimidated to counsel families due to the complexity of the issues and the intensity of the struggles.

   a. How does my admission impact your thoughts about using this book? Does it encourage or discourage you? Why?

   b. If you have family counseling experience, as you reflect back on your past counseling of families, has family counseling been easier or harder than individual counseling? How competent or incompetent have you felt as a biblical family counselor? If you have not yet provided family counseling, as you think ahead to counseling parents and children, are you excited, intimidated, or both?

4. You read several important summaries about the focus of *Gospel-Centered Family Counseling*. For each one (repeated below), do you agree or disagree? How might these premises impact and change your family counseling ministry?

   a. Children need good, godly parenting more than they need good, godly counseling.

   b. The biblical family counselor must never replace the parents as the primary shepherds in the home.

   c. Biblical family counselors are counseling parents to be their children's best biblical counselors and parental shepherds.

   d. Counsel the family → Counsel the parents → The parents shepherd their children → Counsel individual family members primarily within the context of counseling the family.

   e. Biblical family counseling is not individual counseling with an audience.

5. Through the Maturing as a Biblical Family Counselor components of this book, you will have the opportunity to engage in hundreds of training exercises.

   a. Some of those exercises will require you to take an honest, biblical look at your life. How willing are you to do that?

   b. If you are going through this material in a small group lab, how prepared are you to share about your life with those in your training group? What could your group do to make this training experience safe, encouraging, and mutually edifying?

PART 1

A Theological Primer for Biblical Family Counseling

CHAPTER

ONE

God-Dependent Families

Introduction: No, We Can't Skip the Theology Stuff

A pastor once called me after viewing the summaries of my family counseling training on my website. "Bob, I really like your training outline," he began. "Just one thing, though. Could we skip the theology stuff and get right to the practical material?"

Before we jump all over my pastor friend, maybe we could all be honest. We've had similar thoughts, right? Especially if we've been taught theology in a way that is only academic and not related to our hearts, lives, and relationships in a practical way.

So I shared a bit more with this pastor about how my family seminar relates theology to family life and counseling and how that builds a dynamic foundation for the how-to section. Hearing this, he was happy to have me present the theological part of my training. Afterward he expressed how pleased he was that we had built that practical theological groundwork.

In family or parental counseling we are often more like my pastor friend than we are willing to admit. A troubled family enters our office. What do we do? Where do we turn? Often we move right to Ephesians 6:4, "Fathers, do not exasperate your children; instead, bring them up in the training and instruction of the Lord." Or if we are focused on the children, perhaps we turn directly to Ephesians 6:1, "Children, obey your parents in the Lord, for this is right." Vital verses, of course. In fact, I will build on Ephesians 6:4 in its broader theological contexts as I develop our first three chapters. And that is my point: we must understand, teach, and counsel Ephesians 6:1–4 (and other family and parenting passages) *within their theological framework*.

The apostle Paul penned Ephesians to equip the church to maturely love Christ and others. Given this relational purpose, we might wonder why in the world Paul spends only one verse (Eph. 6:4) talking about parenting. The answer: Paul expends his energy throughout his entire epistle divulging more and more of the character of God (Father, Son, and Holy Spirit) so that we might develop more and more of the character of Christ. Theology matters. Who God is matters. Truth about Christlike character matters. If we fail to understand this, then we are destined to become like Manoah and his wife—demanding a parenting manual instead of depending upon every word that comes from the mouth of God (Matt. 4:4).

Give Me a How-To Parenting Manual!

We all want a how-to manual for parenting. It's a natural desire. And in Judges 13, Manoah and his wife—Samson's parents—are no exception. Imagine the excitement Manoah's wife experiences when, after she had been childless for years, the angel of the Lord appears to her with this promise:

> You are barren and childless, but you are going to become pregnant and give birth to a son. Now see to it that you drink no wine or other fermented drink and that you do not eat anything unclean. You will become pregnant and have a son whose head is never to be touched by a razor because the boy is to be a Nazirite, dedicated to God from the womb. He will take the lead in delivering Israel from the hands of the Philistines. (Judg. 13:3–5)

Her mind is racing as she hurries to find Manoah. Her words gush out of her overflowing soul as she tells her husband of her encounter.

> A man of God came to me. He looked like an angel of God, very awesome. I didn't ask him where he came from, and he didn't tell me his name. But he said to me, "You will become pregnant and have a son. Now then, drink no wine or other fermented drink and do not eat anything unclean, because the boy will be a Nazirite of God from the womb until the day of his death." (13:6–7)

Manoah can no longer contain himself. He is probably thinking, "What? We've waited all these years to have a child. Then an ambassador from God comes and he doesn't leave us a parenting manual? This man must come back!" That's the message of Manoah's prayer in Judges 13:8: "Then Manoah prayed to the LORD: 'Pardon your servant, Lord. I beg you to let the man of God you sent to us come again to teach us *how to* bring up the boy who is to be born.'"

That is the normal prayer of every Christian parent. "Please, Father, teach me, guide, me, direct me, instruct me *how to* raise my child."

In Manoah's case, we are told that God heard his prayer. The messenger of God returned. He handed Manoah the latest edition of *12 Steps to Raising*

Your Children for Yahweh and then left. Manoah, his wife, and their son, Samson, lived happily ever after . . .

Then again, perhaps it happened like this. The angel of the Lord comes again to Manoah's wife. Again she races to find her husband. "He's here, Manoah! The man who appeared to me the other day has returned. God has answered your prayer."

Manoah follows his wife, races to the man, and asks, "Are you the man who talked to my wife?"

"I am," he says.

So Manoah asks, "When your words are fulfilled, what is *to be the rule* that governs the boy's life and work?" (13:12). There it is again: a second request for a how-to manual. How shall we order our parenting? What list of rules will lead, guide, and direct us step-by-step?

The angel of the Lord answers, "Your wife must do all that I have told her. She must not eat anything that comes from the grapevine, nor drink any wine or other fermented drink nor eat anything unclean. She must do everything I have commanded her" (13:13–14).

Manoah's jaw drops. "Huh? What's that? Couldn't you leave us a scroll or papyri manual? What about a list? Some steps? Something?"

Rather than giving Samson's parents a checklist, the angel of the Lord exhorts them toward a lifestyle: a God-dependent, God-glorifying, God-trusting, God-surrendered lifestyle. That is the cultural meaning of the Nazirite vow that Manoah, his wife, and their son were to fulfill. It was a commitment to consecrate and dedicate their life to God through a living faith embodied by a daily trust in God alone. The sustenance of the day was the fruit of the grapevine. To choose not to drink it was to live according to the words of Jesus in Matthew 4:4: "It is written: 'Man shall not live on bread alone, but on every word that comes from the mouth of God.'"

Manoah and his wife desired what all Christian parents desire: "Father, teach me how to parent my child." Our Father answers our prayer, but in his way, not ours. His parenting manual has one rule, one commandment:

Parent, be Christlike by being God-dependent.

God's Parental Prime Directive

This is the same message we receive from Paul in Ephesians. Paul pens 131 verses about gospel-dependent living in Ephesians 1–5 before he offers us one verse on parenting—Ephesians 6:4.

When I counsel parents, they often expect me to take them straight to Ephesians 6:1–4. Initially they are a tad surprised when we start by exploring gospel-centered principles like our life purpose as parents and children to glorify God (Eph. 1), our lifelong need for Christ because of our guilt before

God (Eph. 2), our lifelong dependence upon Christ for grace from God (Eph. 2–3), and our lifelong power for growth through God's Spirit (Eph. 3–6).

Judges 13 and Ephesians 1–6 convey the same parental prime directive from God:

> *To become a more powerful parent, we must become a more godly person—a person dedicated to dependence on God.*

GRACE-Focused Family Living and Family Counseling

You may be wondering, "But I thought this book was marked by practical principles for family counseling. How does that fit into all this God-dependence and theology stuff?"

In this training manual, we will build upon a gospel-centered focus of Christ-dependence by examining five marks of GRACE-focused families. However, these five marks would be nothing more than steps and how-to principles if we didn't ground them in hearts surrendered to Christ. Without dependence on Christ, our application of these principles would be results-driven. We would end up being pharisaical counselors counseling pharisaical parents raising pharisaical kids.

God calls us to be gospel-centered family counselors counseling grace-focused parents raising grace-saturated kids. Notice who is in the middle of that sentence—*grace-focused parents*. This returns us to the themes I emphasized in the introduction:

- Children need good, godly parenting more than they need good, godly counseling.
- The biblical family counselor must never replace parents as the primary shepherds in the home.
- Biblical family counselors are counseling parents to be their children's best biblical counselors and parental shepherds.

Through these first three chapters, we will build on Ephesians 6:4 in the larger context of Paul's letter to develop five marks of GRACE-focused family living and family counseling (fig. 1.1). These five marks provide a biblical theology of the family. They become the goal of our biblical family counseling. They become the targets we aim toward and the markers that indicate when family counseling has been "successful."

Figure 1.1

Five Marks of GRACE-Focused Family Living and Family Counseling

G God-Dependent Families: Parental Dedication—The Workout Room (Eph. 5:18; 6:10–18)

R Revelation-Based Family Wisdom: Parental Discernment—The Study (Eph. 5:15–17; 6:19–20)

A Accepting and Affirming Grace Relationships: Parental Devotion—The Playroom (Eph. 6:4: "Do not exasperate your children; instead, bring them up . . .")

C Care-Fronting the Heart: Parental Discipline—The Family Room (Eph. 6:4: "in the training of the Lord")

E Equipping for Life: Parental Discipleship—The Living Room (Eph. 6:4: "in the instruction of the Lord")

Maturing as a Biblical Family Counselor
No, We Can't Skip the Theology Stuff

1. In your life and ministry, how do you balance theology and life? In other words, how do you ensure that you are relating theology to life—as God always does in his Word?

2. In working with troubled families:

   a. Have they had a tendency to expect you to race to Ephesians 6:1–4 and skip over the rest of Paul's teaching? If so, how have you addressed this?

   b. In biblical family counseling, what are several ways that you could use Ephesians 1–5 as a vital foundation for Ephesians 6:1–4?

3. Manoah and his wife wanted a how-to manual. God exhorted them toward a lifestyle—a God-dependent, God-glorifying, God-trusting, God-surrendered lifestyle.
   a. Which do parents want when they come to you for counseling—a how-to manual or a God-dependent lifestyle?

b. How can you empathize with a desperate parent's longing for quick answers while also helping them see that God, not answers, is their primary need?

c. "To become a more powerful parent, we must become a more godly person, a person dedicated to dependence on God." How can you convey that truth to a desperate parent without coming across as too heavenly minded to be of any earthly good?

4. You read, "God calls us to be gospel-centered family counselors counseling grace-focused parents raising grace-saturated kids." We will develop this idea throughout the book, but for now consider these preliminary questions:

a. How might a gospel-centered family counselor be different from a pharisaical family counselor (i.e., one who focuses on lists, steps, rules, the letter of the law, quick and easy answers)?

b. How might a grace-focused parent be different from a pharisaical parent?

c. How might grace-saturated children be different from children raised in a pharisaical, results-driven, law-based home environment?

GRACE-Focused Family Living and Counseling Mark #1
God-Dependent Families: Parental Dedication—The Workout Room

I was recently counseling two parents, Colton and Paige, whose teenage son was a prodigal. After hearing their story and empathizing with their hurts, I asked, "Tell me some of the prayers you've been praying about all of this . . ." They were honest enough to say, "We've become so exhausted by this situation that we've just about stopped praying. We're hoping to get your insights and encouragement . . ."

A Spirit-Dependency Sandwich

It would be easy to jump to judgment: "How could you stop praying?!" Rather than doing that, we turned together to Ephesians 5–6 for some of the encouragement they desired. I began by explaining that Ephesians 5:21–6:9 contains a "household code"—Paul's biblical portrait of how members of a household (husband and wife, parent and child, master and servant) were to relate in his day.

I then asked Colton to read Ephesians 5:18: "Do not get drunk on wine, which leads to debauchery. Instead, be filled with the Spirit." Then I asked Paige to read Ephesians 6:10 and 18: "Finally, be strong in the Lord and in his mighty power. . . . Pray in the Spirit on all occasions with all kinds of prayers and requests."

I didn't even have to ask them what they noticed. They got it. It was Paige who said, "*Before* and *after* Paul talks about family living, he talks about being filled with the Spirit, being strong in the Spirit, and praying in the Spirit."

I replied, "That's right. Paul understands the temptation to give up when family life exhausts us. So he sandwiches and surrounds his discussion of the home with Spirit-dependence. Paul's emphasizing our need for *strength from above*. Based on the context, it's perfectly legitimate for us to paraphrase Ephesians 6:10 like this: 'Mom and Dad, finally and always be strong in the Lord and in his mighty power.' Colton and Paige—the same power that raised Christ from the grave (Eph. 1:19–23) is available to the two of you as you parent your son."

I continued, "And think about how important your God-dependence is to your son. Right now he's depending on anything and anyone but Christ. What does he need the most from you? He needs to see you depending on God—filled with the Spirit, strong in the Spirit, praying in the Spirit. That model has greater potential of drawing and attracting your son to Christ than any principles or steps I could ever suggest."

The Big Idea

As Manoah learned in Judges 13, the first mark of GRACE parenting is God-dependence. Since we are talking about the home, I like to think of this as going into *the workout room*—the spiritual exercise room. So here is the big idea for our first mark of grace-focused parenting:

> *Parenting requires supernatural empowerment. Christ's resurrection power enlightens us to scout our opponent and equips us as we put on our parental spiritual armor.*

Scouting Our Opponent

When tension arises in our homes, our temptation is to see our family member as our enemy. We see the prodigal child as our opponent, the angry husband as our adversary, or the contentious wife as our antagonist.

Paul puts a stop to this false perception by identifying our true enemy—Satan. "Parents, put on the full armor of God so that you can take your stand against your family's enemy—the devil and his schemes. Parents, your struggle is not against your own flesh-and-blood children, but against the rulers, against the powers of this dark world, and against the spiritual forces of evil" (Eph. 6:11–12, author's paraphrase).

Counselor, one of our primary callings in family counseling is to unite the family against their common enemy—the devil. Satan is the family's diabolical and deceitful foe. When the battle rages in the home, equip family members to wage war *together* against Satan rather than fighting against each other.

I recall one case where every family member viewed the middle son, Jim, as the bad kid, the troubled family member, the problem child. Even Jim viewed himself this way. The older sister was the good girl. The younger brother was the compliant son. But Jim was the enemy preventing family harmony—at least that was how everyone saw him at first. Family tension began to melt away when Mom and Dad began to view Satan as their true enemy and Jim as a son, a brother-in-arms, a fellow soldier. This did not mean they faked things and pretended. At times Jim acted like an AWOL soldier, and his parents addressed that. When Jim began to see himself once again as a meaningful, cherished part of the family, much of his motivation for going AWOL was dissolved by grace.

Empowering Parents to Put On Their Workout Gear: The Parental Armor of God

Paul identifies six pieces of workout gear that every parent must put on. "Therefore, parents, put on your full parental armor of God—envelop and arm yourself from head to toe, so that you can stand your parental ground" (Eph. 6:13, author's paraphrase).

Putting On Parental Armor #1: The Belt of Truth—Family Integrity

By "truth" Paul is not talking about the objective truth of the gospel—he covers that in 6:17 with the sword of the Spirit. Throughout Ephesians, Paul uses the idea of truth in the sense of integrity, sincerity, authenticity, and transparency—applying God's truth to daily life. Truthfulness in relationships is the commitment to practice no deceit, no hypocrisy. Family truthfulness means honestly and courageously facing whatever is true about my family.

When our son, Josh, was in kindergarten, his teacher told us about a behavioral problem Josh was having. My immediate, fleshly tendency was to worry about my precious reputation: "I'm a pastor-counselor and my kid is having struggles!" My pharisaical temptation was to jump all over Josh so he would never act out again—so that I would not look bad! That is parental hypocrisy, not parental sincerity.

God's Spirit confronted me with my need for the parental belt of truth. So Shirley and I began to ponder this question: "Are there any things that we are doing or failing to do that may be contributing to Josh's struggles?" We were learning to address the first parental application question that family counselors help parents to prayerfully ponder:

- Parents, are you putting on the parental belt of truth, honestly and courageously facing whatever heart issues might be associated with the struggles in your family?

Putting On Parental Armor #2: The Breastplate of Righteousness— Moral Purity

The breastplate covered and protected the most vulnerable portion of a warrior's body—the chest and abdomen. It was known as the heart protector.

Paul connects the idea of heart protection to heart righteousness. In Ephesians 5:3–14, Paul equates righteousness with moral purity—pursuing purity of heart through Christ's grace and the Spirit's empowerment.

Heart purity secures us against the disabling wound and fatal thrust of our spiritual assailant—the devil. If we harbor sin in our heart, refusing to confess it and failing to take it to the Lord for his cleansing and for victory over it, that sin becomes a defect in the protective covering and leaves an opening through which Satan's dagger can pierce our heart.

Since we are focused on GRACE parenting, we are not talking about personal or parental perfection but parental maturation. The grace of Christ teaches us to say no to unrighteousness and yes to heart purity (Titus 2:11–13). The breastplate of righteousness suggests a second parental application question that biblical family counselors explore with parents:

- Parents, are you putting on the parental breastplate of righteousness, humbly taking any known sins to Christ for his grace to forgive and to the Spirit for his power to overcome?

Putting On Parental Armor #3: The Shoes of Peace—Restful Soul

In order to promote facility of motion over all types of terrain, Roman soldiers were accustomed to putting on shoes thickly studded with nails. In the military battles of the day, proper footwear spelled swiftness of movement that led to victory over the enemy.

Likewise, the peace of God lightens our conscience with grace so we can run the race of parental life without the weight of guilt and the burden of satanic condemnation. In Ephesians 2:14, Paul explains that Christ is our peace. The hostility between us and God has been abolished. The wrath of God has been crucified on the cross. We are now reconciled to God. All is right between us and our Father. When there is no discord between my heavenly Father and me, then the disturbances of my soul are hushed. It is wonderful, restful, and empowering to be forgiven. Peace with God provides the third parental application question that counselors and parents probe together:

- Parents, are you putting on the parental shoes of peace, putting off Satan's lying condemnation and putting on the gospel of Christ's peace so that you are energized to engage your children in the freedom your family has in Christ?

Putting On Parental Armor #4: The Shield of Faith—Trusting Heart

The Roman shield was almost the size of a door and was designed for protection against enemy arrows. When an enemy's fiery arrows collided with a shield, the points were blunted and the flames extinguished.

Our faith alone in Christ alone through grace alone similarly helps us to extinguish the flaming missiles of the evil one. The devil's quiver is full of fiery darts that kindle doubt, worry, hatred, condemnation, defeat, discouragement, anger, wrath, and rage. Satan targets our parental hearts and minds and tempts us to give up in despair and give in to rage.

When parents are tempted to quit caring, the shield of faith blocks that temptation from penetrating their heart. In faith we entrust our soul to God. We envision ourselves taking our most treasured possession and depositing it into our Father's care for safekeeping. The shield of faith suggests the fourth parental application question for counselors to discuss with parents:

- Parents, are you taking up the parental shield of faith? When your children hurt you, are you handing your soul over to God for his care and safekeeping?

Putting On Parental Armor #5: The Helmet of Salvation—Heavenly Hope

No Roman soldier would think of advancing into battle without a helmet. The helmet protected the head from the blows of a broadsword.

Spiritually, Paul labels this a helmet of salvation—forgiveness of and victory over sin past, present, and future. We are fighting a war that Christ has already won for us. Our victory is secure and assured.

But sometimes the individual family battles make us feel as though we are on the losing side. The helmet of salvation protects us from such doubts. Being conscious of our final victory provides us with a future hope that is resilient even through times of turmoil. So counselors interact with parents about a fifth parental application question:

- Parents, are you putting on the parental helmet of salvation? Is your heavenly hope providing earthly strength as you live today in light of your final victory in Christ?

Putting On Parental Armor #6: The Sword of the Spirit—Gospel Wisdom

The Roman soldier carried a short but deadly double-edged sword. With it he not only defended himself but also raced forward into the ranks of the enemy.

Paul tells us to repel and attack the prince of darkness by drawing the sword of the Spirit—the Word of God—the most lethal weapon in the fight for the family. Christ demonstrated the power of God's Word to thwart Satan's cunning attacks. When he was tempted in the wilderness, Jesus responded each time with the words "It is written" (Matt. 4:1–11). He models for us that parents do not live on bread alone but on every word that comes from the mouth of God.

The written Word of God (Scripture) is centered on the living Word of God (Christ) and his gospel victory narrative. The gospel narrative provides us with gospel wisdom—a strikingly distinct perspective on life and relationships. Gospel wisdom teaches us to live like Christ by dying to self and living for others. Parents who want to come after Christ must deny themselves, take up their cross daily, and follow Christ—by losing their lives. Thus our sixth and final parental application question asks:

- Parents, are you taking up the parental sword of the Spirit: do you make parental decisions based on the world's short-term perspective or based on gospel wisdom—dying to self, living for Christ, and sacrificing for your children?

Acknowledged Weakness: God-Dependent Parents and God-Dependent Counselors

Families come to us *divided* and *depleted*. Families, especially parents, need supernatural empowerment. Christ's resurrection power helps families to deal with their divisions by scouting out their true enemy—Satan. Supernatural empowerment helps families to deal with their depletion through putting on the family armor of God—their spiritual workout gear.

When we attempt to teach truth to weak and malnourished parents, they often end up even more discouraged and exhausted. They try in their own limited strength to apply what we are teaching them about family living, but they just can't do it.

Thus the first lesson we must teach parents is that they don't have to depend on their own strength. In fact, they are powerless unless they arm themselves with Christ's resurrection power and the family armor of God.

So we direct weak parents to the spiritual workout room of God-dependency. In the flesh, the worldly workout room is where we become strong in self—self-sufficient, self-trusting, self-focused. Tough. Impenetrable. Invulnerable. In the Spirit, the spiritual workout room is where we become strong in Christ—Christ-sufficient, Christ-trusting, Christ-focused.

Ironically, acknowledged weakness is exactly where parents need to be. We need to help parents hear and heed the assurance Christ gave to the apostle Paul: "My grace is sufficient for you, for my power is made perfect in weakness" (2 Cor. 12:9). We need to help parents apply Paul's response: "Therefore I will boast all the more gladly about my weaknesses, so that Christ's power may rest on me. . . . For when I am weak, then I am strong" (2 Cor. 12:9–10).

We do this by exploring God's Word together. But perhaps even more, we communicate this truth of God-dependency as we live out God's Word as counselors—as we acknowledge *our* weakness. Mothers, fathers, children— they all need to see us raising empty palms to God, crying out to him for help and hope. They need to see us as their counselor admitting that in and of ourselves we are incompetent to counsel. They need to witness us living out the reality that only in Christ alone, by grace alone, through faith alone are we competent to counsel their family.

Maturing as a Biblical Family Counselor
God-Dependent Families

1. A Spirit-Dependency Sandwich

    a. How could you use Ephesians 5:18 and 6:10–18 to help parents see and apply the truth that God never meant for them to apply Ephesians 6:1–4 in their own strength?

b. How could you use Ephesians 6:10–18 to help parents and children understand that their ultimate enemy is not each other but Satan?

2. Use the following questions to interact with parents about each piece of the parental armor of God (Eph. 6:10–18).

   a. *Putting On Parental Armor # 1: The Belt of Truth—Family Integrity.* Are you putting on the parental belt of truth, honestly and courageously facing whatever heart issues might be associated with the struggles in your family?

   b. *Putting On Parental Armor # 2: The Breastplate of Righteousness—Moral Purity.* Are you putting on the parental breastplate of righteousness, humbly taking any known sins to Christ for his grace to forgive and to the Spirit for his power to overcome?

   c. *Putting On Parental Armor # 3: The Shoes of Peace—Restful Soul.* Are you putting on the parental shoes of peace, putting off Satan's lying condemnation and putting on the gospel of Christ's peace so that you are energized to engage your children in the freedom your family has in Christ?

   d. *Putting On Parental Armor # 4: The Shield of Faith—Trusting Heart.* Are you taking up the parental shield of faith? When your children hurt you, are you handing your soul over to God for his care and safekeeping?

   e. *Putting On Parental Armor # 5: The Helmet of Salvation—Heavenly Hope.* Are you putting on the parental helmet of salvation? Is your heavenly hope providing earthly strength as you live today in light of your final victory in Christ?

f. *Putting On Parental Armor # 6: The Sword of the Spirit—Gospel Wisdom.* Are you taking up the parental sword of the Spirit? Do you make parental decisions based on the world's short-term perspective or based on gospel wisdom—dying to self, living for Christ, and sacrificing for your children?

TWO

Parenting Like
Our Heavenly Father

Introduction: Self-Help or Scripture-Wisdom?

During my parenting seminars, I introduce the four sessions on parental discernment, devotion, discipline, and discipleship with a couple of scenarios. One concerns a three-year-old child having problems handling his emotions—and losing it in public. The other describes a thirteen-year-old girl having problems handling her emotions—and losing it in public.

In both cases, I describe the typical response of the firm disciplinarian parents who insist that the correct response is parental discipline that teaches the child self-control and parental respect. Then I describe the typical response of the accepting affirming parents who contend that the correct response is to nurture and empathize with the child because he or she is communicating a need for acceptance and affection.

Then I ask the group to discuss which, if any, of the parents are right. Often we have a three-way split among the attendees, with some siding with the disciplinarian approach, some siding with the accepting approach, and some saying neither approach is correct.

Finally, I ask them the question that is central to these first three chapters: "What is your *biblical* basis for siding with the firm disciplinarian parents, the accepting affirming parents, or neither?"

If they are honest, and if we are honest, we often base our parental and counseling responses on how we were raised, on our personality, on our feelings, or on the current secular parenting theory that is all the rage. Even when we turn to Scripture to answer parenting questions, we tend to turn to those passages that support our internal inclination.

So here is the big idea for counselor wisdom and parental discernment that addresses all five marks of GRACE parenting:

The art of GRACE parenting revolves around interpreting the meaning behind our child's behavior based on a biblical understanding of how God fearfully and wonderfully made our children and on how God models biblical parenting.

A child's behavior contains a message to parents that parents must decipher before responding. The most effective parents are those who use God's Word as a lens to see into the hearts of their children. That is why the room we are using to portray parental discernment is *the study*. GRACE-focused parents enter the study (or library) to examine God's Word in order to understand their children.

As biblical family counselors, if we are to help parents understand (parental discernment) how to love (parental devotion), correct (parental discipline), and equip (parental discipleship) their children, then we must follow a revelation-based approach to family wisdom. This builds upon the first mark presented in the previous chapter. God-dependent families and God-dependent counselors are dependent upon God not only for strength but also for wisdom. Instead of searching the parental self-help section of Amazon, we search for the Christ-help and Scripture-wisdom provided in God's Word.

Maturing as a Biblical Family Counselor
Self-Help or Scripture-Wisdom?

1. "Counselor, know thyself" is good proverbial wisdom. Whether as parents or counselors, we all tend toward some natural, basic, almost ingrained approach to parenting.

   a. Even if it is only 51 percent to 49 percent, do you tend more toward the firm disciplinarian approach or the accepting affirming approach?

   b. More importantly, where did you learn your approach? What factors in your upbringing, experience, personality, or training might lead you toward your preferred tendency in child-rearing?

2. Here is the most important question: What is your biblical basis for siding with the firm disciplinarian parents, the accepting affirming parents, or neither?

3. How could the following summary statements impact how you counsel parents?

   a. The art of GRACE parenting revolves around interpreting the meaning behind our child's behavior based on a biblical understanding of how God fearfully and wonderfully made our children and on how God models biblical parenting.

   b. A child's behavior contains a message to parents that parents must decipher before responding.

   c. The most effective parents are those who use God's Word as a lens, microscope, or MRI to see into the hearts of their children.

   d. GRACE-focused parents enter the study (or library) to examine God's Word in order to understand their children.

GRACE-Focused Family Living and Counseling Mark #2
Revelation-Based Family Wisdom: Parental Discernment—The Study

The bookends surrounding Ephesians 6:4 remind us of our need for wisdom from above. In Ephesians 5:15–17, right before talking about family living, Paul insists that we reject foolishness "but understand what the Lord's will is." Paul then concludes his teaching on family life with an admonition to pray for wisdom to know how the gospel shapes all of life (Eph. 6:18–19). As we enter the study, we are seeking biblical counseling wisdom and parental discernment about two primary questions:

- What are our children's God-designed longings?
- What are a parent's God-modeled callings?

Our Children—Designed for Our Father's Holy Love

How did our Creator design our children? Just like he designed us—with a longing to know him as our heavenly Father. In Romans 8:15, Paul informs us that the essence of our relationship to God involves having received a Spirit of sonship by which we cry out, "Abba, Father, Daddy!" All of us—children, parents, and counselors—long for our Father in heaven.

J. I. Packer summarizes this well:

> The revelation to the believer that God is his Father is in a sense the climax of the Bible. Believers deal with God as their Father. "Father" is the name by which they call him. . . . If you want to judge how much a person understands Christianity, find out how much he makes of the thought of being God's child, and having God as his Father. If this is not the thought which prompts and controls his whole outlook in life, it means he does not understand Christianity very well at all.[1]

Our Father of Holy Love

Who is this Father God? What is his core nature? Throughout the Bible, the image of God as Father unites the concepts of *holiness* and *love*. "Be holy, because *I am holy*" (1 Pet. 1:16). "Whoever does not love does not know God, because *God is love*" (1 John 4:8). God's fatherly love and holiness are equally infinite, equally eternal, and simultaneously displayed. We can begin to envision God's holy love using the summary in figure 2.1.

Figure 2.1

God: Our Heavenly Father of Holy Love

Holy	Love
Sovereign King	Caring Shepherd
Truth	Grace
All-powerful rule/strength	Unfailing care/covenant loyalty
Just	Merciful
Wrath	Compassion
Sternness	Kindness/tenderness/forgiveness
Righteousness	Relationship
Standards/boundaries/rules	Involvement/acceptance
Transcendent—God above us	Immanent—God with us

Psalm 62:11–12 explains that these two overarching attributes of God encapsulate the essence of his infinite nature:

> One thing God has spoken,
>   two things I have heard:
> "*Power* belongs to you, God,
>   and with you, Lord, is unfailing *love*."

What the psalmist captures with words, Isaiah portrays with pictures.

> See, the *Sovereign* LORD comes with *power*,
>   and he rules with a mighty arm.
> See, his reward is with him,
>   and his recompense accompanies him.
> He tends his flock like a *shepherd*:
>   He gathers the lambs in his arms
> and carries them close to his heart;
>   he gently leads those that have young. (Isa. 40:10–11)

Our Father is our sovereign Shepherd of Holy Love whose almighty arms rule over us in protective power (holiness displayed in sovereignty that guards us) and whose tender arms comfort us with gentle care (love). He is the Father we all long for.

Answering the Soul Questions Our Children Are Asking

When our children are upset or discouraged, their two most common cries are:

- You don't love me!
- You're not fair!

It is normal to cringe with exasperation when we hear these statements. However, it helps if we remind ourselves that a child's sense of love and justice comes from God, who made them in his image, revealed himself through holy love, and designed them to long for his (and our) holy love. From infant to young adult, from toddler to teen and every age in between, children ask by their actions:

- *Are you loving and accepting?* (reflecting the longing for unfailing love): Do you love me? Are you safe? Do I have to work for and earn relationship with you?
- *Are you just and strong?* (reflecting the longing for uncompromising holiness): Is anyone in charge? Can I get my own way without cost? Are there safeguards?

Parental responses and counseling wisdom require that we think through the framework of these two biblical categories. Children's behavior contains a message that adults must decipher before we respond. The *art* of GRACE parenting and counseling comes in discerning which question is being asked by which behavior. The *skill* of GRACE parenting and counseling often involves answering both questions simultaneously.

Are You Loving?: Counseling Parents to Respond to Their Children's Thirst for Unfailing Love

Solomon says it plainly when he explains that we all long for unfailing love (Prov. 19:22). Biblical counselors can help parents address their children's longing for loyal love by pondering three parental pathways.

PARENTAL PATHWAY #1: PARENTS POINT THEIR CHILDREN TO CHRIST

Every parent will be a finite, flawed, and sometimes failing model of unfailing love. God calls parents to strive—in his strength—to be "loving enough" that their children trust them. And their parental prayer should be that they increasingly transfer that trust from themselves to Christ.

So counselors remind parents to constantly remind their children that their ultimate Good Shepherd is *not* the parent but Christ. And parents are to constantly give God the glory by admitting that at their best they are "Jesus with skin on," giving their children a small taste of Christ's infinite grace.

PARENTAL PATHWAY #2: PARENTS REMAIN INVOLVED WITH THEIR CHILDREN REGARDLESS OF PERSONAL COST

When my daughter Marie was three, she had a tendency to leave her toys everywhere. I would come home from a long day of pastoral counseling and trip over toys that cluttered every room in our small home. My inclination was to answer only one question: "Is anyone in charge?" (Yes. Me!) My wife Shirley's inclination was to answer the two questions above simultaneously: "Bob, Marie feels lonely in her room. She wants to be around us. I'm working with her to have an area in the living room where she plays. And I'm working with her to pick up her toys when she's done."

My immaturity and selfishness were evident. Shirley's maturity and sacrifice were remarkable. It cost Shirley time, energy, and effort—a price she was willing to pay to communicate to Marie that she was loved.

PARENTAL PATHWAY #3: PARENTS COMMUNICATE THAT THERE IS NOTHING THEIR CHILDREN CAN DO TO CAUSE PARENTS TO LOVE THEM MORE OR LESS

I coached wrestling for over two decades, and I always enjoyed our annual awards banquet. One young man had an especially successful season. After the banquet, I said to his father, "You must be very proud." His response was convicting. "Sure I am. But I would have been just as proud if he had never won a match or if he had never wrestled." What a great job of communicating loyal grace-love. This dad was demonstrating that his love could not be earned and therefore could not be lost.

Biblical counselors help parents to see their kids through the cross of Christ. Children need to know that when they mess up the living room or mess up their lives, they are not loved any less. They also must know that when they clean up the living room or clean up their lives, they are not loved any more.

Are You Just? Counseling Parents to Respond to Their Children's Thirst for Uncompromising Holiness

If we stopped with the first three parental pathways, then our counsel would highlight God's love while minimizing his holiness. Our counsel would be the counsel of the accepting affirming parents; in the absence of the counsel of holiness, it would end up being permissive counsel.

And it would neglect the fact that God designed children to long for uncompromising holiness. Children need parents to be a small taste of God's loving discipline: "the Lord disciplines the one he loves, and chastises every son whom he receives" (Heb. 12:6 ESV).

Biblical counselors can help parents address their children's longing for uncompromising holiness—parental strength—by pondering three additional parental pathways.

PARENTAL PATHWAY #1: PARENTS ESTABLISH THE KIND OF BOUNDARIES NEEDED TO PROTECT THEIR CHILDREN FROM PERSONAL HARM AND LIFELONG IMMATURITY

God created us with an innate desire for protective boundaries (Gen. 2:16–17). A childhood without boundaries sets a person up for adulthood without the full capacity to establish one's own boundaries. This person finds it hard to say no to their feelings and desires. A childhood without boundaries also tends to lead to an adult with a weakened capacity to yield to God's boundaries. This person finds it hard to say yes to God, because they perceive God's boundaries to be punitive rather than protective.

Parental Pathway #2: Parents enforce the types of consequences needed to teach their children the painfulness and ugliness of sin

Parental consequences cause children to bump up against parental moral authority now as a small taste of what it will be like one day to bump up against God's moral authority. Satan whispers to children that there is pleasure in sin—forever. Christ and Christlike parents teach that, while there may be temporary pleasure in sin, there is greater joy forever in righteousness and there are painful temporal and lasting consequences for sin.

Parental Pathway #3: Parents risk their children's displeasure at them for consistently setting boundaries and enforcing consequences

While God designed children to long for uncompromising strength, children rarely appreciate parental boundaries and consequences. While it is normal for parents to want their children to like them, it's ungodly for parents to be controlled by the idol of being their children's best bud, being the coolest, nicest parent, being the "good cop" parent.

With tears of joy in his eyes, a parent in our small group recently shared what his adult son said about his upbringing: "Dad, I bucked you every time you disciplined me. I used pouting, name-calling, and even shaming to get back at you. But you didn't give in or back down. When I think of you now, I picture a strong man—and I want to be like you with my kids."

Designed to Reflect Our Father's Holy Love

Since God designed children to long for his holy love, it should be no surprise that God calls parents to reflect his holiness and love. A basic rule of biblical GRACE parenting states:

As God is to us, so we seek to be to our children.

Our Father's model of parenting involves a perfect blending of holiness and love. Parents must seek to imitate this model that we have in God the Father. An image of God is being developed in our children's minds that is derived from how we relate to them. As our parental model, God the Father is not indulgent and permissive—love without holiness. God does not compromise his holiness in order to spare and spoil us. Neither is he vindictive and condemning—holiness without love. God does not suppress his love in order to crush and destroy us.

A comprehensive, biblical view of God delivers us from false caricatures of him and of godly parenting. Images of justice (holiness) without mercy (love) picture a God or parent who is too strict (firm disciplinarian parents) and a child who feels unloved and uncared for. Images of mercy (love) without justice (holiness) picture a God or parent who is too lenient (accepting affirming parents) and a child who is without standards, boundaries, and safeguards.

Styles of Parenting

In family counseling, I have found it helpful to assess styles of parenting based on the biblical truth that God is our Father of Holy Love and on the biblical calling for parents to reflect our heavenly Father to their children. Having said that, I readily acknowledge that the styles of parenting found in figure 2.2 are not divinely inspired. Instead, they are my current best attempt to translate our Father's holy-love parenting into a practical family counseling approach that provides something of a biblical parenting GPS for both the counselor and the parents.

There are, of course, unlimited variations within each of the four styles of parenting depicted in figure 2.2. The four styles seek to assess the relative balance or imbalance a parent maintains in expressing holiness and communicating love. The vertical axis represents the level of parental holiness conveyed to children: righteous standards, godly character, consistency, strength, protection, guidance, training, and accountability. The horizontal axis represents how well or poorly parents convey biblical love: parental involvement, sacrifice, relationship, grace, devotion, acceptance, empathy, and care.

How parents combine or fail to combine these key ingredients into their relationship with their children determines their respective style of parenting. Figure 2.2 labels these styles of parenting as pharisaical, godly, neglectful, or permissive/possessive. As we examine each of these homes, we can ask ourselves several core counselor diagnostic questions:

- What might it be like to live in this home?
- What impact might such a home have on a child?
- What influence might this home have on the development of a child's image of God?

Diagnosing Pharisaical Parenting: High Holiness/Low Love—The Yes/No Home

Matthew 23 conveys the mood of this home. Parents put heavy burdens and cumbersome loads on their children but are unwilling to lift a finger to help their children. Parents major on minor rules and minor on rich relationship.

Figure 2.2

Styles of Parenting

High Holiness
"Yes, I am strong."

Pharisaical Parenting	**Godly Parenting**
The Yes/No Home	**The Yes/Yes Home**
Frightens their children	Fellowships with their children
Dictatorial	Christlike
Harsh	Care and control
Law	Grace
Tons of rules, little relationship	Relationships and rules
Neglectful Parenting	**Permissive/Possessive Parenting**
The No/No Home	**The No/Yes Home**
Flees their children	Fears their children
Distant	Spoiling and rescuing
Aloof	Pampering and hovering
Abandoned	Selfish relationship
Few rules, little relationship	Few rules, lots of relationship

Low Love
"No, I am not supportive."

High Love
"Yes, I am supportive."

Low Holiness
"No, I am not strong."

This is the yes/no home—"Yes, we are big and powerful and will crush you with consequences. No, we are not grace-giving, forgiving, and caring." In this home, there is pressure to measure up to external standards. Children feel an obligation to succeed for their parents—to make their parents look good. This home is controlling, rule-based, and rigid. Involvement is conditional. "I'll accept you and be pleased with you only if you are obedient, bright, and successful."

Children feel as if no matter what they do, it is never enough—*they* are never enough. They feel profoundly inadequate. Some children respond with perfectionism, phobias, and obsessive-compulsive behavior. Others respond like compliant robots and become people-pleasers. Still others are sad and depressed. Some simply rebel and reject their parents' faith.

Apart from the grace of God breaking in, a child in this home struggles to see God as loving. "God is above me, but he is not near me." To them, God is full of truth but empty of grace. Their relationship with God is one of distance, obligation, works, perfectionism, and emptiness. With their parent and with God, they feel like they are constantly trying to stand on a pedestal yet relentlessly being pushed off. "The only path to God is perfect obedience, and I will never measure up." Some give up. Some try harder—endlessly.

Diagnosing Neglectful Parenting: Low Holiness/Low Love—The No/No Home

Ezekiel 34:1–6 and Matthew 18:2–14 illustrate this home. Children are like sheep without a shepherd. They are neither accepted nor accountable. Selfishness is the word that best describes this model of parenting. The parent comes first. Such parents are low in conveying love, intimacy, involvement, and acceptance. The home is chaotic, cold, and harsh. Unpredictability is the only thing the child can predict. Norms are nonexistent or inconsistent. The home is random and capricious. Parents avoid responsibility for their children. Children are on their own—if they are to be parented, they must parent themselves (and often have to parent their parent).

Not surprisingly, the child feels like an orphan. The lack of parental care and control typically leads to a selfish, empty, and angry child, unless the child surrenders to God. Joseph Stalin, Adolf Hitler, Fidel Castro, and many other dictators grew up in such homes. Rage over emptiness frequently leads to rage toward others.

Defiant and distant are two characteristics of children raised in this type of home. "Since I've never had anything, now I'll get whatever I can, wherever I can, however I can!" And the image of God? "What God? Don't give me that religion stuff. It doesn't work. God doesn't care about me and I don't care about him!" If they do sense God at all, he seems far above them and distant from them.

Diagnosing Permissive/Possessive Parenting: Low Holiness/High Love—The No/Yes Home

We find an example of this type of home in 1 Samuel 2:12–30, which tells the story of Eli's weakness and his sons' wickedness. Eli, like many permissive/possessive parents, honored and feared his children more than he honored and feared God. This home says, "No, I'm not strong. But yes, I am loving." However, this love has been emptied of biblical love. The relationship is selfish because the parents *need* the children to like them. Children are spoiled and rescued, pampered and hovered over. The child becomes an idol, a god to be served.

Apart from the intervention of God, children in this home feel a deep sense of entitlement. They experience a lack of empathy for others but great empathy for themselves. As a result, some children in this home feel fearful, childish, and helpless—nothing was ever expected of them, and they do not expect anything of themselves. Other children in the no/yes home follow a very different path that says, "I'm the center of the universe. Cater to me." They become spoiled and demanding.

Unless they surrender to God, they will see God like Santa or a kindly old grandpa who spoils them. God is their genie in a bottle, their butler, their valet.

Diagnosing Godly Parenting: High Holiness/High Love—The Yes/Yes Home

This is the home all Christian parents strive for. Scriptural examples abound—when we see God as our sovereign shepherding Father (Ps. 23; Isa. 40:10–11; Luke 15). This is the yes/yes home. Parents convey by their actions, "Yes, I am strong; yes, I am supportive." While imperfect, parents in this home strive to provide their children with small tastes of God's holy love—and seek to consistently direct their children to God for his infinite holy love. The home is safe, stable, secure. There is fellowship, flexibility, and follow-through. There are rules and boundaries shared with love and grace.

Children in this home have a wonderful opportunity to grow up with a sense of security and responsibility. As in Ephesians 4:11–16, the combination of truth and love prompts maturity, unity, and humility. They serve not out of guilt but from gratitude for grace. They strive not to earn favor but because they are at rest in God's favor and their parents' favor and desire to give their best in service for others.

Their image of God? He is their sovereign Shepherd. Their God is the father of the prodigal, who runs to them, forgives them, celebrates with them, puts the family clothes on them, and empowers them to go in grace and give up sin.

Maturing as a Biblical Family Counselor
Revelation-Based Family Wisdom

1. Whether counselor, parent, or child, none of us maintains a perfect image of our perfect God.

   a. When your view of God gets unbalanced, do you tend more toward emphasizing God's holiness and minimizing his grace? Or do you tend more toward emphasizing God's love and minimizing his truth/holiness?

   b. How can passages like Isaiah 40:10–11 and Psalm 62:11–12 help you maintain a biblical view of God in your Christian walk and as a biblical counselor?

---

2. By their actions, children ask two primary questions of their parents: "Are you loving and accepting?" "Are you just and strong?" How can an awareness of these two questions impact your counseling of parents? Your counseling of children/teens?

3. Review figure 2.2 and the styles of parenting discussed on pages 45–48.

   a. In the home you grew up in, which parental style was most prominent? What impact did it have on you? On your image of God?

   b. If you are a parent, prayerfully ponder your style of parenting. In those times when you are not reflecting godly parenting, which style of parenting do you reflect? What impact might this be having on your child(ren)? How could you move toward more godly parenting?

   c. How might you begin to counsel a family with the pharisaical parenting style?

   d. How might you begin to counsel a family with the neglectful parenting style?

   e. How might you begin to counsel a family with the permissive/possessive parenting style?

   f. How might you begin to counsel a family where the parents are pretty consistently implementing a godly parenting style, yet the children/teens are deeply struggling?

GRACE-Focused Family Living and Counseling Mark #3:
Accepting and Affirming Grace Relationships:
Parental Devotion—The Playroom

In Ephesians 6:4, the apostle Paul teaches the truth we just highlighted: God designed children to receive parental holy love.

- Love / Devotion: "[Parents], do not exasperate your children; instead, bring them up [i.e., raise them tenderly] . . ."
- Holiness / Discipline: ". . . in the training of the Lord"
- Equipping / Discipleship: ". . . and in the instruction of the Lord"

No one reading Ephesians 6:4 in the twenty-first century can fully appreciate how groundbreaking such words were in Paul's day. Rome had a law called *patria potestas*, which means "the father's power." The father maintained absolute authority over his children. They could be sold as slaves; they could be forced to work in chains; they could receive the death penalty as punishment for disobedience.

Paul steps into this cultural evil and family disgrace and commands parents not to exasperate their children but to bring them up tenderly in the nurture of the Lord. To exasperate means to irritate, to make bitter, to provoke to anger. Instead, Paul calls parents to "bring up" their children. The phrase means to raise them tenderly and lovingly by nourishing them to maturity—we are to *shepherd* our children like the Good Shepherd shepherds us. John Calvin summarized this verse with the idea of parents fondly cherishing their children.

Paul practiced what he preached in relationship to his children in the faith.

Just as a nursing mother cares for her children, so we cared for you. Because we loved you so much, we were delighted to share with you not only the gospel of God but our lives as well. . . . For you know that we dealt with each of you as a father deals with his own children, encouraging, comforting and urging you to live lives worthy of God, who calls you into his kingdom and glory. (1 Thess. 2:7–8, 11–12)

The Big Idea

Though the vast majority of parents deeply love their children, a surprising percentage of children and teens do not feel genuinely loved. Frequently we experience a parent-child communication gap. Children simply do not hear and perceive things the way we adults do. Paul says as much in 1 Corinthians 13:11, where he notes that when he was a child, he reasoned as a child; when he became an adult, he reasoned as an adult.

The *Kinder Cookbook* is a splendid example of this. It was written by a kindergarten class at a Christian school to mothers on Mother's Day. The introduction put it well: "This *Kinder Cookbook* is compiled with your children's favorite dishes. The recipes were written according to the way your child has seen you prepare these dishes." Let's see how a child's perception of the adult world compares to reality . . .

- Fruit Cocktail: Buy fruit cocktail at the store. Put it in a pan and cook for 14 hours. Put on plate and eat.
- Hot Dogs: Put 3 hot dogs in the microwave on a paper towel. Cook for 60 minutes. Put on a bun with mustard and ketchup.
- Fried Eggs: Put 2 cups of grease in a pan. Crack one egg in the pan. Flip it over. Let it cook for 1 minute.
- Chocolate Milk: Put ½ cup of milk into a glass. Add ½ cup of chocolate. Stir it and drink it.

Clearly, children's perception of reality is different from a parent's communication of that reality. So here is *the big idea* for mark #3 of GRACE-focused parenting:

> *Parents must learn to bridge the parent-child communication gap so that they convey the shepherding love in their hearts in a way that touches their children's hearts.*

We just saw that *by their actions* children ask questions like, "Am I loved with a love that cannot be earned and cannot be lost?" Now we are learning that *by their attitudes and actions* parents answer their children's questions with, "You are loved with a grace-like accepting and affirming love." This is why we describe this section using the imagery of *the playroom*—parents can best communicate love during daily interactions as they live and relate together in their children's world. Here then are ten parental actions and attitudes that counselors can discuss with parents to help homes become a place of grace.

Five Parental Actions and Attitudes for Communicating Grace-Like Accepting Love

Grace-like acceptance communicates to children that nothing they do can make parents love them more or less. Counselors can help parents consider five parental attitudes and actions that communicate this to their children.

1. Parents convey the attitude of honest acknowledgment and strong involvement.

The formula for communicating grace acceptance is based on Christ's relationship to us:

Honest Acknowledgment	Strong Involvement
"While we were yet sinners . . ."	". . . Christ died for us."

We might assume that grace acceptance means pretending that children are perfect. In actuality, that is the false formula of the permissive parents who wink at their children's sinfulness. Godly parents say, "Son/daughter, I see who you really are—sins, faults, imperfections, and all—and I love you as much as ever." When we are seen by another at our worst and we are still loved, that is when we experience profound acceptance.

2. Parents admit their own sins, faults, and imperfections.

When we are wrong, we ought to admit it to our children. When we have sinned against them, we ought to seek their forgiveness. Rather than hiding our imperfections, we should acknowledge that we are jars of clay. We are all fallen, sinful people who are finite, frail, and imperfect. Our honesty about our sins and imperfections will send a message to our children that they can sin and find grace, they can mess up and have hope, and they can be imperfect and that's normal.

3. Parents must deal realistically with their children.

This is the flip side of principle #2. Parents should not wink at misbehavior or ignore issues of the heart. Remember the principle of honest acknowledgment. Remember how Paul expressed love in 1 Thessalonians 2:11–12. He urged his children to live lives worthy of God—and when our children are not living worthy of God, we face that honestly with Christ's grace.

4. Parents choose to remain involved with hope.

When kids struggle spiritually with rebellion against God and against their parents, the temptation is to give up in discouragement or to give in to frustration. If God is God, then giving in to feelings of being overwhelmed is not an appropriate grace response. Counselors help parents cling to and communicate Christ's hope even in the worst of circumstances: "We've seen it all; we've seen Christ overcome it all. We love you and we know Christ will help us all work through this together."

5. Parents express love as the battle rages.

The fleshly response to family tension involves defending, attacking, or retreating. It is like the flight, fight, or freeze response to fear and anxiety. The Spirit-empowered response involves tearing down defenses, empowering the other person, and moving toward them in a deeper level of involvement.

What does it look like to express love as the battle rages? Sometimes it means calling a temporary timeout so parents and kids can cool down. Other times it involves a parental apology for losing control. It might involve a hug that breaks the tension. At times it involves verbalizing what is happening: "We're pretty upset at each other right now, aren't we?" Most times it could involve prayer: "Could we stop and ask God to help us love each other as we work through this?"

Five Parental Actions and Attitudes for Communicating Grace-Like Affirming Love

Grace affirmation communicates to children that they are fearfully, wonderfully, and uniquely designed by Christ, and that therefore their identity and worth are found in, through, and for Christ. Family counselors can help parents ponder five parental attitudes and actions that communicate this to their children.

1. Parents ask and answer the question, Whose are you?

The world asks the question, Who am I? The Christian asks a richer, deeper question: Whose am I? Our identity is a grace identity based on being created by Christ our Creator (Col. 1:15–17) and re-created by Christ our Savior (Col. 1:18–23).

Every child at every age and stage will wrestle with their identity and worth. Is our identity based on whether the middle school girls consider us part of the in group, or is it based on our relationship to the Shepherd-King? Is our identity based on being the most compliant kid in the youth group, or is it based on our relationship to the Shepherd-King?

2. Parents communicate that their child is Christ's opus, his poem.

Psalm 139:13–18 teaches that God fearfully and wonderfully made each of us—*uniquely*. Ephesians 2:10 teaches that we are Christ's workmanship, his opus, his poem. Christ is writing a great and grand grace story out of every child's life. Counselors help parents help their children find the title to their life story, or the title to the chapter they are going through now. "Son, what Lord of the Rings–like story is God wanting to craft out of your life as you go through this?" "Sweetheart, what amazing poem is Christ writing for all the world to see as you face this with him?"

3. Parents help their children identify their unique DNA.

Since God fearfully and wonderfully handcrafted each of us to be his one-of-a-kind poem, then part of the parental role is helping children discover God's unique design for them. Counselors encourage parents to help their children discover their interests (rather than just mimicking parental interests). Parents help their children assess areas of strength and encourage their development. They assist them to identify unique temptations or "thorns in the flesh" and how to address them biblically.

4. Parents speak life words, not death words.

If children are God's poem, then as parents we must be very careful what we say about them and to them. Life and death are in the power of the tongue (Prov. 18:21). Death words demean, mock, minimize, guilt, shame, and condemn.

Life words express appreciation for a child's uniqueness and special contributions. Life words encourage—they place courage into. Life words affirm and commend. Paul speaks life words to his son in the faith, Timothy, who struggled with timidity. "My son, fan into flame the special gifts of God that he's given you. You've not been given a spirit of timidity, but God's Spirit of power, love, and wisdom" (2 Tim. 1:6–7, author's paraphrase).

5. Parents welcome age-appropriate contributions from their children.

In our sin-sick world, it is understandable that we want to and need to protect our children. Yet we can overprotect them to the extent that they become fearful, anxious, and doubtful of their abilities. Counselors encourage parents to welcome contributions from their children, whether in terms of work around the house or ministry in the community. Parents need to learn to allow their children to be involved in age-appropriate activities. "Everybody's doing it" is not a free pass. On the other hand, if every other mature Christian parent is allowing every other teen a certain area of freedom, then perhaps a parent will want to consider whether they are being too protective and controlling. Parents affirm their children's worth in Christ when children sense that they are trusted to act their age.

Maturing as a Biblical Family Counselor
Accepting and Affirming Grace Relationships

1. "Parents must learn to bridge the parent-child communication gap so that they convey the shepherding love in their hearts in a way that touches their children's hearts." How can this big idea for mark #3 of GRACE-focused parenting impact your family counseling?

2. As a biblical family counselor, how could you help parents implement each of the following five parental actions and attitudes for communicating grace-like accepting love?

    a. Parents convey the attitude of honest acknowledgment and strong involvement.

    b. Parents admit their own sins, faults, and imperfections.

    c. Parents must deal realistically with their children.

    d. Parents choose to remain involved with hope.

    e. Parents express love as the battle rages.

3. As a biblical family counselor, how could you help parents implement each of the following five parental actions and attitudes for communicating grace-like affirming love?

    a. Parents ask and answer the question, Whose are you?

b. Parents communicate that their child is Christ's opus, his poem.

c. Parents help their children identify their unique DNA.

d. Parents speak life words, not death words.

e. Parents welcome age-appropriate contributions from their children.

CHAPTER

THREE

Parenting with Grace and Truth

Introduction: A Parental Prayer

By the end of this chapter, we will have concluded our theological introduction to biblical family life. We have based our summary on Ephesians 6:1–4 within the larger context of all that Paul says throughout Ephesians.

In Ephesians 5:21–6:9, Paul shares his household code—his instructions on biblical family life. He concludes his teaching by commending parental prayerfulness: "Finally and always, parents, pray in the Spirit on all occasions with all kinds of parental prayers and requests. Parents, with this in mind, be alert and always keep on praying for all people—especially your children" (Eph. 6:18, author's paraphrase).

This is a vital reminder to us as biblical family counselors. Counseling is not only truth-telling. Counseling is sharing gospel truth in love—in the context of a caring relationship for the purpose of loving family relationships. The goal of counseling is not simply the accumulation of information. The goal of family counseling with parents is the heart application of truth that transforms.

As Paul left the Ephesians with a plea to prayerfulness, so biblical counselors pray that the parents we counsel would embody the type of prayerful attitude modeled in the following prayer.

A Parental Prayer: "Fuel Me, Father"

Fuel me, Father, for I am on empty. I cannot parent on my own.
My resources are limited; yours are infinite.
My wisdom is so small; yours is so incredible.
My love is so inconsistent; yours is so unchanging.

My discipline is so harsh one moment, so lax the next; yours is so
   perfect.
My discipleship is so meager; yours is so majestic.

Father, I need you. My kids need me to need you.
I kneel before you this day, this moment,
empty palms and expectant eyes raised to you.
Give me this day my parental daily bread—
parental dedication that is God-glorifying by being God-dependent,
parental discernment that is based on the revelation of your Word,
parental devotion that reflects your fatherly affection and affirmation
   in Christ,
parental discipline that challenges my child's heart,
and parental discipleship that equips my child for the race of life.

I know that you alone are the perfect Parent and that I will not parent
   perfectly today.
So I pray that you will empower me to be a GRACE parent
and that you will be my children's ultimate Parent.
Please empower me to parent my children like you parent me.

Love,

Your Ever-Dependent Child

I am sure you can see the outline of these first three chapters embedded
in this prayer. And that is purposeful. As biblical family counselors, if the
parents we counsel personalize this type of prayerful attitude, then God has
used us to counsel them to counsel their children.

Maturing as a Biblical Family Counselor
A Parental Prayer

1. How could praying Ephesians 6:10–18 in a family or parental context empower parents
   and impact children?

   "Finally and always, parents, pray in the Spirit on all occasions with all kinds of parental prayers and
   requests. Parents, with this in mind, be alert and always keep on praying for all people—especially
   your children."

2. How could these summaries of what counseling is and is not impact your approach to biblical family counseling?

    a. Counseling is not only truth-telling. Counseling is sharing gospel truth in love—in the context of a caring relationship for the purpose of loving family relationships.

    b. The goal of counseling is not simply the accumulation of information. The goal of family counseling with parents is the heart application of truth that transforms.

3. Reread and then take time to pray the parental prayer "Fuel Me, Father."

    a. Whether or not you are a parent, there is much application that every Christian could make from this prayer. How could you apply this prayer to your life?

    b. As a biblical family counselor, how could you help parents not only to pray this prayer but to live this prayer?

4. We conclude this section with a reminder: our goal is to counsel parents so they can counsel their children. How does this goal shape or reshape your focus as a biblical family counselor?

GRACE-Focused Family Living and Counseling Mark #4
Care-Fronting the Heart: Parental Discipline—The Family Room

Recall how Ephesians 6:4 teaches that God designed children to be discipled in the context of parental holy love:

- *Love / Devotion.* Parent your children tenderly for the purpose of conveying to them a small taste of God's shepherding love, which encourages loving trust in God and sacrificial love for others.

- *Holiness / Discipline.* Parent your children in the discipline of the Lord for the purpose of conveying to them a small taste of God's sovereign holiness, which encourages respectful submission and joyful surrender to God.
- *Equipping / Discipleship.* Parent your children in the instruction of the Lord for the purpose of passing on the torch of faith in Christ from one generation to the next.

Children ask by their actions, "Am I loved with a love that I cannot earn and cannot lose?" Parents respond by their attitudes and actions, "You are loved with a grace-love."

Children also ask by their actions, "Can I get my own way without cost?" Parents answer, "No, because you are loved with a holy love."

The Big Idea

Paul encourages parents to tenderly shepherd their children in the sovereign and holy discipline *of the Lord*. In Hebrews 12:5–11, we find a fourfold description of what the Lord's discipline looks like. Our heavenly Father's discipline is:

- *Personal.* He disciplines us as his children out of love and for our good.
- *Purposeful.* He disciplines us so that we might share in his holiness.
- *Painful.* He brings painful consequences for heart foolishness.
- *Potentially productive.* He designs his discipline to produce a harvest of righteousness and peace for those trained by it.

Since parental discipline is to follow the model of the Father's discipline, we can state the big idea for mark #4 of GRACE-focused parenting like this:

Parents are ambassadors for God's moral order, sent to lovingly teach their children the consequences for foolishness by care-fronting their heart with the prayerful hope that their children will increasingly reflect Christ.

Think of that word "care-fronting." Out of shepherding care and love, parents challenge and confront their child's heart. Parents do so in the context of daily family life, so, continuing our room imagery, we picture the discipline aspect of parenting as taking place in *the family room.*

Parental Discipline Is Personal: It Begins and Ends with Love

If we're being honest, we can admit that we've all been there. We try and try to patiently teach and discipline our children, but their rebellion and lack of responsiveness and respect tries our patience. In our attempts not to exasperate them, we become exasperated! At that moment, we are tempted to discipline them not out of love for their good but out of our unholy anger because of our frustration. We can keep being honest by acknowledging the hypocrisy of disciplining our children out of unholy anger so that they can become more holy!

Solomon explains that "the one who loves their children is careful to discipline them" (Prov. 13:24). The Hebrew word translated as "loves" means to be deeply desirous of, to be loyally affectionate to, to tenderly delight in. This reminds us of another proverb that describes God as a father who disciplines the son he delights in (Prov. 3:12). The word "delight" means to take pleasure in. In parental discipline, are we taking more pleasure in venting our frustration than in our child? When we refuse to discipline, are we taking more pleasure in our comfort and ease than in the hard work of shepherding our child's heart?

First, biblical counselors help parents to understand that they communicate love in discipline through their emotional control as they discipline. Notice I did not say "through feeling no emotions." Rebellious children will prompt a host of parental feelings. We use time-outs as a discipline method, but sometimes we need parental time-outs *before* we discipline our children. We take time with God to calm our spirit before we address our child's spirit.

Second, biblical counselors teach that parents express love in discipline through an age-appropriate explanation of the rules, of the violation, and of the consequence.

Third, parents show love in discipline through a provision of acceptance. Think about what would have happened in the heart of the prodigal son if, when he returned home in repentance, his father had shunned him instead of running to him, throwing his arms around him, and reaffirming his loyal love to him . . .

Parental Discipline Is Purposeful: We Discipline Heart Foolishness

All parents have probably said it: "I feel like every time I turn around, I'm disciplining my kids for something new!" If we're not careful, we can become like pharisaical parents, disciplining our kids for a host of legalistic rules that are more about ourselves—our sense of control and comfort. God disciplines us so that we might share in his holiness—and holiness is first and foremost a heart issue. In Matthew 23:13–26, Jesus care-fronted the Pharisees because they focused on external behavior—the outside of the cup—rather than on the more important heart matters of justice, mercy, and faithfulness—the inside of the cup.

Solomon concurs with this heart focus: "Folly is bound up in the heart of a child, but the rod of discipline will drive it far away" (Prov. 22:15). We do not aim our discipline simply at attempts to change external behavioral issues. We focus our discipline on internal heart foolishness.

Proverbs 28:26 provides the clearest, most pointed scriptural explanation of heart foolishness: "Those who trust in themselves are fools." Solomon identifies heart foolishness with all the self sins: self-sufficiency, self-sovereignty, self-centeredness.

Psalms 10 and 14 describe these foolish self sins by depicting the fool saying in countless ways, "I don't need God! I will not submit to God! I can make my life work quite well apart from God! I'm not accountable to God!"

Listen to the heart of the fool in Psalm 10: "In all his thoughts there is no room for God" (v. 4). The fool says, "Nothing will shake me, I'll always be happy and never have trouble" (v. 6). "He says to himself, 'God will never notice. . . . He won't call me to account'" (vv. 11, 13).

In wise parental discipline, parents look for patterns of behavior that indicate a foolish attitude of the heart—the inside of the cup. Parents seek to discern and address behaviors and attitudes that communicate foolish heart messages like:

- Selfishness and self-centeredness: "Life is all about me. Life is not all about Christ."
- Self-sufficiency: "I can make life work on my own. I don't need God."
- Self-sovereignty: "I can get my own way without cost. I'm not accountable to God."

Parental Discipline Is Painful: Parents Bring Painful Consequences for Heart Foolishness

Foolishness is the core conviction that I can make my life work apart from God. It is the belief, played out in a child's behavior, that I can get my own way without cost. Foolish children (and parents) believe that we can live autonomously—do our own thing—and reap pleasure.

Biblical discipline seeks to confront and challenge these core convictions. So biblical counselors work with parents to design parental discipline to teach the truth that *pain and not pleasure is the consequence of sinful foolishness.* Experiencing painful consequences for wrong beliefs is meant to teach that there is a holy God to whom we are accountable now and to whom we will one day give personal account.

Consider consequences in the physical realm. When you touch a hot stove, your hand experiences intense pain and you remove your hand. In the physical realm we tend to experience immediate painful consequences. Contrast this with the spiritual realm. Galatians 6:7 teaches that we will reap what we sow. But there is a catch. Consequences are often *delayed* in the spiritual realm. Hebrews 11:25 acknowledges that there is pleasure in sin *for a season*. Because spiritual consequences tend to be delayed, our foolish hearts tend to think we can get away with our selfish ways. Ecclesiastes 8:11 clearly communicates this reality: "Because the sentence against an evil deed is not executed speedily, the heart of the children of man is fully set to do evil" (ESV). Peter notes that God is a patient and gracious Judge and that time-oriented human beings tend to foolishly misinterpret God's graciousness as slackness or permissiveness (2 Pet. 3:8–11).

Imagine you are counseling a parent whose teen has stolen a video game. Secretly bringing it home, he enjoys hours of pleasure with his stolen treasure. Inside his foolish heart he thinks, "This is awesome! No one caught me. I made out like a bandit. I got what I wanted for nothing. And I sure am enjoying every second of it!" Because the consequences in the spiritual realm are often delayed, this teen is reinforcing his sinful belief that he can get his own way, reap pleasure, and not experience pain.

As a family counselor, you explain that parental discipline involves demonstrating the reality of God's spiritual moral order. Parents must give their children a small taste *now* of what it will be like to bump up against God and his holy moral order in the day of judgment. Thus kids bump up against parental discipline as an anticipation of the consequence of bumping up against the future discipline of God. Parental consequences inflict temporary pain now to help children sense the eternal holiness of God, repent, and avoid the worse pain of alienation from God.

Parents are God's moral ambassadors. Their role is to fill the time delay between human disobedience and divine consequences. In parental discipline, parents are making the long-term consequences of God's spiritual rule more immediately felt.

So the parent you are counseling comes home from work and notices their teen playing with his new (stolen) video game. After a little conversation and detective work, the truth slowly begins to leak out. Your biblical counsel to the parent might sound something like this:

- What would it be like to discuss the issue candidly with your son, highlighting God's perspective and what a Christlike response would look like? And what if you decided together that you'll go with your son to the store, where he's required to not only return the game and confess that he stole it but also to use money from his part-time job to pay back *double* the cost of the game?

- Your son now has the opportunity to develop a new set of core convictions. He could think to himself, "Wow! It cost twice as much than if I had just bought this in the first place. And I had the added embarrassment of confessing that I stole it. It sure is right that crime doesn't pay. I guess it's true what the Bible says—we reap what we sow and God will not be mocked."

Parental Discipline Is Potentially Productive: Responses to Heart Discipline

Of course, there are other potential responses to this discipline scenario. Rather than softening his heart, this son might harden his heart—against God and his parents. So it's important for counselors to help parents recognize that their role is to respond to foolishness with heart-focused consequences. However, parents must understand that they cannot control their child's heart response. In Hebrews 12, we see that even God's perfect discipline can be responded to either wisely or foolishly. Hebrews 12:5–6 says that some of God's children make light of his discipline—they despise it, reject it, and refuse to be internally changed by it. Others lose heart when they are disciplined by God—they give up, grow weary, and quit trying to live a godly life. Even the most godly and wise parental discipline is only *potentially* productive.

Fortunately, the news is not all bad. Hebrews 12:9 tells us about two potentially positive responses to godly discipline. Children can respond with *respect* and *submission*—they respect and honor their parents as representatives of God's holiness, and they willingly submit from the heart to parents as ambassadors for God's moral order. The end result of that heart attitude is a harvest of righteousness and peace (Heb. 12:11).

As biblical counselors, we help parents grasp this biblical truth:

- Parent, assume responsibility for how you administer discipline—in love with a focus on wisely instituting consequences that address heart foolishness. Do *not* assume responsibility for your child's response. Instead, humbly and hopefully pray that your child will respond by growing increasingly like Christ.

Maturing as a Biblical Family Counselor
Care-Fronting the Heart

1. "Parents are ambassadors for God's moral order, sent to lovingly teach their children the consequences for foolishness by care-fronting their heart with the prayerful hope that their children will increasingly reflect Christ." In what specific ways might this big idea for parental discipling impact your parental and family counseling?

2. Picture yourself counseling a family where the parents are struggling to bring consistent biblical discipline to a consistently rebellious preteen. How could you work with the parents to help them implement each of the following biblical principles of discipline?

    a. Parental Discipline Is Personal: It Begins and Ends with Love

    b. Parental Discipline Is Purposeful: We Discipline Heart Foolishness

    c. Parental Discipline Is Painful: Parents Bring Painful Consequences for Heart Foolishness

    d. Parental Discipline Is Potentially Productive: Responses to Heart Discipline

3. Discipline can be frustrating. How could you use this principle, derived from Hebrews 12:5–11, to help parents understand what they are and are *not* responsible for in parental discipline?

    "Parent, assume responsibility for how you administer discipline—in love with a focus on wisely instituting consequences that address heart foolishness. Do *not* assume responsibility for your child's response. Instead, humbly and hopefully pray that your children will respond by growing increasingly like Christ."

In our theme verse—Ephesians 6:4—Paul coaches parents on how to coach their children in the faith: by bringing them up in the instruction of the Lord. The word "instruction" has the idea of training for life, coaching children in the faith.

The apostle John speaks for every Christian parent: "I have no greater joy than to hear that my children are walking in the truth" (3 John 4). Our passion as parents is to pass on the baton of faith to our children, as Lois and Eunice did with Timothy. "I am reminded of your sincere faith, which first lived in your grandmother Lois and in your mother Eunice and, I am persuaded, now lives in you also" (2 Tim. 1:5).

The Big Idea: Parental Coaching Clinic

But what parental practices best encourage children to make parental faith *their* faith, and then to live out their faith in loving worship of God and loving ministry to people? Deuteronomy 6:4–9 provides a parental coaching clinic on:

- *Parental Modeling*: "Hear, O Israel: The LORD our God, the LORD is one. Love the LORD your God with all your heart and with all your soul and with all your strength" (6:4–5).
- *Parental Formal Teaching*: "These commandments that I give you today are to be on your hearts. Impress them on your children" (6:6–7).
- *Parental Informal Training*: "Talk about them when you sit at home and when you walk along the road, when you lie down and when you get up. Tie them as symbols on your hands and bind them on your foreheads. Write them on the doorframes of your houses and on your gates" (6:7–9).

We glean the big idea of mark #5 from this passage:

> *Parents pass on the baton of faith active in love by walking the talk (parental modeling), by relating God's eternal truth to their children's daily lives (parental formal teaching), and by spiritual coaching (parental informal training).*

Walking the Talk: Parental Modeling

We have come full circle—we began our discussion in chapter 1 with Manoah and his wife needing to be God-dependent disciples. Now we turn to Moses, who begins his lesson on parental discipleship by calling on parents to *be disciples*.

Example Precedes Instruction

In Deuteronomy 6:4–5, Moses teaches parents the need to spend time with their children, during which they live out a pattern of Christlikeness that their children can witness, be drawn to, and imitate. How do parents drive out foolishness and instill wisdom? Teaching is part of it, but example must precede instruction.

As parents, we undermine our kids' natural resistance to following Christ by puzzling them with our core commitment to Christ. I recall one rebellious adolescent girl telling me in counseling that she had fought and fought against her parents' faith. But their example of loving her and of loving foster children was something she just could not fight. It was what God used to soften her heart—toward him and toward her parents.

Parental Role Models

What are parents to model? Consider four questions biblical counselors can explore with parents.

1. *How well do I model the joy of relationship with Christ?*
   Is church a chore or a joy? Is time in the Word a deep thirst of my heart or a rule I must follow?

2. *How well do I model a heart relationship with Christ?*
   In my sinful imperfections as a person, spouse, and parent, do my children witness me being a repentant, humble Christ follower? Do they witness any evidence of my panting after God like a deer pants after water?

3. *How well do I model trusting and obeying God?*
   When the layoff comes, when the diagnosis is shared, when the conflict at work arises, while my kids may see my worry, do they also see my prayerful dependence? Do my teens recognize my conviction that God is good even when life is bad?

4. How well do I model sacrificially loving people—including my children?

The apostle John confronts us with the truth of the hypocrisy of saying we love God while we don't love people. Do our kids see us setting a Philippians 2:1–11 example of Christlike, other-centered living?

Relating God's Eternal Truth to Children's Daily Lives: Parental Formal Teaching

Living like Christ without teaching our children about Christlike living is similar to lifestyle evangelism without sharing our faith. Our neighbors may see that there is something different about us, but they may never understand the connection between who we are and who Christ is. In evangelism and in parental discipleship, God calls us to combine our walk and our talk.

Parents Teach As Their Life Arouses Questions

Modeling and teaching go hand in hand. As kids see their parents model a growing Christian life, imperfect though it may be, they become more open to what parents have to say. Some people believe that more is caught (seeing our modeling) than taught (hearing our teaching). Deuteronomy 6:6–7 teaches that the two go together: "These commandments that I give you today are to be on your hearts." Parental modeling—what is caught. Then Moses continues, "Impress them on your children." Parental formal teaching—what is taught.

Imagine you're having dinner and your teen son says, "I heard from Mom that you guys decided not to get the new car and you're giving the money toward the City Life Center's new ministry. But you *really* wanted that car, Dad! What's up with that?" Now is the perfect time to teach about how much Christ sacrificed for us and about how God calls us to live for others . . .

Powerful Parental Teaching Relates God's Story to the Child's Story

When training counselors, I always tell (and show) them that biblical counselors must listen to *two stories*. We listen first to our counselees' painful, troubling earthly story. We hear them well, joining with them, empathizing with them, and understanding what they are going through to the best of our ability. All the while we are also listening to God's eternal story. And we invite our counselees on a journey with us to sense where God is in the story, to ponder what Christ is up to in the story, and to pray about how God's Spirit is leading us to live through and for God in our story.

It's the same with children. Counselors help parents understand that whatever devotional time they have as a family, whatever passage they read together, they always relate truth to life—God's truth to their daily life, God's eternal story to their earthly story.

Counselors disciple parents so that if they are talking with their children about worry, anxiety, and fear from Philippians 4, then the parents talk about their own fears and worries. Then they probe the passage together as a family to explore how God wants each family member to handle those troubling emotions and distressing situations. God tells us to address anxiety by remembering that he is always near (Phil. 4:5), by presenting our requests to God with prayers and petitions with thanksgiving (4:6), by guarding our hearts and minds with the peace of God (4:7), by thinking on what is true (4:8), by putting into practice those truths (4:9), and by reminding one another that the God of peace is always with us (4:9). Counselors demonstrate that in this one passage—powerfully and personally related to a child's fears—parents have a month's worth of devotional time together.

Spiritual Coaching: Parental Informal Training

Many counselors teach parents the importance of parental modeling—walking the talk. Many interact about how vital devotional times are—formal parental teaching. But counselors less frequently discuss the third parental lesson in Deuteronomy 6: passing on the baton of faith—spiritual coaching through informal training.

Discuss Truth in Natural Settings

Right after Moses says to "impress them on your children" (formal teaching), he adds, "Talk about them when you sit at home and when you walk along the road, when you lie down and when you get up." These are informal, ongoing spiritual conversations.

Moses is saying that parents need to keep their eyes open to everyday opportunities to discuss life from God's perspective. As biblical counselors, we might say to parents:

- You're driving home from picking up your daughter at middle school and she starts talking about being bullied. You listen, you care, and you discuss Christ's caring presence . . .

- You're at the zoo and your elementary-age son is amazed at the huge neck of the giraffe. You start discussing the awesome creativity of our amazing Creator . . .

Counselors equip parents to help their children see that all of life is under God's sovereign control and that everything is sacred. Parents communicate that God's Word is all-embracing. There is no neutral ground in life; it is all to be lived for him. Parents want children to learn that God's Word provides sufficient wisdom to address everything they will face. This is why God encourages parents to talk about truth in the dailyness of life.

Give the Gift of Stories

Counselors, families, churches, and Christian schools have a tremendous responsibility for the quality of the stories and images we provide as gifts and guides for children and teens. When our kids were young, we told them "wise and joyful" stories—made-up stories that they were in, with a realistic challenge to face and difficult obstacles to overcome through Christ's strength. As they got older, they read great stories like the Chronicles of Narnia.

Not everything they read or saw was directly Christian. In fact, a great teaching point would be to watch a movie and detect Christian themes, as well as discussing non-Christian messages and what the Bible has to say about them. Wise parents help their children to think about life with wisdom from God's Word. This is what it means for biblical counselors to equip parents to equip their children for life.

Maturing as a Biblical Family Counselor

Equipping for Life

1. The apostle John speaks for every Christian parent when he writes, "I have no greater joy than to hear that my children are walking in the truth" (3 John 4). What would it feel like, look like, and sound like for you as a biblical family counselor to empathize with Christian parents who are experiencing the opposite of this—prodigal children who are not walking in the truth?

2. What would it sound like for you to interact with parents about the three foundational parental discipleship principles outlined in Deuteronomy 6:4–9? Parents pass on the baton of faith active in love by walking the talk (parental modeling), by relating God's eternal truth to their children's daily lives (parental formal teaching), and by spiritual coaching (parental informal training):

   a. Parental modeling

   b. Parental formal teaching

   c. Parental informal training

3. How could you explore these four parental modeling questions with parents?

   a. How well do I model the joy of relationship with Christ?

   b. How well do I model a heart relationship with Christ?

   c. How well do I model trusting and obeying God?

   d. How well do I model sacrificially loving people—including my children?

4. Parents seem to move between the extremes of focusing almost exclusively on formal teaching or on informal training. As a family counselor, how could you help parents to balance both of the following elements of biblical parental discipleship?

   a. Parental formal teaching: relating God's eternal truth to children's daily lives

   b. Parental informal training: spiritual coaching

PART 2

Practical Training for Biblical Family Counselors

How to Develop 22 Family Counseling Relational Competencies

FOUR

Our Family Counseling GPS for Family Suffering, Sin, and Sanctification

Introduction: Bridging Family Theology and Family Counseling

Theology matters. The theology of family life from chapters 1–3 matters. It serves as a foundation for our methodology of biblical family counseling that will unfold in chapters 5–13.

Another vital aspect of family life matters: family suffering, sin, and sanctification. If every parent lived out the five marks of GRACE parenting and if every child responded to such godly parenting in godly ways, then there would be no need for this equipping manual. Sadly, parents and children sin. Which also means that parents and children suffer and need growth in grace—sanctification. In this "bridge" chapter, we explore the nature of family suffering, sin, and sanctification, and the implications these family struggles have on family counseling. All the practical family theology in the world *still needs to be applied in the family counseling relationship*. This is why the subtitle of this book is *An Equipping Guide for Pastors and Counselors*.

As we noted in the book's introduction, individual counseling is messy enough. And family counseling is exponentially messier. So we need a GPS—Gospel Positioning Scripture—wisdom to know where to start and where to head. Biblical family counselors need the prayer Paul prays in Philippians 1:9–11.

> And this is my prayer: that your love may abound more and more in knowledge and depth of insight, so that you may be able to discern what is best and may be

pure and blameless for the day of Christ, filled with the fruit of righteousness that comes through Jesus Christ—to the glory and praise of God.

Picture Mitch and Carla and their thirteen-year-old son, Liam. To observe them at church, they appear to be the all-American family. However, to hear the three of them describe what happens behind closed doors is another story indeed. They cannot get along. The smallest incident—such as cleaning a room to Mom and Dad's specifications—can turn into World War III. If only room cleaning was the only issue. Everything is an issue! Mealtime. Grades. Bedtime. Curfew. Friends. Attitude. Body language. Attire. And that's just the external stuff. Mom and Liam are both so distraught that Liam is dealing with anxiety issues and Carla is struggling with sadness bordering on depression. In their frustration, Dad has punched holes in walls, Mom has thrown the fine china, and Liam has slammed his door so hard it came off its hinges.

What is a biblical counselor to do? Some would advise referring them to outside help. And certainly a team approach is valid and would be valuable. It would be wise for Carla and Liam to see a physician to address any possible medical issue potentially related to their anxiety and depression struggles. Involving advocates, co-counselors, youth pastors, mentors, and friends would all be viable options. But is the final answer really to refer out?

If we do not refer, then where do we start with this family? What are our goals? How do we move from point A to point B . . . or Z? How do we even determine what points B and Z are?

As their family counselor, we need biblical wisdom to know how we can help their love abound more and more in knowledge and depth of insight. We need *a scriptural plan* to help them discern what is best, pure, blameless, righteous, and glorifying to God. We need a GPS that provides a map to guide us as we seek to understand their family dynamics, diagnose their heart issues, and prescribe God's wisdom for their specific family situation.

We also need a family counseling GPS to help us know how to empathize with the pain that each of them is experiencing (chaps. 6–7). We need a scriptural GPS to know how to help them see their troubling family life through the hope-filled lens of Scripture (chaps. 8–9). We need a gospel-centered GPS to know how to see and gently expose sin while encouraging family repentance and reconciliation (chaps. 10–11). And we need a biblical GPS to know how to help them change through Christ—how to relate like Christ, parent like Christ, and be a son who honors Christ and his parents (chaps. 12–13). In this chapter, we introduce you to this biblical family counseling GPS.

Maturing as a Biblical Family Counselor
Bridging Family Theology and Family Counseling

1. None of us have been parented in a home or are parents in a home where the five marks of GRACE parenting are perfectly expressed. However, we can learn from families where "grace is the place."

   a. What family (it could be your family of origin, it could be your home now, it could be a neighbor, coworker, or church member) has seemed to model well (not perfectly) any or all of the five marks of GRACE parenting?

   b. In your experience (either as a pastor or counselor or as an observer of families), which of the five marks of GRACE do parents seem to get right the most? Which do they seem to struggle with more often?

2. In this chapter we are going to address family suffering, family sinning, and family sanctification (growth in grace). Based on your experience as a pastor or counselor or as an observer of families, answer the following questions:

   a. What are some of the greatest areas of family suffering, pain, loss, hurt, and grief?

   b. What are some of the greatest areas of family besetting sin?

   c. Where do most families seem to need the most growth in grace and family sanctification?

3. How could praying Philippians 1:9–11 shape your focus and prepare your heart as a biblical marriage counselor?

4. Where in the world would you start with Mitch, Carla, and Liam? More importantly, what biblical GPS, model, or map would you follow as a guide to counseling them?

Family Suffering, Sin, and Sanctification

Family Suffering

If we are to counsel Mitch, Carla, and Liam, we need to put ourselves *in* their situation and story and *into* their souls—identifying with their deepest suffering. Biblically, what is the deepest suffering of a parent? Of a child? We discover the answers to these questions when we consider a foundational principle:

> *What God calls a parent to offer indicates what*
> *God designed a child to thirst for.*
> *What God calls a child to offer indicates what*
> *God designed a parent to thirst for.*

The Soul Suffering of Parents

In Ephesians 6:1–3, God calls children to offer their parents *honoring love.* In verse 2, Paul chooses a Greek word for honor that means to have an inner attitude of high regard for someone. The Hebrew word for honor that is used in the Old Testament relates to the marketplace and scales. People fixed the value of an item by estimating its weight. Things of value were "weighty." Highly esteemed individuals were regarded as having great worth, significance, and weight. The Old Testament word for dishonor is often translated as "curse," and its root means to take lightly. It implies holding a person in low esteem—they are a "lightweight." When a child dishonors a parent, they are regarding and treating them as small, puny, irrelevant, and insignificant.

"Honor" is a relational word. When a son cursed his father in the Old Testament, he communicated both lack of respect (honor) and lack of relationship (intimacy, love). When children in the New Testament disobeyed their parents, they communicated an attitude of disrespect and disloyalty. *Dishonoring distance* is the opposite of honoring love. Picture the prodigal son disgracing and distancing himself from his father.

God designed parents to thirst for intimacy and respect from their children. Parents do not *demand* this, but they legitimately long for it—for their children to value them, hold them in high regard, be proud of them, and desire close relationship with them. Parents can pursue their heavenly Father as their Spring of Living Water (Jer. 2:13) and yet still be heartbroken by their children. "A wise son brings joy to his father, but a foolish son brings grief to his mother"—meaning anguish that rips the heart apart (Prov. 10:1). Sorrow floods the parent of a foolish child (Prov. 17:21, 25). Shame and disgrace overwhelm the parent of a dishonoring child (Prov. 19:26).

God created parents for the parental paradise of receiving honoring love from their children. Many parents live in the parental desert of receiving dishonoring distance from their children. Created for paradise and living in a desert, parents naturally experience grief and disgrace, emptiness and shame. In chapters 6–7, we will learn how to identify with and enter this parental soul suffering.

The Soul Suffering of Children

We learned from Ephesians 6:4 that God calls parents to offer their children holy love. God designed children to long for unfailing love (Prov. 19:22)—loyal love, holy love. Parents are to bring up their children by rearing them tenderly in the nurture (devotion, love) and instruction (discipline, discipleship, holiness) of the Lord. God designed children to receive parental tenderness and strength, security and stability, care and control, unfailing love and uncompromising holiness.

When they do not receive parental holy love, the Bible says children are prone to become exasperated (Eph. 6:4) and discouraged (Col. 3:21). Exasperated means they are provoked to irritation, resentment, anger, and bitterness. Discouraged means they are goaded to become sullen, morose, disheartened, dispirited, listless, broken in spirit, and losing heart. In chapters 6–7, we will learn how to identify with and enter this soul suffering of children.

Family Sinning

Family sin starts with the failure of parents to offer their children holy love and continues with the failure of children to offer their parents honoring love. James 4 teaches us that the problem is exacerbated by how family members sinfully respond to being sinned against. It is the proverbial vicious cycle. But family sin cannot be addressed until it is acknowledged—by exposing the log in each family member's eye . . .

Exposing the Log in My Eye

Sit a troubled family in front of you, tell them about the lack of holy love and honoring love, and here is what you will hear: "Yes! That's right. Mom and Dad mess up like that all the time!" or "You tell him, Pastor. Liam dishonors us all the time!"

The failure to offer holy love and honoring love are substantial problems in troubled families. Sin's deceitfulness and blindness are substantial obstacles toward progress in family counseling. God calls us to see to it that no one "has a sinful, unbelieving heart that turns away from the living God" (Heb. 3:12). How do we do that as biblical family counselors? By encouraging one another daily so that no one is "hardened by sin's deceitfulness" (Heb. 3:13).

Sin blinds us to our faults, to the log in our own eye, to our sinful role in our family struggles. Parents and children need the light of Scripture to expose their spiritual blindness.

This is a central family counseling issue: parents and children come to us so hurt by each other that they are blind to and deceived about their own family faults. They focus on what their parent or child is doing wrong or not doing right. They mercilessly judge each other. Our calling in family counseling is to help them take the log out of their own eye.

> Why do you look at the speck of sawdust in your [family member's] eye and pay no attention to the plank in your own eye? How can you say to your [family member], "Let me take the speck out of your eye," when all the time there is a plank in your own eye? You hypocrite, first take the plank out of your own eye, and then you will see clearly to remove the speck from your [family member's] eye. (Matt. 7:3–5)

When asked the question "What's the reason for your family problems?" all of us as family members are sinfully hardwired to answer with: "My parents/our children are the cause of our family problem!" "It's him!" "It's her!"

We are all slow to apply Matthew 7:3–5—slow to see the large log in our own eye, and slow to focus on our own issues. Instead, we are quick to see the speck in our family member's eye and quick to focus on them as the root cause of all our family fights and quarrels. When I am more concerned about my family member's issues than my own heart issues, our family will never become a Christlike, Christ-centered home.

What Really Causes Our Family Fights and Quarrels?

In James 4, James asks and answers the pivotal family diagnostic question, "What causes the fights and quarrels among you?" (4:1). The fact that James asks this question indicates that in the midst of family tensions we are poor judges of the root source of our relational conflicts. We need the light of

Scripture to understand the heart issues lurking beneath our family struggles. Consider this family counseling paraphrase of James 4:1–4.

> *What causes your family fights and quarrels?* Don't they come from within *you*—from *your* self-centered demands and *your* sinful responses to *your* unmet parental/child desires that battle within *you*? *You* desire and demand *your* happiness, *your* agenda, *your* kingdom, but *you* do not get what *you* want from *your* parents/child.
>
> In response, *you* covet—*you* manipulate: "I'll do whatever I can to get you to meet my needs." When that doesn't work, in anger and frustration, *you* lash out—*you* retaliate: "You hurt me; I'll hurt you!" But you still can't get what you want.
>
> That's why you quarrel and fight. Your family issues are ultimately rooted in a spiritual issue in *your* heart and in *your* relationship to God. You do not have because you do not ask God *humbly*. Instead, you keep subtly demanding *your* will be done, *your* kingdom come.
>
> Even when you do get around to asking God, you do not receive, because *you* ask with wrong, selfish motives—that you may spend what you get on *your own* pleasures. You become a taker, a consumer, a demander, instead of a sacrificial giver.
>
> You know what that makes you? *A spiritual adulterer!* That's right. You forsake God, your Spring of Living Water, and you try to make your family member come through for you as your messiah. You try to make your parent/child do for you what only God can do, what only the Savior can do—quench the deepest thirsts of your soul. But no family member makes a good savior. So you end up turning to broken cisterns—your imperfect, finite parent/child—who holds no thirst-quenching water.

God's Real and Raw Description of Our Family Warfare

God pulls no punches when he talks about our relational boxing matches. He describes them as fights and quarrels. Revelation 12:7 uses the word "fight" to describe our feverish warfare with Satan. In James 3:13–17, the word depicts evil, bitter, selfish turf wars that are demonically inspired. This is a great reminder to family members that their parent or child is not their enemy; Satan is. God calls parents and children to fight together against Satan.

The word translated as "quarrels" means vicious verbal battles. Paul uses the same word in 2 Timothy 2:23–24 to picture argumentative debates. In John 6:52 it depicts sharp disagreements. Paul uses it again in 2 Corinthians 7:5 to portray harassing conflicts and in Titus 3:9 to highlight hurtful interactions. This sounds familiar to family counselors: verbal battles and debates filled with resentful, sharp, cutting words that hurt, harm, and harass.

God's Insight into Our Family Fights: The Problem in My Family Is *Me*

James answers his own question with a rhetorical question about the source of our fights: "Don't they come from your desires that battle within you?" (4:1). In other words, the problem in my family is *me*!

The battle begins in my heart as I wrestle with who is on the throne of my home—Christ or me.

The home is a battleground between two kingdoms: the kingdom of God and my kingdom of self. Family life is always a war between the kingdom shaped by Christ, with its agenda focused on holiness and glorifying God, versus the kingdom shaped by self, with its agenda focused on my happiness and satisfaction.

I Fight You When I Demand That You Fulfill Illegitimate, Misdirected Desires

James diagnoses two types of family heart sins. First, he points to misdirected, illegitimate desires. This is the meaning of the Greek word for "desire" used in James 4:1—*hedonon*—from which we get our English word "hedonist." In our fallen state, we have an insatiable demand for self-gratification that wages war within our soul. We sinfully corrupt good desires into illegitimate demands.

Think again about Mitch, Carla, and Liam. In counseling with Mitch and Carla, it did not take long to detect that their legitimate desire for Liam to lovingly respect them had morphed into an illegitimate demand that he perfectly obey them so they looked good and felt at peace. Liam could make a million changes—and he tried—but his parents' root issue was not Liam's dishonoring distance (as painful as that was). Their root issue was their demand that their son become their polished trophy that they could show off on the mantel of their parental ego.

In counseling with Mitch and Carla, my goal was *not* to kill their legitimate desire for honoring love. God put that longing into their parental souls (Eph. 6:1–3). My desire was to help them recognize how they had transformed their desire into an illegitimate demand.

I Fight You When I Mishandle My Unmet Legitimate Desires

James, as a biblical soul physician, identifies a second root source of family conflicts: "You covet but you cannot get what you want" (James 4:2). The Greek word translated as "want" is a neutral term that can refer either to legitimate longings or to sinful lusts. In context, James is talking about legitimate, God-designed desires that go unmet. I fight you when I mishandle my unmet legitimate desires. These are not corrupt desires but a corrupt response to unmet desires.

Mitch and Carla legitimately desire Liam's honoring love. When Liam fails to fulfill his biblical calling (Eph. 6:1–3), his parents are going to hurt and thirst. "Hope deferred makes the heart sick"—depleted, empty, weak, faint (Prov. 13:12). In their thirst and emptiness, Mitch and Carla could humbly call out to God, their Spring of Living Water, for his compassion, healing hope, and strength to love sacrificially.

They could recognize that the family is not a container for their happiness. They could be consumed by kingdom thoughts and remind each other, "The home is a receptacle for receiving God's grace and for sacrificially giving Christ's grace. Our broken son is a God-given opportunity to be grace-givers." Or, like a lot of us, they could respond sinfully to the unmet desires and unquenched thirsts of their soul.

Our Sinful Responses to Unmet Family Desires

Put yourself here. Picture it. Feel it.

> I deeply desire something from my child—and it's a legit, biblical desire placed in my soul by God. But I'm not receiving it. My hope is deferred. My heart is depleted. How will my hurting, hungry heart respond to my child and to my Savior?

Sinfully Responding to My Child with Manipulation

James emphasizes two potential sinful responses when we can't get what we want: we kill and we covet (James 4:2). Let's start with the second response—coveting. The Greek word can have a positive meaning, as in desiring or coveting a spiritual gift (1 Cor. 14:1). As it's used here in James, however, it has the negative meaning of jealously, zealously insisting upon, demanding, clinging to, and desperately needing something. When this occurs in our heart, even a good desire can become an idol. To use an image from Jeremiah 2:13, a good desire becomes a broken cistern that holds no water. We foolishly choose our broken family member over God, the Spring of Living Water. We replace the Creator with the creature.

Carla in particular thirsted for her son's respectful love but could not sip a drop of it. In her heart she was saying, "I must have your respectful love in order to survive! I'm not receiving it. Rather than take my emptiness to God, I'm going to demand that you be god for me."

This hints at another aspect of this word "covet." In covetous zeal, I exert myself *on my behalf*. I expend my energy *manipulating* you to meet my need. "I want what I want and I want it now!" Carla imagines and creates an arsenal of manipulative ways to seek to obtain from Liam what her soul desperately longs for.

Sinfully Responding to My Family with Retaliation

James says we not only manipulate, we also retaliate—we kill! In 1 John 3:15, John links the word "kill" with murderous hatred, a seething rage. We might imagine Mitch, Carla, and Liam each secretly thinking, "No matter what I do, I can't get you to come through for me. Fine! See if I'll come through for you. You've hurt me. Now it's your turn to feel the pain!"

I am not suggesting that most family members have a clear awareness of this underlying agenda. Remember that sin blinds and deceives us. Only the Word of God used by the Spirit of God through the people of God can melt hardened hearts and give sight to blind eyes.

What has James taught us? Our family expectations are not rooted in the gospel. They are rooted in self. My unstated and sometimes unrecognized family expectation is that my family member will make me happy, make me feel good about me.

Sinfully Responding to My Savior with Idolatry

James now guides us on a vital mindset shift. Ultimately, *our sin in our home is due to sin in our heart*. Our sin against one another is eventually traceable to sin against God. Our social sin flows from our spiritual sin. "You do not have, because you do not ask God" (James 4:2). "Ask" is the key word. It means to humbly ask on loan, to ask submissively.

We do not ask God, because we think we can self-sufficiently manipulate others into meeting our needs. We do not ask God, because we go back to the first sin in the garden—we doubt God's good heart. We imagine God to be a thou-shalt-not god who is withholding something good that we need and desire (Gen. 3:1–3).

My biggest problem in my family is me—putting myself on the throne of my kingdom of self and trusting myself more than I trust God.

Sinfully Responding to My Savior with Carnality

According to James, when we do finally get around to asking God, we ask amiss. "When you ask, you do not receive, because you ask with wrong motives, that you may spend what you get on your pleasures" (James 4:3). The Greek word *kakos*, translated as "wrong motives," means impure, corrupt, carnal motives. James is indicating that most of our family prayers are hedonistic, carnal, and self-serving, rather than other-centered and God-glorifying. Rather than living a life of ministry, we live family life as a consumer. Our belly has become our god (Rom. 16:18; Phil. 3:19).

James is teaching me that I do not need to be rescued from my family. *I need to be rescued from myself!* I need to be rescued from my self-centered, demanding, carnal heart.

Sinfully Responding to My Savior with Spiritual Adultery

In verse 4, James moves to imagery that seems out of context, unless we are versed in the Old Testament portrayal of sin as spiritual adultery. "You adulterous people, don't you know that friendship with the world means enmity toward God? Therefore, anyone who chooses to be a friend of the world becomes an enemy of God" (James 4:4).

When I demand that my family member be god for me, I have become a false worshiper. I love my family more than I love God. Or perhaps more accurately, I think I *need* my family more than I need God. Spiritual adultery is my frantic, frustrated effort to survive and thrive without needing God. Who seems better equipped to quench my thirst than my family? But family members make horrible God substitutes. Even at their best, parents and children are broken cisterns that can hold no water. They pale in comparison to God, the Spring of Living Water (Jer. 2:13). The root source of my family fight is my flight from God and my fight with God.

Family Sanctification: God's Prescription for Family Harmony— Relational Repentance

James, inspired by God, clearly gets the cause of our fights and quarrels. He also understands God's prescription for family harmony. Family conflict will be halted only by repentance of the self sins: selfishness, self-sufficiency, and self-trust.

This is why James transitions from spiritual adultery to the scriptural truth that "God opposes the proud but gives grace to the humble" (James 4:6 ESV). When we see that our demanding heart is the core problem in our home, then we become *desperate for Christ's grace*. Then we begin to look at our family member with *grace eyes*. And we begin to realize that *there is no family problem so deep that the grace of Jesus isn't deeper*.

Teaching on family responsibilities, roles, and communication falls not simply on deaf ears but on cold hearts, unless those hearts are thawed by Spirit-prompted repentance.

> Come near to God and he will come near to you. Wash your hands, you sinners, and purify your hearts, you double-minded. Grieve, mourn and wail. Change your laughter to mourning and your joy to gloom. Humble yourselves before the Lord, and he will lift you up. (James 4:8–10)

This is relational repentance—coming near to God. It is the spiritually adulterous parent or child returning to God. It is the prodigal son coming to his senses and returning to the Father. Repentance is a *change of relationship*—relational return to God as our refreshing Spring of Living Water.

Maturing as a Biblical Family Counselor
Family Suffering, Sin, and Sanctification

1. Regarding family suffering:

    a. When parents receive dishonoring love from their children, they experience grief and disgrace, emptiness and shame. How would you seek to empathize with and comfort hurting parents?

    b. When children do not receive parental holy love, they become exasperated and discouraged, provoked to irritation, anger, and resentment, and goaded to be sullen, disheartened, and dispirited. How would you seek to empathize with and comfort hurting children? How would you seek to equip parents to empathize with and comfort their hurting children?

2. James teaches two core truths about family conflict: I fight you when I demand that you fulfill my illegitimate, misdirected desires, and I fight you when I mishandle my unmet legitimate desires.

    a. Share illustrations of each of these types of responses—from your family life or from your family counseling experiences.

    b. Role-play or write out a scenario involving each of these sinful family responses. How do you provide biblical family counseling in each scenario?

3. James teaches three central ways we sin against God: idolatry, carnality, and spiritual adultery.

    a. Share illustrations of each of these types of responses—from your family life or from your family counseling experiences.

    b. Role-play or write out a scenario involving each of these sinful family responses. How do you provide biblical family counseling in each scenario?

Where do we start with Mitch, Carla, and Liam? Any wise counselor is going to say we start by listening to their story. Agreed. Assume that we have done that. Then any biblical counselor would say we focus on their heart issues, not just on surface behavioral matters. Agreed. But whose heart issues do we focus on first? And which heart issues—the heart of their hurt and their suffering? Or the heart of their hurting each other and their sinning? What is our biblical guide?

Two Guideposts for Biblical Family Counseling

In *Gospel-Centered Family Counseling*, we follow a GPS derived from God's Word and the history of Christian soul care. It provides two guideposts and four compass points for biblical family counseling.

Our biblical approach to family counseling will address both family suffering and family sin, both hurting hearts and hard hearts, both comforting and confronting. In the words of Frank Lake, "Pastoral care is defective unless it can deal *thoroughly* with the evils we have suffered as well as with the sins we have committed."[1]

Guidepost #1: Biblical Family Counseling for Suffering

Clearly, Mitch, Carla, and Liam are each suffering. What does the Bible offer them in their family pain? Among the many New Testament words for spiritual care, *parakaleo* ("to comfort, encourage, or console") predominates, appearing 109 times. In 2 Corinthians 1:3–11, Paul pictures God as the Father of compassion and the God of all comfort (a noun form of the verb *parakaleo*). Paul then teaches that the best comforters are those who go to God for comfort: "who comforts us in all our troubles, *so that* we can comfort those in any trouble with the comfort we ourselves receive from God" (2 Cor. 1:4).

The word *parakaleo* emphasizes personal presence—one called alongside to help. It also highlights the idea of empathy and suffering with another person or a family—weeping with those who weep (Rom. 12:15). The English word "comfort," when broken down, pictures well the biblical idea: co-fortitude. Shared sorrow is endurable sorrow.

In parakaletic family counseling, we seek to turn Mitch, Carla, and Liam's desolation into consolation through hope in God. The word "encouragement," when broken down, pictures the idea well: en-courage—to put courage into. Encouragers come alongside to help struggling, suffering family members through personal presence coupled with scriptural wisdom that directs the family's gaze and focus to God's eternal perspective.

When Christ ascended, he sent the Holy Spirit to be our *Parakletos*—our Comforter and Advocate called alongside to encourage and help us in times of suffering, trouble, grief, injustice, and hardship. The Spirit performs his ministry by being in us and by revealing truth to us (John 14:16–17). As the Spirit of Truth, his ministry is the exact opposite of Satan's, who is the father of lies (John 8:44). Satan is called the accuser (Rev. 12:10), and his core strategy is to speak lying words of condemnation to us. The Spirit is called Encourager and Advocate, and his ministry is to speak gospel truth in love about our justification and reconciliation in Christ.

Think about what Paul is saying to *you*. You don't need a PhD in family systems therapy to become a competent parakaletic family counselor. You have the resource planted within you—the *Parakletos*, the Holy Spirit—so that you can comfort and encourage Mitch, Carla, and Liam to hope in God and believe that God is good even when their family life is bad.

Guidepost #2: Biblical Family Counseling for Sin

In Romans 15:14, Paul says that the Christians in Rome are competent to counsel, instruct, and disciple. Here he uses a form of the Greek word *noutheteo*, which occurs eleven times in the New Testament. Jay Adams, the founder of the National Association of Nouthetic Counselors (now the Association of Certified Biblical Counselors), describes nouthetic counseling as "confronting for change out of concern."[2]

Noutheteo emphasizes inner heart change leading to relational change. The foundational meaning of the word comes from the root *noeo*, meaning to direct one's mind, to perceive, and from *nous*, which refers to the heart, the mind, the seat of spiritual, rational, and moral insight and action. The mind is the place of practical reason leading to moral action. The stress is not merely on the intellect but also on motivation and affections. *Noutheteo* means to impart understanding, to set right, to lay on the heart. Nouthetic impartation of truth can take on many forms, such as encouraging, urging, spurring on, teaching, reminding, admonishing, reconciling, guiding, and advising.

Paul uses *noutheteo* in Colossians 1:20–29 to describe one aspect of his multifaceted pastoral ministry. God commissioned him to present Christ's gospel of grace to people (1:20–25), infusing people with the hope of who they are in Christ (1:26–27), with the goal of presenting them mature in Christ (1:28), through personal, passionate, persistent involvement in their lives (1:28–29), by Christ's resurrection power (1:29).

Paul is saying in Romans 15:14 that believers like you are competent to disciple family members like Mitch, Carla, and Liam toward communion with Christ and conformity to Christ through the personal ministry of the Word—biblical family counseling. Through loving nouthetic ministry, they can internalize the truth that God is gracious even when their family relationships

Comprehensive and Compassionate Biblical Family Counseling

Parakaletic Biblical Family Counseling for Suffering Family Members

- **Sustaining**: Like Christ, we care about each other's hurts.
- **Healing**: Through Christ, it's possible for us to hope in God together.

Nouthetic Biblical Family Counseling for Sinning Family Members

- **Reconciling**: It's horrible to sin against Christ and each other, but through Christ it's wonderful to be forgiven and to forgive.
- **Guiding**: It's supernatural to love each other like Christ, through Christ, and for Christ.

are sinful and that his grace that saves is also his grace that sanctifies and changes their family.

Four Compass Points for Biblical Family Counseling

While family counseling can be complex and messy, we will keep our GPS as simple as possible. As a map has the four compass points of north, south, east, and west, so our biblical family counseling model has the four compass points of sustaining, healing, reconciling, and guiding. Figure 4.1 illustrates this for us.[3] For each of our compass points, we will first explore what it looks like in individual counseling. Then we will make the transition to what it looks like in family counseling.

Biblical Compass Point #1—Sustaining: "Like Christ, we care about each other's hurts."

Sustaining involves joining with others in their suffering—comforting them as we weep with them. We grieve together, empathizing with them and compassionately identifying with them in their pain. Sustaining gives the other person permission to grieve. It communicates the biblical truth that *it's normal to hurt* when our fallen world falls on us. Sustaining enters the other person's troubling earthly story of suffering and despair.

I use a rather macabre image to capture the essence of sustaining ministry: *climbing in the casket*. I have developed this picture from 2 Corinthians 1, where Paul says he does not want his brothers and sisters in Christ to be ignorant about the hardships he had suffered. Paul writes, "We were under great pressure, far beyond our ability to endure, so that we despaired of life itself.

Indeed, we felt we had received the sentence of death" (2 Cor. 1:8–9). When Paul despaired of life and felt the sentence of death, he wanted the Corinthians to climb in his casket—to identify with what felt like a death sentence.

It is important that we learn to offer Mitch, Carla, and Liam our sustaining comfort. However, remember a vital principle that we will repeat often: *family counseling is not individual counseling with an audience.* If Mitch and Carla watch me comfort Liam, and then Liam watches me sustain his parents, that's good—but it's not best (remember Phil. 1:9–11). What is best is when they begin to communicate to each other, *"Like Christ, we care about each other's hurts."* Ponder how extraordinary that is. The three of them have been at each other's throats. They are causing each other's hurt. They are focused almost exclusively on their own pain. But in Christ, they can move to deep heart change where they start caring deeply about each other's pain—pain they have often caused.

Recall two of our premises for family counseling: (1) Children need good parenting more than they need good counseling. (2) Parents should be their children's best biblical counselor. The onus, responsibility, and privilege of family sustaining and comforting should fall first and foremost *on the parents.* We seek to empower the parents to start the chain of empathy. The age and maturity of the children in the home will factor into our level of expectation that a child empathizes with parents.

In chapters 6 and 7, we will learn biblical family counseling competencies that can help family members climb in each other's casket, give each other permission to grieve, and weep with each other. They will become each other's best parakaletic biblical counselor by sustaining each other in Christ through restoring each other's trust in the Father of compassion. We do this by asking ourselves the sustaining question, "How can I help this family find their gospel comfort in Christ so they can comfort each other?"

Biblical Compass Point #2—Healing: "Through Christ, it's possible for us to hope in God together."

In biblical counseling through healing, we journey with sufferers to Christ, encouraging them to live today in light of Christ and his eternal hope. When bad things happen to God's people, Satan attempts to crop Christ out of the picture. He tempts families like Liam, Carla, and Mitch to conclude, "Our home is bad. God is sovereign. So God must be bad too." God calls us to *crop Christ into their picture.* We have the privilege of journeying with Liam, Carla, and Mitch so they listen together to God's eternal story of healing hope in Christ alone. We move with them to the place where they can say with conviction, "Life is bad, but God is good. He's good *all* the time—the cross of Christ forever proves this."

To balance the sustaining image of climbing in the casket, I capture the essence of healing ministry with *celebrating the empty tomb*. Earlier we read 2 Corinthians 1:8–9. I purposefully stopped before the end of verse 9. Paul continues, "But this happened that we might not rely on ourselves but on God, who raises the dead." Paul does not remain in the casket, because Jesus did not remain in the tomb. Because of Christ's resurrection, it is always possible to hope!

Consider again the subtle yet vital mindset shift we must make in family counseling compared to individual counseling. Liam, Carla, and Mitch meet with me one hour a week, which means they are apart from me the other 167 hours in the week. It is not enough for me to be the one who points each of them individually to Christ's healing hope.

This is why, in chapters 8 and 9, we will learn biblical family counseling competencies that will help family members say, *"Through Christ, it's possible for us to hope in God together."* They must become each other's biblical en-couragers—putting Christ's courage into their dis-couraged hearts and dis-couraged marriage. What an amazing change this is. Liam, Carla, and Mitch have been crushing each other's hearts. Now, we have the joyful privilege of equipping them to be soul physicians for each other—doing open heart surgery on each other and infusing each other with hope in God! We do this by asking ourselves the healing question, How can I help this family find their gospel encouragement in Christ so they can encourage each other?

Biblical Compass Point #3—Reconciling: "It's horrible to sin against Christ and each other, but through Christ it's wonderful to be forgiven and to forgive."

People come to us not only hurting but also hurtful. They not only need biblical comfort and encouragement through parakaletic sustaining and healing; they also need biblical discipline and discipleship through nouthetic reconciling and guiding.

In reconciling, God calls us to expose sin humbly yet firmly—speaking gospel truth in love (Eph. 4:15). Like the early Christians, we are aware of the deceitfulness of sin, so we commit to being sure that no one has a sinful, unbelieving heart that turns away from the living God (Heb. 3:7–19). Like the prophet Nathan did with King David, we have the ability to paint pictures that say, "You are the one! See your sin in all its horrors!" Like the Puritans, we are able, when necessary, to load the conscience with guilt so that hard hearts are softened by God's Spirit of truth.

Biblical reconciling does not stop with the exposure of heart sin. God also calls us to be skillful at magnifying grace—to communicate that where sin abounds, grace mega-abounds (Rom. 5:20). We not only communicate that it's horrible to sin but also convey that it's wonderful to be forgiven. In biblical reconciling, we communicate that God is gracious to us, even when we are sinful. We don't just load the conscience with guilt; like the Puritans, we lighten the conscience with grace.

To communicate reconciling, I use the image of every Christian as a *dispenser of grace*. Grace is God's medicine of choice for our sin. Grace is God's prescription for our disgrace.

What does this look like in *family* counseling? In chapters 10 and 11, we will learn biblical family counseling competencies that will help family members like Carla, Mitch, and Liam confess their sin to Christ and to each other, receive Christ's forgiveness, and forgive each other. In addition to each of them realizing that it's horrible to sin, they communicate to each other that *it's horrible to sin against Christ and each other.* They begin to take the family mote out of their eye (Matt. 7:1–5) and begin to accept responsibility for their own sinful responses (James 4:1–4). Because they each have been recipients of Christ's great grace, they also begin communicating to each other that *through Christ, it's wonderful to be forgiven and to forgive.*

Nothing is more wonderful than watching Christ's amazing grace melt the hurting and hard hearts of family members. We do this by asking ourselves the reconciling question, How can I help this family find their gospel restoration in Christ so they can forgive each other, reconcile with each other, and have their family restored in Christ?

Again, the greatest responsibility for this depth of repentance and forgiveness falls upon the parents. As they become living models of receiving and giving Christ's grace, they richly impact their children for Christ.

Biblical Compass Point #4—Guiding: "It's supernatural to love each other like Christ, through Christ, and for Christ."

In biblical guiding, we help people discern how God empowers them to put off the old sinful ways and put on the new ways of the new person in Christ. We help them practice the biblical spiritual disciplines that connect them with Christ's resurrection power (Phil. 3:10). We assist them in thinking through the implications of their identity in Christ and what Christ has already done for them (the gospel indicatives), and the implications of commands to obey Christ out of gratitude for grace (the gospel imperatives). We practice what first-century Christians practiced in spurring one another on to love and good deeds (Heb. 10:19–25).

In family counseling, we help family members live out the truth that *it's supernatural to love each other like Christ, through Christ, for Christ.* Their family love reflects Christ's love, their love is empowered by Christ, and their love has glorifying Christ as its ultimate goal. The grace that saves them is also the grace that empowers them to grow. Their growth in grace involves responding to and availing themselves of Christ's resurrection power—the same power that raised Christ from the grave is in them (Eph. 1:15–23; Phil. 3:10).

The picture I use for guiding is *fanning into flame the gift of God*. Our role is not to place power within our counselees. Our role is to stir up and fan into flame the gift of God *already* in them, just as Paul stirred up the gift of God in Timothy (2 Tim. 1:6–7).

In chapters 12 and 13, we will learn biblical family counseling competencies that will help parents like Mitch and Carla be their children's spiritual directors. They equip each other to put on the full family armor of God so that instead of fighting each other, together they fight against Satan—in Christ's strength. Through the Spirit's power they live out Ephesians 6:1–4 by loving each other like Christ. We do this by asking the guiding question, How can I help this family discover and apply gospel wisdom from Christ and his Word so they can discern together what is best and pure and glorifying to Christ?

Family Counseling as "Spaghetti Relationships"

Reviewing our GPS, you might think family counseling is a nice, neat, easy, linear process where you quickly move directly from sustaining, to healing, to reconciling, to guiding. That's not the case.

I often call counseling "spaghetti relationships." It is mixed up and messy. Yes, sustaining, healing, reconciling, and guiding provide a comprehensive map or GPS. However, the trek, the family counseling journey, is filled with detours, mountains, valleys, road closures, obstacles, and even accidents. So do not imagine a straight line and do not see sustaining, healing, reconciling, and guiding as a straitjacket. View family counseling as a creative and artistic endeavor led by the Spirit as you and the family dance together.

Maturing as a Biblical Family Counselor
Our Biblical Family Counseling GPS

1. Regarding the *two guideposts*: We all tend to be a tad more inclined toward focusing on either comforting the suffering or confronting the sinning. Which are you more inclined toward? How could you further develop your skillfulness in the other?

---

2. Regarding the *four compass points*: We all tend to be a tad more inclined toward one of these four: sustaining, healing, reconciling, or guiding. Which are you more inclined toward? How could you further develop your competencies in the other three?

3. Family counseling is not individual counseling with an audience. This means our calling as biblical family counselors is not just to sustain, heal, reconcile, and guide each family member. Instead, we are to *equip them* (especially the parents) to sustain, heal, reconcile, and guide *each other*. You will develop these skills in subsequent chapters. So respond to the following questions based on your current understanding and competency.

   a. "Like Christ, we care about each other's hurts." How important do you think it is to help family members (especially parents) live this out? How hard do you think this will be? What skills do you think you need to develop?

   b. "Through Christ, it's possible for us to hope in God together." How important do you think it is to help family members (especially parents) live this out? How hard do you think this will be? What skills do you think you need to develop?

   c. "It's horrible to sin against Christ and each other, but through Christ it's wonderful to be forgiven and to forgive." How important do you think it is to help family members (especially parents) live this out? How hard do you think this will be? What skills do you think you need to develop?

   d. "It's supernatural to love each other like Christ, through Christ, and for Christ." How important do you think it is to help family members (especially parents) live this out? How hard do you think this will be? What skills do you think you need to develop?

CHAPTER

FIVE

Infusing HOPE in the Midst of Hurt

Resurrection-Focused Family Counseling

Introduction: Informing or Infusing Hope?

When Kevin and Melissa stopped me after a church service, I could see the exhaustion in their eyes. After listening for just a few minutes, I was exhausted too. Their family was in chaos. Not the chaos of teens struggling with addiction or being promiscuous. This was the chaos of three undisciplined, out-of-control children ages seven and under.

"Our kids are running our home," Melissa shared with exasperation in her voice. "We've read all the right books. We've been to parenting seminars hosted by experts. We pray about it. We try discipline. We try everything. Nothing is working. Can you help us?"

By then we had made our way to my church office. We didn't have a lot of time that morning. I prayed with Melissa and Kevin. I empathized with their frustrations and concerns. Then I think I surprised them. "When can the six of us meet together this week?"

Kevin's jaw dropped. Then he spoke. "Pastor Bob, you want us to bring our children—ages seven, five, and three—*with us* to the counseling appointment? You heard our description, right?"

"Yes, I heard your description. And yeah, I would like you to bring your children. If it's chaotic, then at least I'll get a firsthand picture . . ."

When the six of us met three days later—it was chaotic. I certainly gained an up-close-and-personal look at what Kevin and Melissa were experiencing, what their parenting was like, and how their children responded (for better or worse) to their parents' parenting (or lack thereof).

My guess is you would love to hear exactly how I counseled Melissa and Kevin. However, my purpose for introducing them to you is more focused. Melissa and Kevin were at their wits' end. Yes, they needed counsel in terms of wisdom and guidance. But they also needed hope. Recall that they had read all the parenting books and gone to all the seminars. They had *info*. Like many families at the start of counseling, they needed an *infusion of hope*. In this chapter we learn how to infuse HOPE for families like Melissa, Kevin, and their three young children.

H Having Hope as a Family Counselor

O Offering Hope to Hurting Families

P Prompting Parents to Tap into God-Given Resources

E Encouraging the Family to See Signs of Christ on the Move

Maturing as a Biblical Family Counselor
Informing or Infusing Hope?

1. Imagine that you heard this scenario: "Our kids our running our home. We've read all the right books. We've been to parenting seminars hosted by experts. We pray about it. We try discipline. We try everything. Nothing is working. Can you help us?" What would be running through your mind?

2. Where would you start with Kevin and Melissa? What would you listen for? What would be the focus of your initial sharing?

3. Would you have counseled Melissa and Kevin alone, or would you have brought the whole (chaotic) family into the session(s)? Why or why not?

4. When you see broken family after broken family—whether it is abusive parents, prodigal young adults, promiscuous teens, or out-of-control young children—how do *you* maintain *your* hope in God? How do you keep from becoming discouraged or overwhelmed?

Having Hope as a Family Counselor

I have counseled families for almost four decades now. I have not seen it all, but I have seen a lot. I have counseled families like Kevin and Melissa's, with children out of control and parents unable to shepherd. But I have seen much worse, much more difficult, much more devastating and disheartening family situations: sibling sexual abuse, parental sexual abuse, or sexual abuse by a non-family member; parental physical abuse; young children with inconsolable fears and uncontrollable phobias; very young children with anger and rage that is shocking; depressed and suicidal teens; depressed and suicidal moms; physical altercations between parents and teens; the death of a parent or child; addicted or enslaved family members; families crushed by infidelity; hurting families with loved ones who are cutting, self-harming, or battling eating disorders. You get the picture.

So why address all of this? Why introduce such family pain? Because we need to be honest and candid. The family counselor can feel overwhelmed and overcome. This is why our starting point is having hope as a family counselor.

Family counseling begins long before we first meet the family—any family. Our family counseling starts with *us*—with our attitude toward God, life, and families. To infuse hope, we must have hope in God.

We live the narrative we believe. Do we believe the Bible's grand redemptive narrative of creation-fall-redemption-consummation? If we do, then we know that though families sin because of the fall, God can and does redeem families in this life, and he does promise a final, glorious consummation in the next life. God's redemptive narrative is a hope-filled, resurrection-focused narrative.

None of this denies the reality of sin and the fall. Biblical counselors grasp the horrors and ugliness and evil of the fall's impact on families. We do not pretend. We never wink at sin. Still, we never stop at sin, because God does not stop there.

If we believe that sin superabounds above grace, then we will see only family problems and failure. On the other hand, if we believe that where sin abounds, Christ's grace superabounds (Rom. 5:20), then we will see life through eyes filled with redemptive hope and resurrection power.

If we believe that life, suffering, and sin are just too intense and too ingrained in some families, then we will see life only through problem-saturated lenses. On the other hand, if we believe that God is faithful and therefore will provide a way to bear, endure, and triumph even in family temptation (1 Cor. 10:13), then we will see family problems as God's opportunity to reveal more of his grace and power.

If we believe that family life is so bad that it negates the goodness of God and his good purposes, then we will despair of ever helping distraught families. On the other hand, if we believe that God is good and that he is a rewarder and not a hoarder of his good gifts (Heb. 11:6), then we will seek to see how we can stir up and fan into flame the gifts of God within each family member (2 Tim. 1:6–7).

When families approach us with their family horror stories, in addition to feeling deep pain with them, we can be asking *ourselves* questions filled with resurrection hope, such as:

- What is God up to in this family? What great redemptive work is he planning to do? How may God be weaving good out of evil (Gen. 50:20) and be creating beauty from ashes (Isa. 61:1–3)?
- Through Christ's strength (Phil. 4:13, 19), what do these parents have to offer each other? What do they have to offer their children?
- What unique resources do these parents possess from God that I can fan into flame (2 Tim. 1:6–7) to empower them to encourage their kids?
- In what specific ways has God fearfully and wonderfully made this family (Ps. 139:13–18) with just the right mixture of gifts and personalities so that they can become a unique reflection of his grace?
- God has called me to minister to this family for such a time as this (Esther 4:14). What unique resources, biblical wisdom, and ministry and family life experiences is God wanting to draw out of me so that I can minister his grace to them?
- Hmm . . . the very fact that they have contacted me tells me that they have not given up all hope. I wonder how they have cooperated with God to maintain hope in the midst of their family turmoil . . .

Maturing as a Biblical Family Counselor
Having Hope as a Family Counselor

1. If you have already started your ministry as a family counselor, describe (confidentially) some of the most horrific and disheartening family situations you have faced. If you have yet to do any family counseling, describe (confidentially) some of the most horrific and disheartening family situations you have been aware of (or perhaps experienced yourself).

2. Reflecting back on your answer to question 1, how have you been able to hope in God even in the midst of those horrible family situations?

3. As you focus on hoping in God, remember that God helps us to grasp his love and power *together with all the saints* (Eph. 3:16–21). Family counselors need encouragers. Who are your Ephesians 3:16–21 and Hebrews 10:24–25 encouragers?

4. How could God's Spirit use passages like Genesis 50:20; Esther 4:14; Psalm 139:13–18; Isaiah 61:1–3; Romans 5:20; 1 Corinthians 10:13; Ephesians 3:16–21; Philippians 4:13, 19; 2 Timothy 1:6–7; and Hebrews 11:6 to help you hope in God as you counsel troubled and broken families?

5. What additional passages and biblical principles do you cling to (or could you begin clinging to) in order to keep having hope as a biblical family counselor?

Hurting families need *empathetic encouragement* (you will learn more about this concept in chapters 6–9 under family sustaining and healing). Empathy communicates that I hear your hurt and I hurt with you in your hurt. Encouragement conveys that even in the midst of your hurt, you can find God's hope and help, his comfort and power.

If a hurting family comes to you and you encourage them without empathizing with them, they will feel unheard. They will see you as a pie-in-the-sky counselor. They will perceive you to be so heavenly minded that you are of no earthly good.

If a hurting family comes to you and you empathize with them without ever encouraging them, they will feel heard but likely will still feel hopeless. They may see you as caring but lacking in a God perspective. They may perceive you as so earthly minded as to be of no heavenly good.

Hurting families need empathetic encouragement—hope in the midst of their hurt. We infuse hope through interactions that acknowledge the pain and problems (empathy) while directing families to God's powerful personal presence (encouragement).

Infusing Hope throughout Counseling

When do you infuse hope? In one sense, *always*. It is not a stage in counseling. It is a biblical mindset of compassionate faith—a faith that feels pain while sensing God's personal presence.

Recall the image in chapter 4 of family counseling as spaghetti relationships. It is messy, mixed up. Counseling is not neat and linear. So empathetic encouragement is not something we offer at the onset of counseling and then set aside. While vital at the start of family counseling, infusing hope through empathetic encouragement never goes out of style, which is why we will revisit this competency several times in chapters 6–9.

Infusing Hope during Initial Contacts through Trialogues

A hurting family contacts you. You listen, empathize, pray, and arrange a first meeting. Your first contact is almost over and your first meeting may not be for a week. How do you leave them? What concrete acts of hope can they participate in?

To answer these questions, I need to introduce the concept of *trialogues*. One of the great advantages of the personal ministry of the Word (biblical counseling) is the ability to engage in back-and-forth conversations about how biblical principles and scriptural passages relate to life. I call these trialogues.

In a monologue, I speak to the counselee or family. In a dialogue, we talk to each other. But in a trialogue, there are three conversation partners: me, the counselee/family, and God through his Word. Trialogues are another way of picturing gospel conversations—we converse about the difference the gospel and Scripture make in the particulars of a family relationship. I encourage the use of two types of trialogues.

- *Spiritual Conversation Trialogues*: We engage the family members in thinking about the application of relevant scriptural principles.
- *Scriptural Exploration Trialogues*: We engage the family members in discussing specific application of pertinent biblical passages.

Consider two example trialogues we could engage in with Melissa and Kevin right after our brief meeting in the church sanctuary and then in my pastoral counseling office.

- Many parents and families report that the act of asking for help starts a positive chain reaction. It's a biblical principle. When we are weak, then in Christ we are strong. God gives grace to the humble. God hears the cry of the needy. So, over the next few days, I want the two of you to be on the lookout for and jot down any positive changes in your family relationship that God is helping you to make.

This trialogue focused on pondering and applying scriptural principles: spiritual conversation.

After we agreed to meet (all six of us!) that coming Wednesday evening, I asked them to search God's Word related to their family situation. I then engaged them in a trialogue focused on exploring and applying a specific biblical passage—scriptural exploration.

- Between now and Wednesday, jot down the passages you've been exploring. And jot down where you see God's love, concern, comfort, and compassion for each of you and for your family. Also jot down the promises God gives you in his Word that you can begin claiming and applying . . .

Infusing Hope through Initial Paperwork

While a detailed Personal Information Form (PIF) is very helpful, I have found that hurting families often do not have the mental or emotional energy to share such exhaustive information before the first meeting. Plus, in some church cultures, the idea of completing a lengthy form before getting to talk to a pastor feels too clinical. So I typically reserve the longer PIF for after

> ### Figure 5.1
>
> ## Family Counseling Goals and Focus: Parents
>
> 1. What are the top two or three areas in **your** heart, actions, attitude, and way of relating to your children that **you** want help changing so that you can be more Christlike and your family relationships can be more Christ-honoring?
> 2. What are the top two or three strengths that you see **in each of your children** that you want to affirm?
> 3. What are the top two or three aspects **of your family life** that you want help changing so that your family can be more Christ-honoring?
> 4. Please read **Ephesians 3:14–21**. Let's create a **vision** for your family based on that passage.
>   a. Think ahead three months. As God does exceedingly, abundantly above all that you could ask or imagine in your heart and in your family, what **two or three amazing changes are you envisioning, praying for, and hoping for**?
>   b. What **needs to happen** in **your heart** and in **your family relationships** so that through Christ's strength these amazing changes start to occur?
> 5. What else do you want us to know, think about, or focus on in our times together?

our first meeting. Before our first meeting, I ask the parents each to complete a one-page, five-question sheet (Family Counseling Goals and Focus Form) and return it to me before we meet. See figure 5.1 for the five questions I ask parents. On the actual form, each question leaves space for a one-paragraph response. If the family issue includes teens, they complete figure 5.2.

I have yet to have a family member not complete this form. I have found that this form alone gives us enough to interact about for weeks of resurrection-focused family counseling. Notice a few aspects of the Family Counseling Goals and Focus Form:

- It starts with the mote in their eye (question 1): "the top two or three areas in *your* heart." Family members come to us focused on the faults of their children or parents. Question 1 focuses first on one's own issues.
- It starts with an assumption of change and growth: "that *you* want help changing."
- It starts with a Christ-centered focus: "so that you can be more Christlike and your family relationships can be more Christ-honoring."

Figure 5.2

Family Counseling Goals and Focus: Adolescents

1. What are the top two or three areas in **your** heart, actions, attitude, and way of relating to your parents that **you** want help changing so that you can be more Christlike and your family relationships can be more Christ-honoring?

2. What are the top two or three strengths or positive characteristics that you see **in your parents** that you want to affirm?

3. What are the top two or three aspects **of your family life** that you want help changing so that your family can be more Christ-honoring?

4. Please read **Ephesians 3:14–21**. Let's create a **vision** for your family based on that passage.

   a. Think ahead three months. As God does exceedingly, abundantly above all that you could ask or imagine in your heart and in your family, what **two or three amazing changes are you envisioning, praying for, and hoping for**?

   b. What **needs to happen** in **your heart** and in **your family relationships** so that through Christ's strength these amazing changes start to occur?

5. What else do you want us to know, think about, or focus on in our times together?

- It asks for strengths to affirm in one's children or parents (question 2). Even in the messiest families, family members have always been able to identify some strengths in their children or parents.
- It does *not* ignore problems (question 3). It asks for the top two or three family problems that each family member wants us to address.
- It casts a future vision by asking the Ephesians 3:14–21 question about what God can do in their family above all that they ask or imagine (question 4a). This is the most important, hope-inducing question on the form. I have never had a family member—including teens—be unable to answer this.
- It connects Christ's strength and their heart change as the biblical foundation for family hope (question 4b).

Infusing Hope during the First or Early Counseling Meetings

You will find additional vignettes and illustrations of empathetic encouragement in subsequent chapters. Here are examples that are particularly helpful in early meetings.

- What you're describing has to be excruciating. Yet here you are asking for help. How have you and your family members found the strength to keep clinging to Christ in the midst of all of this?
- From everything you've described, you all have been enduring this for some time. I've heard people describe God as a "time God"—he doesn't come too early or too late, he actively intervenes at just the right time. Of course, his timing and ours are frequently different.

  » What has it been like for each of you as you have waited on God?
  » What would it look like for God to show up and intervene now?
  » Where, even in the midst of the mess, might you already be seeing some signs of God's powerful presence in your family?

Maturing as a Biblical Family Counselor
Offering Hope to Hurting Families

1. We infuse hope through interactions that acknowledge the pain and problems (empathy) while directing families to God's powerful personal presence (encouragement).

   a. Which do you tend more toward—the empathy aspect or the encouragement aspect?

   b. Is it a new competency for you to include both empathy and encouragement? If so, how can you develop this further?

2. In *Gospel-Centered Family Counseling*, you will read numerous trialogues—*spiritual conversation trialogues* where you engage family members in thinking about the application of relevant scriptural principles, and *scriptural exploration trialogues* where you engage family members in discussing specific application of pertinent biblical passages.

---

a. Is this concept of a trialogue new for you? If so, how will you develop the competency of trialoguing as opposed to monologuing, where you teach *at* instead of talking *with*?

b. While it is a little early to assess the concept of trialogues, what are your initial thoughts? Agree? Disagree? Excited to learn more and see more examples? Skeptical?

3. Refer back to figures 5.1 and 5.2.

a. Which of the questions resonate with you the most? Which seem like the most helpful initial questions to ask?

b. If you had only four or five initial questions to ask, what questions would your Family Counseling Goals and Focus Form include?

4. Ponder a situation you are working through in your own life, marriage, or family. Create an Ephesians 3:14–21 vision.

a. Think ahead three months. As God does exceedingly, abundantly above all that you could ask or imagine in your heart and in your life, marriage, and family, what two or three amazing changes are you envisioning, praying for, and hoping for?

b. What needs to happen in your heart and in your life, marriage, and family so that through Christ's strength these amazing changes start occurring?

Now the family sits in front of you. Or now the young children roam the room and just about ruin your office. And the parents try to control their children while they also try to make you think they are maintaining their parental self-control.

Be prepared. All your pre-session, hope-focused interventions will not magically or biblically wipe away all their hurt or clear up all their family blemishes. Now is when you take the resurrection-focused questions you are already asking yourself, and the questions you have asked them to complete on their Family Counseling Goals and Focus Form, and you interact about them with the family.

"Kevin and Melissa, as you predicted, it's a bit chaotic right now. Over the next several weeks, we're going to think biblically about how to deal with the chaos you're feeling in your souls and the chaos we're witnessing in my office. But before we look at specific biblical parenting principles, I'm thinking that what you might need is *faith* in God's work in your hearts, so that you have *hope* that God can help you to love your children with his holy *love*.

"Kevin, let's start with you. As you think about your wife, what are the unique gifts, talents, abilities, and strengths that God has given Melissa, that she can use to shepherd your children? Swivel your chair around so you're facing Melissa and share those with her."

After Kevin shares, then you continue. "So, Kevin, what would it look like for you to fan into flame Melissa's gifts? How can you help her, encourage her, and empower her as her parental partner?"

Then you interact with Melissa. "Melissa, what was it like to hear Kevin affirm those parental strengths in you?"

After Melissa shares, then you follow up. "Melissa, what would it look like for you to fan those gifts into flame—to tap into Christ's resurrection power so that you could shepherd your children well?"

After Melissa shares, then you shift focus. You ask her to share about Kevin's unique parental gifts from God. You ask her about fanning them into flame. Then you ask Kevin what it is like to hear of his wife's confidence in his giftedness from God. And you ask Kevin how he could tap into Christ's power.

About now you might be thinking, *But all this time those kids are running wild and ruining your office!* I hope they don't, because I love my office and all my knickknacks.

But here's the power of *family* counseling. Now you say, "So, you've been encouraged a bit by each other. Let's see about the two of you together stepping into this chaos and parenting your kids right now in my office. Maybe before we do that, or as we do that, let's each pray—maybe short prayers, because we need to keep our eyes on the kids."

"Now, Kevin and Melissa, using the parental knowledge you already have from all the books and seminars, and using the unique God-given resources you just affirmed in each other, what might it look like to shepherd your kids right now?"

You talk together about what it might look like. Then you release them to act, to shepherd, to parent *in front of you*. You may coach a bit. You may help a bit. You may affirm a lot. Who knows exactly how it might go—it is just the first meeting. But you have accomplished a lot.

- You have added God's perspective on who they are in Christ—their unique giftedness and resources.
- You have encouraged them to affirm and encourage each other and to fan into flame each other's parental gifts.
- You have connected their information about parenting to their infused hope in God's work in their family life.
- You have encouraged them to work together as parents.
- You have observed them—in the parental moment in your office—stepping into chaos.

Depending on what has just happened, you might move to any of the family counseling areas we are about to explore: sustaining, healing, reconciling, or guiding.

- *Sustaining*: Maybe this first attempt seems to them like an embarrassing disaster. So you offer sustaining empathy. "Okay. That was tough. I can tell that you feel like it didn't go so well. Let's talk about what you're each feeling right now—anger, embarrassment, frustration, defeat . . ."
- *Healing*: Maybe the first attempt went semi-well and semi-not-so-well. So you offer healing encouragement. "Okay, there were some good things and maybe some things you'd like to see happen differently next time. But God does his best work in bringing order out of chaos, in bringing light into darkness. So, what could we all learn from this first attempt . . . ?"
- *Reconciling*: Maybe you observed some sinful anger in the parents or some sinful disobedience in the children. "Okay, it looks like the kids can really get you going, Kevin. Seems like you went from trying to corral them to getting kind of upset with them. Am I right. . . ? Maybe not right now, but in upcoming meetings, let's plan to talk about what's going on in your heart . . ."
- *Guiding*: Maybe it went somewhat well and somewhat poorly. "In future meetings, let's look at some of the good parenting and

shepherding that just happened and figure out how to do more of that . . . And let's examine some of what didn't work so well and think through biblical principles that you could apply in situations like this . . ."

What if it is a single-parent situation? Then you and the single parent trialogue about God-given resources. If you follow the valuable process of having a co-counselor or an advocate present, they also can speak into the unique resources God has given that specific parent.

Maturing as a Biblical Family Counselor
Prompting Parents to Tap God-Given Resources

1. To fan into flame the unique God-given resources of another person, we need to be the type of people who understand the unique ways God has fearfully and wonderfully made and equipped us.

   a. Reflect on Psalm 139:13–18. What are your unique, God-given gifts, abilities, strengths, weaknesses (God uses us in our unique weaknesses too), and personality traits?

   b. Reflect on 2 Timothy 1:6–7. How could you fan into flame and stir up the unique gifts of God within you? How can God use those unique qualities in your life as a family counselor? In your family life?

2. On a scale of 1 to 10, with 1 being low and 10 being high, how well do you recognize the unique gifts of others? How well do you fan those gifts into flame?

3. What are the benefits, what is the value, of having spouses affirm and fan into flame each other's unique parental gifts?

4. This section briefly touched on the value of having a co-counselor or an advocate (a friend or family member of the counselee) in each session.

   a. Have you counseled with a co-counselor? If so, what have the benefits been? If not, how do you think it might help to have a co-counselor with you?

   b. Have you counseled with an advocate present? If so, what have the benefits been? If not, how do you think it might help the family counseling process to have an advocate present?

Encouraging the Family to See Signs of Christ on the Move

Churches offer premarital counseling, but they rarely offer pre-parental counseling.[1] So, having engaged in little preventative parental counseling and little parental discipleship, families typically come to us problem-saturated. They are not necessarily seeing their own heart sins (see our discussion of Matthew 7 and James 4 in chapter 4). But they are seeing the sins of their family members and the dysfunctions of their family. They have come to you because they are overwhelmed and under-hopeful.

To infuse resurrection hopefulness, we seek to help the family see past, present, and future signs of God at work—Christ on the move in their family's life. While listening well and empathizing compassionately about family hurts and struggles, we also want to draw out *past* victories the family may be blind to.

- Kevin and Melissa, you've shared honestly about times where the kids are king and you two feel helpless to corral them. But surely there are some times when God has given you some level of parental victory and success.

  » Tell me about a couple times of real victory in your family . . .
  » What is different about those times?
  » How are you encouraging each other in those times?
  » How are you tapping into God's strength in those times?
  » How do you think you, your family members, and God could keep this victory going?

We can also explore *present* victories.

- Kevin and Melissa, tell me what things are like when your family is not having these problems.
- What are each of you as parents—and each of your children—doing differently when you do not experience this problem?
- Through Christ's strength, how do you think your family and God can keep these times of victory going and growing?

In figures 5.1 and 5.2, you saw an example related to exploring God's *future* family vision and victory.

- Melissa and Kevin, let's talk about your responses to the Ephesians 3:14–21 question on your Family Counseling Goals and Focus Form. First, let's reread that passage . . .

  » Let's talk about how you each responded to the first part of that question: Think ahead three months. As God does exceedingly, abundantly above all that you could ask or imagine in your heart and in your family, what two or three amazing changes are you envisioning, praying for, and hoping for?
  » And let's talk about the second part of that question: What needs to happen in your hearts and in your family relationships—and in your kids—so that through Christ's strength these amazing changes start to occur?

Maturing as a Biblical Family Counselor
Encouraging the Family to See Signs of Christ on the Move

1. While many churches offer premarital counseling, far fewer churches offer pre-parental counseling.

   a. Why do you think that is?

b. If you were to create a pre-parental discipleship curriculum, what elements would you include?

2. Think about a situation in your family—whether your family of origin growing up, or your extended family now, or your immediate family now if you have children.

   a. Review the trialogues from page 109 about *past* family victories. How would you answer those questions related to the family situation you are pondering? How could your answers provide encouragement to you regarding that situation? How could your answers have changed the way you handled a past situation? How could your answers change the way you are handling a current family situation?

   b. Review the trialogues from page 110 about *present* family victories. How would you answer those questions related to the family situation you are pondering? How could your answers provide encouragement to you regarding that situation? How could your answers have changed the way a past situation was handled? How could your answers change the way you are handling a current family situation?

   c. Review the trialogues from page 110 about *future* family victories. How would you answer those questions related to the family situation you are pondering? How could your answers provide encouragement to you regarding that situation? How could your answers have changed the way you handled a past situation? How could your answers change the way you are handling a current family situation?

SIX

Building a Bridge of Tears

Sustaining in Family Counseling, Part 1

Introduction: Family Pain and Family Empathy

It quickly became clear that Becky (wife/mom), Eric (husband/dad), and Kiara (preteen daughter) were experiencing deep family pain. However, none of the three were framing their issues as *family* pain. Instead, they each saw and felt *their own pain* acutely. Becky and Eric thought they saw their family problem accurately—their daughter was the problem. Likewise, Kiara thought she saw the family problem clearly—Mom and Dad!

Each of them was experiencing individual pain and each of them had individual problems. Eric felt devastated and defeated by the constant unresolved tension in their home. Over time, he came to see and began to address his struggle with impatience and what he eventually described as his simmering temper.

Becky shared that she had a long-term battle against mild depression and contended with a horribly negative outlook on life. Their family's yearlong conflict left her empty, drained, discouraged, and ready to give up on trying to parent.

Kiara disclosed that for several years she had wrestled with constant up-and-down emotions. And she did not deny her recent rebelliousness, though she was quick to link it to her parents' overbearing, controlling, and perfectionistic ways.

Picture yourself hearing this info for the first time. Where do you start? What and who do you focus on? Imagine that you start by infusing hope through empathetic encouragement (chap. 5). The family has an initial sense that they each feel heard and that together they have at least a sliver of hope. Now what?

Now we implement our family counseling GPS by providing family sustaining. Yes, family counselors must pray for family-specific wisdom to discern what is best—remember Philippians 1:9–11. And yes, every situation and family is different—remember family counseling as spaghetti relationships. That said, often what families most need after an infusion of hope is *family sustaining*. They need their counselor to come alongside them and (1) identify with their individual suffering, (2) identify with their family suffering, (3) help them identify with each other's suffering, and (4) equip them to comfort each other with Christ's comfort.

Think of it like this. In our urgent desire to fix the family problem, we can fall into four family counseling errors:

> *Family Counseling Error #1*: Not feeling for/with each family member.

- God calls us to look at each family member through the lens of suffering.
- "Hope deferred makes the heart sick" (Prov. 13:12).
- We look at family members as saints in Christ and sons and daughters of God who are *suffering* as they battle against *sin* on their individual and family *sanctification* journey.
- We need to feel before we seek to fix; we care as a prerequisite for care-fronting.

> *Family Counseling Error #2*: Not feeling for the family as a unit—as a family—failing to experience their *family pain*.

- God calls us to observe, openly join, and orchestrate the family dance and the family dirge.
- We care so deeply that we share not only Scripture but also our very own souls (1 Thess. 2:8).
- We see them, relate to them, and feel for them not only as individuals but as a family.
- We need to understand and connect with the family before we restore the family.

> *Family Counseling Error #3*: Not helping each family member to open the eyes of their heart to their family members' hurts.

- God calls us to venture together across the family chasm.
- They need to weep with their weeping family members (Rom. 12:15).

- We empower them to build bridges of empathy between each other.
- They need to move from focusing exclusively on being hurt to focusing on the hurt and pain of their family members.

Family Counseling Error #4: Not equipping the family to feel for and empathize with each other.

- God calls us to equip the family in mutual empathy.
- They need to comfort each other with Christ's comfort (2 Cor. 1:4).
- We equip them to comfort each other.
- They need to be able to communicate to each other that, like Christ, we care about each other's hurts.

Our focus as we start counseling Becky, Eric, and Kiara is not to dole out scriptural passages like magic bullets that immediately fix every feeling and change every circumstance. Our focus is not on a one-problem, one-verse, one-solution mindset. We focus on empathizing with the family *so that* they can connect with each other and comfort each other with Christ's comfort.

Ponder how much change sustaining seeks to promote. Becky, Eric, and Kiara enter counseling focused almost exclusively on their own pain and on seeing the other person(s) as their enemy. Through family sustaining, they begin to move from caring primarily about their own hurt to caring deeply about their family members' hurts (Phil. 2:3–4). When God does this transformational work in family members' hearts, then they are prepared for family healing, reconciling, and guiding.

At the beginning of counseling, they are saying, "Don't you see how you've hurt me? I'm going to hurt you back! You don't care about anyone but yourself! Fine, I'll just take care of me and forget about you." Through the process of sustaining, they are saying to each other, "Like Christ, we care about each other's hurts." We join with Christ in encouraging families to move toward this colossal change through the family sustaining counseling competencies of LOVE:

L Looking at Families through the Lens of Suffering: Hope Deferred Makes the Heart Sick (chap. 6)

O Observing, Openly Joining, and Orchestrating the Family Dance and the Family Dirge: Building a Bridge of Tears (chap. 6)

V Venturing Together across the Family Chasm: Building Bridges of Family Candor and Compassion (chap. 7)

E Equipping the Family to Comfort Each Other with Christ's Comfort: Sharing Together in Our Savior's Compassion (chap. 7)

Maturing as a Biblical Family Counselor
Family Pain and Family Empathy

1. Think about family pain in your life—growing up, in your adult life, or currently.

    a. What was your *personal* suffering and pain like in that situation—can you put it into words?

    b. Reflect on the suffering and pain *of your family members* in that situation. How hard is it to even think about their pain, given the pain they may have caused you? Can you put into words the pain and suffering they may have experienced or are going through?

2. As a biblical family counselor, how inclined are you toward a "fix it" mentality and a "stop it" focus? Said another way, do you tend to emphasize spotting sin and fixing problems before you focus on seeing suffering and empathizing with family pain?

    a. If so, where did you learn that "fix it" and "stop it" approach?

    b. What are some good, biblical aspects of seeking to help families fix their problems and stop their sinning?

    c. What are some good, biblical aspects of seeking to see family suffering and empathize with family pain?

3. You read about four family counseling errors. Reread those and the descriptions connected with each one below.

    -   *Family Counseling Error #1*: Not feeling for/with each family member.
    -   *Family Counseling Error #2*: Not feeling for the family as a unit—as a family—failing to experience their *family pain*.

- *Family Counseling Error #3*: Not helping each family member to open the eyes of their heart to their family members' hurts.
- *Family Counseling Error #4*: Not equipping the family to feel for and empathize with each other.

  a. How inclined are you toward falling into each of those errors?

  b. How could you grow in doing the opposite of those errors—in doing the bullet points listed under each error?

Looking at Families through the Lens of Suffering: Hope Deferred Makes the Heart Sick

It has become common in the biblical counseling world to encourage counselors to look at Christian counselees through the three lenses of saint, sufferer, and sinner. This threefold analysis seeks to expand biblical counseling beyond primarily seeing counselees as sinners in need of confrontation. Saint/sufferer/sinner is a helpful expansion.

Looking through the Lens of Saint and Son/Daughter

I tend to tweak this even further to saints/sons/suffering/sin/sanctification.

God calls us to look at Christian counselees through the lens of *saints* in Christ and *sons/daughters* of God who are *suffering* in a fallen world as they battle against *sin* while on their individual and family *sanctification* journey.

In our core identity as believers we are *saints*—new creations in Christ (regeneration) and more than conquerors through Christ (redemption), and we are *sons and daughters* of God—forgiven by the Father through the Son (justification) and welcomed home by the Father with the Son (reconciliation).

There is great power in looking at Christian counselees through the lens of salvation—as saints and as sons and daughters of God. As a counselor, I never have to try to put power or newness into a Christian family member. It is already there through Christ. They are new in Christ. Our calling is to stir up and fan into flame the new person they already are. Our calling is to encourage them in daily family life to put off the old dead person who is already crucified with Christ and to put on the new creation in Christ who is already resurrected with Christ. In their core identities, they are not sinners; they are saints who struggle against sin—against the world, the flesh, and the devil.

Looking through the Lens of Family Suffering

Seeing Christian counselees as saints and sons/daughters does not diminish the reality of the suffering that family members endure. Our perfect Savior not only suffered physical agony on the cross; Christ also suffered unimaginable emotional and relational anguish in the garden of Gethsemane (Matt. 26:36–46). Saints suffer significantly.

Counselor Empathy: Affirming and Offending Family Members

Though our ultimate goal is to help family members empathize with one another's suffering, it often is unrealistic to anticipate this initially. Typically, we first need to feel their pain and verbally acknowledge their suffering before they are prepared to do the same for one another. Our counselor empathy can be a catalyst for family empathy. Our empathy can model family empathy. Our empathy can open the eyes of family members to begin seeing that they are not the only hurting people in their home.

But beware. Counselor empathy can prompt hostility from family members. I call this *affirming and offending*. If I empathize with Kiara regarding areas where her parents are failing her and hurting her, then I have *affirmed* her while potentially *offending* them. "What? You're taking *her* side? I thought you were a *biblical* counselor!"

How do we address this? First, be aware of the likelihood. You have now been forewarned. Second, talk openly to family members about *affirming and offending*.

- I want you to know that I'll do everything in my power to be fair. I don't want to take anyone's side. I'm on *your family's* side. But understand that at times I'll let Mom and Dad know that I understand how hurt they are. Other times I'll let Kiara know that I get how much pain she's in. By affirming the pain one of you is going through, my intent is not to offend the other family members . . .

Levels of Counselor Empathy

Without becoming too technical, we can picture three levels of family counseling empathy:

Level 1 Empathy: Understanding Family Members through God's Eyes
Level 2 Empathy: Understanding Family Members through Your Own Eyes
Level 3 Empathy: Understanding Family Members through Their Eyes

LEVEL 1 EMPATHY (FOUNDATIONAL): UNDERSTANDING FAMILY MEMBERS THROUGH GOD'S EYES

In level 1 empathy, we think *theologically* about the thirsts and longings of parents and children. Recall our exploration in chapter 4 of family soul suffering: what God calls a parent to offer indicates what God designed a child to thirst for; what God calls a child to offer indicates what God designed a parent to thirst for.

God calls children to offer their parents *honoring love*. The deepest parental soul suffering that Becky and Eric can experience from Kiara occurs as they receive her *dishonoring distance*. Her disrespect and disobedience crush them. Her retreat from involvement with them causes them agony. Designed for the paradise of honoring love, they are thirsty sufferers in the desert of Kiara's dishonoring distance. As family counselors, we empathize with this parental emptiness.

Think of the apostle John's statement that he has no greater joy than hearing that his children walk in the truth (3 John 4). Christian parents are crushed when the opposite occurs—when their children are prodigals, when they are walking away from their parents' faith, when they distance themselves from their parents and everything dear to them. Foolish children bring their parents grief, anguish, sorrow, bitterness, shame, and disgrace (Prov. 10:1; 17:21, 24; 19:26). As family counselors, we climb in the parental casket of disrespect and disloyalty.

God calls parents to offer their children *holy love*. The deepest soul suffering that Kiara can experience as a child ensues when her mom and dad fail to provide her the strength and support, guidance and care, shepherding and relationship God designed her for. Her hope is deferred and her soul shrinks. Designed for the paradise of godly parental holy love, Kiara is a thirsty sufferer in the desert of her parents' pharisaical parenting (all rules and holiness without grace or love), neglectful parenting (abandonment, rejection, a lack of love and of holiness), or permissive/possessive parenting (fearing her, spoiling her, overprotecting her). As family counselors, we feel a child's soul disappointment.

Paul describes the result of parental failure—children are exasperated (Eph. 6:4) and embittered and discouraged (Col. 3:21). As family counselors, we climb in the casket of the soul brokenness of a child who feels unloved and unsafe, who experiences parental distance and weakness.

LEVEL 2 EMPATHY (FILTERING): UNDERSTANDING FAMILY MEMBERS THROUGH YOUR OWN EYES

We first seek to understand and empathize with family pain through *God's eyes*—this is our foundational understanding. Next, we empathize through *our own eyes*. Our experience is the filter through which we seek to relate to the pain of parents and children. We seek to tap into our own emotional awareness of what it would be like for us to experience and live in such a relational desert.

Many times we can tap into similar painful experiences we've had as a child or as a parent. However, our experience need not be identical. Consider 2 Corinthians 1:3–4. Biblical family counselors need to be the type of people who turn to "the God *of all comfort,* who comforts us *in all our troubles,* so that we can comfort those *in any trouble* with the comfort *we ourselves receive from God."* The infinite Father and the infinite Christ, who sympathizes with all of our weaknesses (Heb. 4:15), can equip us to empathize with and comfort parents and children in their family pain.

LEVEL 3 EMPATHY (FOCUSED): UNDERSTANDING FAMILY MEMBERS THROUGH THEIR EYES

Third, we seek to empathize with family members through *their eyes.* As we sense what it would be like to live in their home, as we feel their pain and taste their unquenched thirst, then we enter their thirst and engage their souls. Right there, right in front of the other family members (affirming and offending), we focus on their experience of their family life.

We *adopt their emotional viewpoint.* We replace our internal frame of reference with theirs. We seek to hear and see and feel what their family pain is like for them.

Then we *express their emotional viewpoint.* We express in our words what we sense they feel in their situation and in their soul. Once we put their pain into our own words, we check in: How does this hit you? Does this resonate with you? Am I on track? How could you better express what you are feeling?

Many times during this process, we will need to encourage the family member to *accept their own emotional viewpoint.* "Hmm. I hear you saying you're fine. Yet I sense the pain in your voice, see the tears welling up in your eyes . . ." We nudge them to acknowledge their soul's experience. We help them to accept and verbalize what they are experiencing. We encourage them to verbalize their personal psalm of lament in our presence and in the presence of their family members. Initially, we focus on drawing out whatever is in their soul. Are they in denial? Are they facing the reality of the pain in their soul?

As you can imagine, this puts it all out there. It can, and likely will, get messy. The truth is, it's *already* messy—in each family member's soul and between the family members. The family can try to sweep the mess under the carpet or they can try to deal with it without you. Or you can all look under the carpet together and deal with the mess together—biblically—through the rest of the sustaining, healing, reconciling, and guiding process.

Our desire in this initial part of our family counseling journey is for each family member to have their experience verbalized (here is what you feel) and validated (I have heard and cared about what you feel). The family is no longer alone on their journey.

As the family counseling process continues, we will want to help each family member *evaluate their own emotional viewpoint*. Emotions are God-given, but they are not God. Emotions are important messages, but they are not all-wise. Over time we want to help individuals explore whether they are accurately assessing how their family members are relating to them. Are their expectations too high or too low? Are they underreacting or overreacting?

Maturing as a Biblical Family Counselor
Looking at Families through the Lens of Suffering

1. God calls us to look at Christian counselees through the lens of *saints* in Christ and *sons/daughters* of God who are *suffering* as they battle against *sin* on their individual and family *sanctification* journey. How could this way of looking at counselees impact your family counseling? What difference might it make?

2. You read about affirming and offending family members.

   a. Have you ever experienced this? What was it like? How did you handle it?

b. If you have not experienced it, how could you handle it in the future if one family member is offended and feels you are taking sides when you empathize with another family member?

3. Of the three levels of empathy, which one are you most experienced with? How could you develop the other two levels of empathy that you are less experienced with?

    • Level 1 Empathy (Foundational): Understanding Family Members through God's Eyes
    • Level 2 Empathy (Filtering): Understanding Family Members through Your Own Eyes
    • Level 3 Empathy (Focused): Understanding Family Members through Their Eyes

4. It gets messy when we have family members express their emotional pain to us in each other's presence. How would you seek to allow for the messiness—getting hurts out into the open while also shepherding family interactions so that emotions are not used as weapons and hurts are not inflamed?

Observing, Openly Joining, and Orchestrating the Family Dance and the Family Dirge: Building a Bridge of Tears

Empathizing with an individual is Counseling 101. For most of us, empathizing with the family as a unit is Advanced Family Counseling 201. It is new terrain, a new way of thinking about counseling. Sustaining in family counseling involves experiencing the family's pain and identifying with their family suffering—seeing, relating to, and feeling for them not only as individuals but also as a *family unit*. We care so deeply for them as a family that we not only share Scripture with them, we connect with them soul-to-soul—our soul to their family soul.

Observing and Seeing the Family as One Unit

Family counseling requires that we view the family through God's eyes. In Genesis 2:24, before God describes the cleaving and weaving together of a husband and wife as one flesh, he describes the man leaving his once primary connection to father and mother. A husband is to leave one primary unit, one place of core loyalty and primary connection, to establish a new home—a new family with a new place of core loyalty and primary connection. God envisions the family as one unit, one entity—the many uniting as one family. What is true in the physical/individual family is also true in the spiritual/universal family. The church is the family of God—one family, one body, united (1 Cor. 12:12–13, 24–27; Eph. 2:19; 4:4–6).

This does not mean that family members lose their individuality. Instead, it means that the individuals join together in oneness to develop a corporate identity and personality—a blended, unique family DNA, family culture, family way, family dance, and family dirge.

Openly Joining the Family Dance and the Family Dirge

If we watch carefully, we can observe the recognizable family pattern of interaction (how they relate, think, and act)—the family dance. If we listen soulfully, we can tune into the unique family frequency and receive the family signals, becoming aware of how they feel (the family emotional state and mood)—the family dirge.

Feel that word "dirge"—the family's pain and lament, their sad song. Like the African American spirituals that expressed individual and group pain in this life as well as future hope through the Giver of life, so families sing their own songs of lament and of hope in God.

In order to empathize with the family, we need to join with them in their collective pain. We seek to hear their shared story and feel their communal pain from their perspective.

Orchestrating Their Family Dance So We Can Experience Their Family Dirge

We do this by attending to their style of relating and their mode of feeling, which is revealed through the dynamics of their interactions and expressions. Central to this is *keeping the family relationship in the room*. Rather than only or primarily listening to stories about the history of how they have related to each other (which can become "he said, she said" or "parents said, children said"), encourage them to relate to each other right now in your presence. Picture yourself as the orchestra conductor or as their dance instructor:

- *Enact*. Get them talking to each other in front of you about their present relationship.
- *Watch and listen for patterns*. What is their family style of relating? What is the tune of their family pain?
- *Share a creative, family-specific depiction of their family dance and family dirge*.

Having observed something of the unique way this family relates (dances) and feels (dirge), soulfully put into words and pictures what you see and sense. Pray for Spirit-guided wisdom to express their family pattern and family pain in their language, at their pace, according to their style. Mimic their family emotional vocabulary, accommodating to them much as a missionary accommodates in culture matters to minister in a given mission field. With Becky, Eric, and Kiara, you might share any of the following examples . . .

- Becky, Eric, and Kiara, you *all* seem so worn out, exhausted, thirsty, depleted. Like it's the thirteenth inning of a tied-up softball game in the middle of a summer heat wave and drought. What do you think? Am I on target? [Kiara plays softball, and Mom and Dad never miss a game.]
- You all seem engaged in a fiercely competitive game of Twister! Family hands and feet intermingled and intertwined everywhere. Everyone racing for the same spot at the same time. And *nobody* even the least little bit happy when someone else lands on their color! Nobody wanting to budge and give up their chosen spot. Does this description fit how you guys may be relating and feeling these days . . . ? [This family used to *love* to play family games.]
- It looks to me like you've formed sides here. In this corner, weighing in at—er, well, I guess I won't give your weight! In this corner, Mom and Dad, and in the other corner, the challenger, Kiara . . . This is MMA at its fiercest. No holds barred. Everyone wanting to force their opponent to tap out . . ." (*Stop. Look around. Shrug shoulders. Wait for them to respond . . .*) [Dad likes to watch mixed martial arts.]

Imagine that you have shared one of these family summaries. And imagine that they have owned the description either outright or by tweaking it somewhat. Now you empathize with their family pain.

- That has to be exhausting. You all—each of you—have to be exhausted. I'm feeling wiped out and on empty just feeling with you . . .

- That's a lot of anger. And when I think about how you guys were two years ago—the cutest, funnest, most connectedest fam out there . . . It makes me so sad . . . right now . . . that I can barely fight back the tears. (*You pause. You wipe tears from your cheeks. And the four of you share a cry together . . .*)

Building a Bridge of Tears

In one sense, I do not like ending a chapter here—with raw emotion exposed but unresolved. Yet this is exactly what this dear family has been facing. And it is exactly what you and I will face as biblical family counselors if we resolve to counsel soul-to-soul.

However, just in case the lack of resolution is too overwhelming for you, I can hint at where we are headed. Having become their therapeutic glue, we can now function as their emotional conduit. We have joined with them in their relational pattern and family pain *so we can begin to assist them to join with each other.*

In fact, have we not already done that? They/we are *crying together*, or at least feeling together, over the sadness of their separation from each other. Their joint memory—our joint memory—of how close they once were is now creating a *bridge of tears*.

Maturing as a Biblical Family Counselor
Observing, Openly Joining, and Orchestrating the Family Dance and the Family Dirge

1. Empathizing with individuals = Counseling 101. Empathizing with the family as a unit = Advanced Family Counseling 201.

    a. How new is this concept for you of empathizing with the family as one entity?

    b. How easy or difficult might it be for you to understand and empathize with family pain?

---

2. You read that we can picture family pain as a family dirge, lament, or sad song.

   a. In your family—either growing up or now—what pain has the whole family experienced? What song or psalm might capture that pain? How have you lamented and dealt with that pain?

   b. In your experiences with other families (counseling, pastoring, being a family friend) how have you sought to hear, empathize with, and walk with families in pain?

3. You read about enacting, watching, and listening for patterns, and sharing a creative, family-specific depiction of the family dance and family dirge. This requires a level of soul connection that is foreign to a more clinical or aloof approach to counseling.

   a. How ready do you think you are for inviting the family to relate and feel in front of you?

   b. What skills and relational competencies would you need to develop in order to be able to accurately capture and share a creative, family-specific depiction of the family dance and family dirge?

4. This chapter ended without resolution and with an introduction to building a bridge of tears.

   a. How comfortable or uncomfortable are you with ending a counseling session without having brought resolution?

   b. How comfortable or uncomfortable do you think you will be with building a bridge of tears—so empathizing with a family that you help them to empathize with each other?

SEVEN

Connecting Families through Christ's Comfort

Sustaining in Family Counseling, Part 2

Introduction: Cultivating Family Unity through Mutual Empathy

Chapter 6 ended a bit like Psalm 88 ends. Known as the "Psalm of the Dark Night of the Soul," Psalm 88 ends without resolution. The psalmist Heman addresses God and concludes with these words: "You have caused my beloved and my friend to shun me; my companions have become darkness" (Ps. 88:18 NLT).

Many of us could not end there. We would have to tack on, "And I hope in you, God!"

Heman hoped in God. His hope was so intense that he felt no need to placate, pacify, mollify, or soothe God. Heman's faith was so strong that he felt no need to pretend, but instead allowed himself the biblical art of venting and lamenting.

Biblical family counselors have much to learn from Heman. As counselors, we should focus on family feeling, not family fixing. Invite families to cry out to God before racing families to supposed quick fixes. Cultivate family unity through encouraging family empathy.

Paul agrees with Heman. Before Paul invites us to the God who works all things together for good (Rom. 8:28), he invites us to the God who intercedes for us with groans that cannot be put into words (Rom. 8:26). Likewise, when Paul talks to the contentious Corinthians about oneness, his pathway is not pretense, denial, and niceness. Instead, Paul insists that we address division in the family of God by each member having equal concern for each other (1 Cor. 12:25) so that "if one part suffers, every part suffers with it" (1 Cor. 12:26).

This is why chapter 6 left us in tears. We began building a bridge of tears with Kiara, Becky, and Eric. We felt for their individual pain *and* joined with them in their family pain. In chapter 6, we learned how to become their therapeutic glue through:

L Looking at Families through the Lens of Suffering

O Observing, Openly Joining, and Orchestrating the Family Dance and the Family Dirge

Now, in chapter 7, they learn how to weep with each other and comfort each other. We learn how to become their emotional conduit through:

V Venturing Together across the Family Chasm

E Equipping the Family to Comfort Each Other with Christ's Comfort

---

Maturing as a Biblical Family Counselor
Cultivating Family Unity through Mutual Empathy

1. Read Psalm 88—the Psalm of the Dark Night of the Soul.

   a. Have you ever felt like Heman did in Psalm 88? When? What was the external situation? What was your soul situation—that is, what was your soul experiencing and feeling?

   b. Were you able to vent and lament? Were you able to be honest and candid with yourself, and were you able to lament frankly to God?

   c. Do you have Heman's faith in God to end a prayer of lament to God without pretense that everything in your soul is immediately all better? "You have caused my beloved and my friend to shun me; my companions have become darkness" (Ps. 88:18 NLT).

2. How could you implement Heman's spiritual lessons in your family counseling ministry?

    a. Focus on family feeling, not family fixing.

    b. Invite families to cry out to God before racing families to supposed quick fixes.

    c. Cultivate family unity through encouraging family empathy.

3. How could you implement Paul's spiritual lessons in your family counseling ministry?

    a. Before Paul invites us to the God who works all things together for good (Rom. 8:28), he invites us to the God who intercedes for us with groans that words cannot utter (Rom. 8:26).

    b. Paul insists that we address division in the family of God by each member having equal concern for each other (1 Cor. 12:25) so that "if one part suffers, every part suffers with it" (1 Cor. 12:26).

Venturing Together across the Family Chasm: Building Bridges of Family Candor and Compassion

We need to expand on points we made in chapter 6.

- Empathizing with an individual is Counseling 101 (chap. 6).
- Empathizing with the family as a unit is Advanced Family Counseling 201 (chap. 6).
- Equipping families to build bridges of empathy between each other is Advanced Family Counseling 301 (chap. 7).

We join with them in their family pain *so that* they begin to learn how to join with each other in their individual and family pain.

Families come to us emotionally raw and emotionally immature. That immaturity may show itself in stuffing feelings—denial, pretense, never honestly opening up, never connecting. Or it may show itself in spearing feelings—throwing emotions at each other, uncontrolled expressions of hurtful and hateful words, never connecting.

One outlier approach to handling emotional communication in family counseling involves letting the fur fly. This method adopts an "anything goes" attitude based on the old adage that all's fair in love and war. There is no organizing, structuring, shaping, or coaching by the counselor.

Another outlier approach to emotions in family counseling involves politeness and pretense, where no emotions are allowed in the counseling room. Practitioners of this method would say, "We only fix problems; we don't feel pain."

Neither extreme helpfully *equips* troubled families to face their problems in effective, long-lasting ways. They need our help to venture together across the family emotional chasm—often the size of the Grand Canyon—by building bridges of family candor and compassion. I like to think of this aspect of family counseling as *organizing the organism*. Becky, Eric, and Kiara are real people with raw problems—the family is a living, breathing, feeling, experiencing organism. At this moment, they are also contentious, chaotic, and disconnected—they need some structuring, coaching, and organizing. In our presence, they need emotional and relational coaching.

We've learned that we want to get the family members interacting in front of us. In chapter 6 that involved observing the family dance and feeling the family dirge. Here in chapter 7, we will discuss how to structure interactions to help family members share with each other candidly and (at least somewhat) calmly, and hear each other (at least somewhat) non-defensively. To prevent something so relational from becoming too technical, we can envision the process as stages in a relational family journey:

a. Explaining the purpose and protective process
b. Structuring the sharing
c. Shaping the listening and responding
d. Shepherding the interaction
e. Debriefing together
f. Inviting the Messiah into the family messiness

Explaining the Purpose and Protective Process

- Eric, Becky, and Kiara, you've just heard how I hurt for each of you. While I hope that's helpful, I'm not always going to be around. What will be much more helpful is if you can learn to hurt with each other . . .

- Before we try that right now with each other, I'd like to share what I've noticed in a lot of hurting families. At first, we try to communicate our hurt in a helpful way. Later, when that doesn't seem to get through to our family members, sometimes we give up and stuff our feelings. Other times we start sharing our hurt in hurtful ways—attacking and putting others down. So what we started as an attempt to draw closer now becomes another reason to grow further apart.

- I'd like to get us back to the place of sharing our hurts in a way that helps you to understand each other, care about each other, weep with each other, and comfort each other. I know. Sounds impossible. But remember the Ephesians 3 passage we started with last week—God can do exceedingly, abundantly above everything we think possible.

- As I have each of you share, I realize that this can be very old territory. You've heard some of these hurts for so long that by this time they feel like complaints or attacks. Remember, there is a difference now. You have a third party here. I'm not simply a referee. I want to be something of a coach to help you know what to do with your family hurts and struggles. How to share. How to listen. How to respond.

- Before we start this process of sharing, could we all stop and pray right now, asking God for his strength to speak truth in love?

Structuring the Sharing

- Kiara, I want us to go back to the most recent blowup you all had. I want you to be honest about what you're feeling. But I also want you to watch your tone. Don't attack. I'd like you to share two things. First, tell Mom and Dad what you wish had happened instead when you came home five minutes late—how you wish you would have responded and how you wish Mom and Dad would have responded. Second, tell Mom and Dad what *you felt* when they responded the way they did. If they could have climbed in your soul as you heard their words to you, what would they have felt?

- I know that's a lot. Let me jot this down on the whiteboard for us.

- Before you share, Kiara, let me give your parents some coaching.

Shaping the Listening and Responding

- Mom, Dad, here's your role. Please don't interrupt Kiara, okay? I know—you have your side of what happened and you have your feelings . . . and you'll get to share that soon. But for now, let's listen quietly until I ask Kiara to give you two a chance to interact.

- While you're listening, I want you to do a couple of things. First—pray. Ask for God's help to listen non-defensively and to feel what Kiara feels. Second, I want you to think about how you could put into words the hurt that Kiara shares. I know—you're hurting too. But for the moment, let's keep our focus on Kiara's hurt.
- Let me jot that down on the whiteboard also.
- Any questions, thoughts, feedback, pushback?

Shepherding the Interaction

It is anybody's guess how this will go. Likely, it will not go smoothly. There may be interruptions—sometimes verbal, sometimes nonverbal, such as facial expressions, sighs of exasperation, and head shaking.

As Kiara shares, you draw her out, you direct her, you redirect her, you coach. You ask clarifying questions.

Then, you remind Becky and Eric of their focused task—to try to get inside their daughter's hurting soul. You will need to keep them focused, coach them, draw them out, and guide them.

Depending on how the sharing goes and how long it lasts, we may now switch roles. Mom and Dad share their hurts and feelings while Kiara listens.

Debriefing Together

As a counselor, be patient. They may have shared this twice—once in the first session and now with a little coaching. But they have had emotional battles like this for a long time. Our goal in this initial interaction is not to fix all the family problems. Instead, it is to start the chain of family empathy.

Applaud those times when any of the family members share candidly and respectfully about their feelings. Cheer on those times when any family members non-defensively hear each other's heart hurts.

Inviting the Messiah into the Family Messiness

We have another family counselor goal—to remind the family of their desperate need for Christ. These interactions are *not* designed to set the family up to fail. They are designed to coach the family to weep with weeping family members.

However, most of us are really lousy at being other-centered. This whole sharing and listening scenario is about much more than teaching communication skills. It is about encouraging servanthood, death to self, other-centered empathy, compassionate climbing in the casket—in other words, sacrificial agape love. It is about challenging family members to express Christlike loving character in the midst of their mess—both their situational mess and their soul mess.

You may conclude the interaction with words like . . .

- That was some good stuff, Kiara, Becky, and Eric. Like I said, high-fives and fist-bumps for several times of sacrificial listening and compassionate caring. Well done.
- Still, it was hard, wasn't it? I get it. We all want to tell our side of the story. We all want the other person to feel our feelings. We all want to be heard more than we want to hear. Even with me right here coaching you through this, it was *not* easy.
- This reminds me of the Spirit-dependent sandwich we talked about in our first meeting. Remember? God surrounds family living verses with passages about depending on the Spirit (Eph. 5:18) and being strengthened in Christ (Eph. 6:10). If change is going to keep happening in this family, if you're going to be able to weep with each other, then you're going to need to invite Jesus into your family's messiness. Jesus is the man of sorrows, acquainted with grief. He's your sympathetic High Priest who is touched with the feelings of your infirmities (Heb. 4:14–16). If you're going to grow in your ability to care about each other during even the messiest times, you're going to need the Messiah every second . . .

Maturing as a Biblical Family Counselor
Venturing Together across the Family Chasm

1. Families tend to handle emotions in one of two extremes. Some stuff them and pretend. Others spear them and hurt one another with them.

    a. In your family—growing up or your immediate family now—what was/is your pattern?

    b. In your family counseling experience, what have you seen most—stuffing feelings or spearing feelings? How do you address each of these in counseling?

2. Family counselors have a tendency toward one of two outlier approaches when it comes to what they encourage families to do with their emotions during counseling sessions. We can encourage the full and free expression of all feelings—get it out there however you have to so we can address it. Or we can discourage any candid expression of feelings because at best we see them as dangerous and misleading; we ignore feelings so we can fix behavioral problems.

   a. Have you seen either of these approaches in family counseling? If so, how has that worked? How has it turned out? What has it accomplished?

   b. This chapter recommended "organizing the organism"—coaching families toward candid sharing of feelings and compassionate hearing of feelings. Have you seen this approach in family counseling? If so, how has it worked? Has it turned out? What has it accomplished?

3. We recommended a relational process of: (a) explaining the purpose and protective process; (b) structuring the sharing; (c) shaping the listening and responding; (d) shepherding the interaction; (e) debriefing together; and (f) inviting the Messiah into the family messiness. Craft a counseling role-play of a family in turmoil (perhaps a family you have counseled or a troubled family you are aware of). How would you word each of these six areas?

Equipping the Family to Comfort Each Other with Christ's Comfort: Sharing Together in Our Savior's Compassion

The New Testament has two primary verses on parenting—Ephesians 6:4 and Colossians 3:21. Both highlight the parents' impact on the emotional state of their children. As we have seen, Ephesians 6:4 commands fathers not to exasperate their children—to irritate them, make them bitter, or provoke them to anger. Colossians 3:21 commands fathers not to embitter their children or they will become discouraged. The word "embitter" means to make mad, arouse toward irritation, and provoke to anger. A person who is discouraged becomes sad, sullen, and morose. We can categorize many emotions under mad and sad—and Paul hits both of these in his family counseling verses.

This is why we are devoting two chapters to family members weeping with each other's emotional pain. We practice parakaletic family counseling—family counseling for suffering—because Paul teaches parakaletic parenting that emphasizes the need for family empathy. God calls us to equip the family in mutual empathy. Family members need to learn how to communicate to each other that, like Christ, we care about each other's hurts.

Families need to comfort each other with Christ's comfort (2 Cor. 1:4). This becomes another central focus of gospel-centered family counseling. As vital as it is for family members to weep with and comfort one another, ultimately they must point one another to the perfect Comforter. They soothe their family soul in the person of their suffering and sympathizing Savior.

Because God's Word highlights the parental responsibility to shepherd children's emotions, we can follow a basic (but flexible) order for family counseling:

- Equipping parents to empathize with and comfort their children
- Equipping parents to empathize with and comfort each other
- Equipping (age-appropriate) children to empathize with and comfort their parents

Equipping Parents to Empathize with and Comfort Their Children

Because God gives parents the ultimate authority and responsibility in the home, they must initiate the chain of empathy. Tremendous parental power is unleashed when parents see the exasperation, embitterment, and discouragement of their children, own their part in it, repent of it, empathize with their children in it, and comfort their children with Christ's comfort.

By starting with parents, we are affirming their biblical authority, because biblical power is always servant leadership. We are respecting the parents' God-given capacity to be good shepherds who lay down their lives for their children. There are several relational competencies family counselors can use to equip parents to comfort their children, beginning with counselor-directed empathy.

Counselor-Directed Empathy

Consider some sample trialogues where the counselor guides the gospel conversation to encourage the parents to sense their children's pain.

- Eric and Becky, I can really sense your heart for Kiara. You want so badly to do what's right. What I think I'm hearing from Kiara is that she feels like she can never measure up. She feels like she has to be perfect or you are, to use her words, "always on her case." Imagine for a minute what it feels like to be Kiara. Place yourself in her shoes, her soul . . .
- Bill and Debbie, you've worked hard to give your kids the best. You have been successful at that. It seems to me that Luke and Isabel are feeling like they have your "stuff" but not *you*. Frankly, they miss *you*. They're lonely. How about the four of you discuss that for a while?

Parent-Focused Empathy

This is where true empathetic equipping launches. We want to equip parents with the relational competencies to empathize with their children in and out of our sessions. We want to empower parents to:

- See into their child's soul and taste their child's suffering.
- Climb into their child's casket.
- Offer their child bold love in the midst of troubling circumstances and distressed emotions.
- Shepherd their child's emotions.

Counselors can equip parents to nurture eight core elements of parental empathy in which parents connect with their child's soul and suffering.

1. Deepening Levels of Involvement with Their Child

This begins with intellectual involvement, where parents develop an awareness and appreciation of their child's circumstances, especially the troubling ones.

- Becky and Eric, I wonder how much you are aware of how troubled Kiara has been these last few months. I think the first place to start may be exploring with Kiara what she's been going through lately. Could you do that right now?

Once parents begin to understand their child's external circumstances, they can move deeper through caring involvement, where they verbalize and validate their child's feelings (as the counselor did earlier with each family member). As parents come to understand what motivates and impacts their children, they can increasingly respond with gentleness and empathy.

- Wow! You've gone a long way, Becky and Eric, toward tapping into Kiara's struggles. Could you express to Kiara right now what you feel for her?

2. Prayer That Identifies with the Troubling Circumstances of Their Child

We should never underestimate the power of parental prayer that identifies with the troubling circumstances of their child and brings them before God. This can start with encouraging the parents to pray for their child during the session.

- You've really begun to connect with Kiara. I sense that you all feel some pain and yet also some hope. Would it be okay if we spent some time praying together now? Specifically, I'm thinking that it would be helpful if the two of you prayed for yourself and for Kiara—praying that you could understand her even more and praying that God would continue to heal her hurts . . .

Encouraging ongoing out-of-session prayer is equally powerful.

- You could deepen this experience if the three of you spent some time this week praying together about all of this.

3. Listening beneath Their Child's Words (Prov. 18:4, 6–7)

A child's words often carry oceans of meaning and betray what is really going on internally. It is through careful listening that a parent discovers the depth of their child's heart. Counselors can start by helping parents to recognize implicit messages. Certain kinds of words kids use are almost always pregnant with meaning. For example, words that are colorful or graphic generally have a lot to say about how a child is thinking about themselves or their world. Imagine that Kiara says to Mom and Dad, "You guys have been so involved with all the church conflict stuff that I feel like I might as well not even be around anymore." Then you might say to Mom and Dad, "Can you put into words the powerful message that Kiara just sent you?"

Parents can also reflect on how their child's words affect them and then allow those words to penetrate and impact them personally. *A mature parent allows their child's words to impact them emotionally but not volitionally.* That is, they feel the impact of the words but do not allow their emotions to control their outward reaction. We help parents by asking questions like:

- How did Kiara's words make you feel?
- What is it about her words that makes you feel so hurt?
- What do you think Kiara is really trying to say to you?
- What is Kiara trying to get you to feel or do by choosing to use these words?
- How can you take your hurt to Christ and then find Christ's strength to respond maturely to Kiara?

4. OPENING DOORS TO THEIR CHILD'S HEART (PROV. 18:13, 15, 17)

Solomon extols the virtue of listening before responding. He also emphasizes active listening. The best way to listen actively is to ask the type of questions that get to the truth in another person's heart.

Asking non-defensive questions. Too often parents are afraid of the truth. So their questions carry an implicit message that warns their child not to answer in a way that might increase the parents' pain or discomfort. For instance, Becky might say, "What do you mean you think we've been ignoring you?" The implicit message: "Don't you dare accuse me of being selfish." When we hear questions like this, we will want to gently expose the implication while suggesting another approach. "Becky, I think that if I were Kiara, I might be hesitant to keep the dialogue going. Do you think you could rephrase that question in a way that is a bit more inviting for Kiara?"

Asking open-ended questions. Open-ended questions encourage a child to talk freely about the source of their concerns or the purpose of their actions. Such questions don't seek clipped, concise answers, nor do they manipulate the child to give the exact answer the parent is looking for. A closed or high-structured question might be, "Are you mad at me?" An open or low-structured question might be, "Could you tell me what you're feeling toward me right now?" We can empower parents in this by:

- Modeling open-ended questions with them and their children
- Teaching them about the difference between open and closed questions
- Gently pointing out when they use closed questions

Asking biblically perceptive questions. To get to the heart of what a child is all about, a parent must ask perceptive questions, questions that are guided by a biblical understanding of what makes kids tick. This is why it is so valuable to use parental discipleship classes in conjunction with family counseling. We teach and encourage parents to ask questions using the lens of longings (desires, dignity) and the lens of foolishness (depravity, sin).

- Sample questions designed to get kids talking about their desires:

  » What do you hope to get out of school this year?
  » What things make school a scary or difficult place for you?
  » If you could wave a magic wand and change anything about your friends or about us, what would you change?

- Sample questions designed to get kids talking about their foolishness:

  » If you could wave a magic wand and change anything about yourself, what would you change?
  » What things are making you the most mad and frustrated these days?

5. Entering Their Child's Pain

Parents need to enter their child's emotional casket. The preceding four points allow the parent to sense their child's pain. Now we want to help them to feel and enter their child's pain.

- Becky and Eric, what do you think it's like emotionally for Kiara right now?
- What would you be feeling if you were in her shoes?
- Have you ever experienced anything like this? What was it like for you?

6. Putting Words to Their Child's Thoughts and Feelings/Hurts (Prov. 15:2, 4; 18:21)

Parents who want to understand and minister to their children must learn how to speak "life words" to them—words that capture and articulate what they are thinking and feeling. Such words help kids make sense of their behavior and normalize their feelings. Here are a few examples of how words like these *verbalize and validate* a child's feelings.

- Eric, could you put words to Kiara's feelings?
- With your guidance, Eric could say to Kiara, "Kiara, it seems to me that you're starving to know that we really value you just for who you are. Much of what you do seems pointed toward getting that one major thirst quenched. But it doesn't seem to be working very well for you. I think that's why you must be feeling so empty lately."

7. INVITING THEIR CHILD TO REFLECT

Kiara is now experiencing a teachable moment. Being careful not to assume a tone of rebuke or judgment, Eric and Becky can challenge Kiara, with your help, to ponder her behavior in light of her feelings.

- Eric and Becky, could you help Kiara make some sense of how she's been relating to you?
- Becky responds, "Well, Kiara, I think I'm beginning to see a pattern. The more involved Dad and I have become in our problems at church, the less involved we've been with you. And I'm wondering if some of your irresponsibility lately has been your way of getting our attention. Makes me think that all three of us may have some changing to do."

8. INVITING THEIR CHILD TO CLING TO CHRIST'S COMFORT

- Eric and Becky, this week could the two of you and Kiara read through, pray through, and talk about applying 2 Corinthians 1:3–11? It's all about finding our comfort in Christ. Verses 8–9 are very real and raw as Paul shares his despair—so don't neglect to talk about the hard stuff. And then talk together and pray together about what it is like to take that to Christ for his comfort . . .

Equipping Parents to Empathize with and Comfort Each Other

We are not always working with a two-parent family. In those situations, it is vital to help the single parent recruit an advocate who can be part of the counseling sessions and be a spiritual friend outside the counseling meetings. Many of the principles below can be applied to an advocate relationship, especially if that advocate is a family member or a close church friend.

When we are working with a two-parent family, then we want to empower the parental unit. Often tension over children either results in or reflects tension between parents. It is not uncommon to need to provide marriage counseling as an adjunct to family counseling. When the need is not so great to warrant separate marital counseling, then we can connect parent to parent during the family counseling.

With or without the child(ren) present, *we want to help parents to taste each other's unquenched thirst for honoring love.*

- *Verbalize what you sense.* "Eric, you seem really disheartened by what Kiara said just now." Saying this in the presence of Becky not only validates Eric, it also helps her to begin tuning into her husband's pain.
- *Encourage on-the-spot empathy.* "Becky, can you put into words what you think it's like for Eric when Kiara responds to him like this?"
- *Get them interacting.* "How about you share together right now what you're feeling . . ."
- *Encourage them to invite Christ into their emotional casket.* "As you talk about this during the week, what will it look like to invite Jesus into all of this? What would it be like right now for the two of you to pray a prayer of parental lament about this?"

Equipping (Age-Appropriate) Children to Empathize with and Comfort Their Parents

It is neither the calling nor within the capacity of a five-year-old to emotionally and spiritually comfort her parents. However, we can encourage older children—on their level and in their language—to understand, empathize with, and comfort their parents in Christ. Even if the kids don't quite get it right, the parents have been affirmed by your working with the child(ren) to understand their parents.

- Kiara, your desire for freedom strikes me as quite normal, quite age-appropriate. To be honest, your approach to it also hits me as a bit . . . well . . . insensitive and even at times mean. If I were your mom and dad, I would feel pretty beaten up by some of your comments. Even those you've shared in this room. Have you noticed your mom's tears while you were talking to your dad? What do you make of her tears?

Maturing as a Biblical Family Counselor
Equipping the Family to Comfort Each Other
with Christ's Comfort

1. The two primary New Testament verses on parenting both emphasize parents exasperating, embittering, and discouraging their children.

   a. What are the parenting implications of this?

   b. What are the family counseling implications of this?

2. This section highlighted eight elements of parental empathy. Create a family counseling scenario. Then, for each of the eight areas below, craft a relevant trialogue.

   a. Deepening levels of involvement with their child

   b. Prayer that identifies with the troubling circumstances of their child

   c. Listening beneath their child's words

   d. Opening doors to their child's heart

e. Entering their child's pain

f. Putting words to their child's thoughts and feelings/hurts

g. Inviting their child to reflect

h. Inviting their child to cling to Christ's comfort

3. How would you help a struggling family like Becky, Eric, and Kiara apply 2 Corinthians 1:3–11 to their situation and souls, so that they can help one another to find their comfort in Christ?

EIGHT

Gospel Hope for Family Hurt

Healing in Family Counseling, Part 1

Introduction: Two Ears and Pivot Feet

In chapters 6 and 7, we empathized with Becky, Eric, and Kiara. More importantly, we equipped them as a family to *empathize with each other* and to *comfort each other* with Christ's comfort.

As we move from sustaining to healing family counseling with Becky, Eric, and Kiara, it is helpful to picture the images of two ears and pivot feet. With one ear, we have been listening to their family's earthly story of suffering and struggle, confusion and conflict, pain and problems. Not wanting to ignore their earthly story, we have kept one foot in the reality of their fallen world. And we have climbed in their family casket of doubt and despair, seeking to draw them to empathize with each other and to communicate that, like Christ, we care about each other's hurts.

But we never stop there. Biblical family counselors do not slam the casket lid shut. With our other ear we listen for resurrection hope. With spiritual eyes we glimpse the light piercing the family casket of darkness. We move with Becky, Eric, and Kiara, pivoting our feet between two worlds—between their earthly story and Christ's eternal, heavenly story of resurrection hope.

If we stop at empathizing with pain, climbing in the casket, and sustaining families in their hurt, then we should not call ourselves biblical, Christian counselors. Likewise, if we refuse to enter the hurt of family pain, we will turn families off with a steady stream of positivity, because they will perceive us as insensitive to their family anguish. So we pivot back and forth between sustaining and healing, between empathizing with their hurt and encouraging them to hope in Christ.

Remember Paul's pattern with the believers in Rome. Initially he climbs in their casket of suffering, entering their groanings that could not be uttered (Rom. 8:17–27). Then Paul enlightens the Roman believers to the truth that God works all things together for good and that they are more than conquerors (Rom. 8:28–39). Suffering, then glory. Groanings about the badness of life, then reminders of God's goodness and encouragement to grow in grace.

Biblical family counseling is both/and: both hurt and hope, sustaining and healing, the earthly/temporal story and the heavenly/eternal story. We walk with messy families in our messed-up world, probing together the good news that God is graciously present with us in this evil world. We place Eric, Becky, and Kiara's very real, truly painful smaller story into God's really real, eternally true larger story. We help them to integrate their story into Christ's eternal story. We take their family story seriously while helping them take God seriously.

We are always joining with families like Eric, Becky, and Kiara to ponder the question, How does your human-size story fit into God's infinite story? As biblical family counselors, we join with parents to enlighten them so they can enlighten their children to Christ's family narrative of resurrection hope. Throughout the family healing process, we are praying that they will learn to say together, "Through Christ, it's possible for us to hope in God together." Biblical family counselors pursue this healing goal as we implement the five family healing counseling competencies of FAITH:

F Framing Family Healing Narratives: Cropping Christ into Our Family Portrait (chap. 8)

A Applying Our Identity in Christ: Co-authoring Our Family Love Story (chap. 8)

I Integrating in Our Victory through Christ: Co-authoring Our Family Adventure Narrative (chap. 9)

T Training in Teamwork on the Family Quest: Journeying Together (chap. 9)

H Honing Homework That Works: Keeping the Change Going (chap. 9)

Maturing as a Biblical Family Counselor
Two Ears and Pivot Feet

1. Which is your more natural tendency—sustaining or healing?

   a. Do you tend more toward *sustaining*: climbing in the casket, the earthly story, empathy, normalizing hurt, and Romans 8:17–27? Or do you tend more toward *healing*: celebrating the resurrection, the eternal story, encouragement, promoting hope, and Romans 8:28–39?

   b. Where do you think this tendency comes from—your personality, your upbringing, your training, your experience, how people have related to you, something else?

   c. If you tend less toward sustaining, how could you further develop those biblical family counseling skills? If you tend less toward healing, how could you further develop those biblical family counseling skills?

2. Think about your family life, either growing up or as an adult.

   a. Has anyone ever stopped at sustaining—that is, climbed in the casket with you but left you there aware of your hurt and without hope? If so, what impact did that have on you and your family?

   b. Has anyone ever skipped sustaining and moved directly to healing—quickly telling you to forget those things that are behind and communicating that God will make it all better if you just trust him and don't worry about your past abuse or present pain? If so, what impact did that have on you and your family?

c. Has anyone ever listened with two ears and used their pivot feet to move with you back and forth between sustaining and healing, helping your family to realize that it's normal to hurt, that you could hurt together, and that it's possible to hope again as a family? If so, what impact did that have on you and your family? If not, what impact do you think it could have had if someone had ministered biblical family sustaining *and* healing to you and your family?

Framing Family Healing Narratives: Cropping Christ into Our Family Portrait

Families like Becky, Eric, and Kiara rarely come to us until after the disaster. Typically, they come to us with darkened lenses because *when life stinks, our perspective shrinks*. All they can see are the negative aspects of their relationships, and they view any positives through skewed eyesight. We could diagnose families with spiritual astigmatism: blurred vision that prevents the light of gospel hope from entering their line of sight.

Hopelessness is not simply a human condition. Satan is a liar, deceiver, condemner, and accuser. He accuses us to one another and to God. He accuses God to us. "If God is so good," the serpent hisses, "then why is he allowing such evil into your family?" Satan seeks to *crop Christ out of the family portrait*. With digital photography, we can crop in and crop out anything we want. Satan is a master at cropping resurrection hope out of our picture.

Families Need Counselors Who Pray for the Opening of Blind Eyes

Biblical family counselors need to be like Elisha. In 2 Kings 6:8–18, Elisha's servant was in full panic mode when he saw that the enraged king of Aram had surrounded Elisha with an army of horses and chariots. Elisha shocked his servant with the words, "Don't be afraid. Those who are with us are more than those who are with them" (6:16). Not seeing anyone on Elisha's side, the servant likely suspected that the prophet had finally lost it. So Elisha prayed, "Open his eyes, LORD, so that he may see" (6:17). When the Lord opened the servant's eyes, "he looked and saw the hills full of horses and chariots of fire all around Elisha" (6:17).

Elisha's Old Testament prayer points to Paul's even more powerful New Testament prayer in Ephesians 1:18–20.

I pray that the eyes of your heart may be enlightened in order that you may know the hope to which he has called you, the riches of his glorious inheritance in his holy people, and his incomparably great power for us who believe. That power is the same as the mighty strength he exerted when he raised Christ from the dead and seated him at his right hand in the heavenly realms.

What do we pray for? We pray that God would crop Christ's resurrection power into the heart-eyes of Becky, Eric, and Kiara. Having climbed in the casket with them, now we celebrate the empty tomb with them. We probe and trialogue . . .

- *Ephesians 1:18–20.* We have wept together about Eric's impatience and temper, Becky's struggles with depression, and Kiara's rebellious heart. Now imagine together what Christ's resurrection power could do in each of these difficult areas.

  » How could the power that raised Christ from the dead impact and change your heart, Eric? How could an eternal perspective help you to take every thought and emotion captive when you're tempted to give in to a short temper?

  » Becky, how could knowing your heavenly hope help you to tap into Christ's infinite power as you battle against depression and negativity? Like David in Psalm 42:5, how could you hope in God when your soul is downcast?

  » Kiara, in that moment when your up-and-down emotions tempt you to lash out at Mom and Dad, what would it look like to call upon the power that raised Christ from the dead?

- *Ephesians 6:10–18.* Because it concludes a section focused on the family, we can paraphrase Paul's words in Ephesians 6 as follows: "*Families,* be strong in the Lord and in his mighty power. *Families,* put on the full family armor of God, so that your *family* can take your stand against the devil's schemes. Your struggle is not against your flesh and blood *family,* but against Satan and the powers of this dark world and against the spiritual forces of evil."

  » Becky, Eric, and Kiara, how might things change if you started seeing Satan as the enemy, rather than each other as the enemy?

  » What might it look like to join together—in Christ's resurrection power and with the family armor of God—to fight against Satan's attacks on your family?

Families Need Parents Who See Life with Spiritual Eyes

The parenting theme repeated throughout the Old Testament is one of parents creatively telling and retelling, applying and reapplying the exodus event to their children (cf. Exod. 15; Deut. 8 and 16). Moses envisioned parents who are incurable storytellers. With imagination, parents were to remind each new generation of God's mighty miracles, great grace, and redemptive power.

In a variety of ways, parents were to be careful that their families never forgot "the LORD, who brought you out of Egypt, out of the land of slavery" (Deut. 6:12). Parents were called to impress these redemptive memories upon their children, talking about them when they sat at home, when they walked along the road, when they lay down, and when they got up. Parents were to place memory markers everywhere—on their hands, on their foreheads, and on the door frames and gates of their homes (Deut. 6:7–9).

God calls parents to stimulate their children's imagination in a variety of ways.

- In song (Exod. 15; Deut. 32)
- Through word pictures and by visual markers (Num. 17:10; Deut. 6:8–9; 11:16–21; Josh. 4:20–24)
- Through psalms (Ps. 90)
- In story form (Num. 33; Deut. 1–3)
- Through celebration (Deut. 16)

We say to Eric and Becky:

- I get it. Right now you barely have faith to believe. But pray, "Lord, I believe. Help my unbelief." Then work together as husband and wife, as mom and dad, to help Kiara to look at her life with spiritual eyes that factor in Christ's saving power.
- What are some creative ways you could help Kiara to remember past times when God has given beauty for ashes in your lives? In her life? In your family's life?
- What family victory stories, what stories of Christ's redemptive power in the life of your family, could you remind Kiara of?

Family Healing Requires Biblical Family Counseling Where the Counselor and Family Join Together in a Heroic Love Story

What is family counseling?

Family counseling is a heroic adventure narrative set in a love story.

The Bible is the greatest war story ever told—the story of the battle that began all battles and the battle that will end all battles. It is the battle of good against evil, of God against the devil. The Bible is the greatest love story ever told—the story of a Father's unrelenting love for his prodigal child. It is the story of a faithful Husband's pursuing love for his unfaithful wife.

Every family's smaller story is plopped smack-dab in the middle of the greatest story ever told. The Father commissioned the family you are counseling to create (grand adventure) and relate (love story). The great divider—Satan—is doing all he can to cause the family to destroy and separate. He was the original weed planter. Now he has planted weeds in their family garden—weeds of discouragement, anger, hatred, competition, and hopelessness. Just read Genesis 4–50 to see the relational weeds that destroyed fallen family after fallen family. We do not ignore the weeds. Neither do we act as if the weeds can defeat us.

We join with the family that sits before us. *We are a guide on a grand adventure set in the middle of a love story.* They are main characters in God's drama of family redemption. Their lives are like Job's life. In Job 1–2, we learn what Job was unaware of—his spiritual battle was on display before the hosts of heaven. The whole world is watching the redemptive drama being played out in our families (Eph. 3:10–11). Who will prevail? Who is worthy of worship (Job 1–2)? Will this family curse God and die, or will this family bless God and live? Will this family believe Christ's truth that the Father has a good heart, or will they believe Satan's lie that God's heart can't be trusted?

We listen together, integrating Christ's larger story into their smaller story.

- *We listen together to their smaller earthly story.* What is the theme of their earthly story? What images and pictures are pervading their minds? What is Satan trying to do to them? How are they seeing themselves? What pain are they suffering? What sins are they committing? What thirsts are they experiencing? What lies are they believing?

- *We integrate Christ's larger eternal story.* What is God up to in this family? How is the Spirit wanting to use what they are going through to shape them into the image of Christ? How can they respond to this in a way that draws them closer to one another and closer to Christ? What grand adventure is God calling them to? What vision does God have of what they will create out of this chaos? What love story is God unfolding in their lives? What vision does God have of how they will experience beauty from ashes?

By the end of sustaining and healing, we pray that faith, hope, and love have conquered the world, the flesh, and the devil. We pray that by *faith* the family acknowledges, "God is good even when our family life is bad." Through resurrection *hope*, we pray that they say, "Even if we don't find relief, we can find God. Our goal is not happiness but holiness: loving God, worshiping God, and being a testimony to an onlooking world of Christ's great grace." We pray that in mutual *love* they communicate, "We feel each other's pain" and "It's possible for our family to hope in God."

We do this through:

- Applying Our Identity in Christ: Co-authoring Our Family Love Story (chap. 8)
- Integrating in Our Victory through Christ: Co-authoring Our Family Adventure Narrative (chap. 9)

Maturing as a Biblical Family Counselor
Framing Family Healing Narratives

1. Families need counselors who pray for the opening of blind eyes.

   a. Sometimes we need to pray for spiritual sight for *our* blind eyes as family counselors. We are eye- and ear-witnesses to so much pain and damage. How do you cling to Christ to keep hoping in the middle of hurting and hardened families?

   b. We used Ephesians 1 and 6 to create trialogues of resurrection hope. Select two or three other biblical passages and create one or two resurrection hope trialogues for each passage.

2. Families need parents who see life with spiritual eyes.

   a. In your life, what are some of the redemptive stories—the stories of Christ's victory in your life and your family—that you cling to as memorial stones to remind you of God's past work?

b. What are creative ways that families can show and tell great family stories of God creating beauty from ashes, of God resurrecting dead things or situations in their family?

3. Family healing requires biblical family counseling where the counselor and family join together in a heroic love story.

   a. Think of a past or current struggle in your life. How does it impact you to know that "the whole world is watching"—that your response bears witness to a watching world that you trust God's good heart?

   b. How could these three prayer goals shape or reshape your focus in family counseling?

      • By faith the family acknowledges, "God is good even when our family life is bad."

      • Through resurrection hope, the family says, "Even if we don't find relief, we can find God. Our goal is not happiness but holiness."

      • In mutual love they communicate, "We feel each other's pain" and "It's possible for our family to hope in God."

Applying Our Identity in Christ: Co-authoring Our Family Love Story

In church history, the healing aspect of biblical soul care does *not* focus on a change in circumstances or on inner healing for damaged emotions. Instead, biblical healing focuses on core spiritual issues: the healing of faith, hope, and love. Family members like Becky, Eric, and Kiara come to us with doubts about God instead of faith in Christ; with despair about their situation and themselves instead of hope in God; and with distance between themselves, God, and each other instead of Holy Spirit–empowered sacrificial love.

Soul-u-tion-Focused Biblical Family Counseling

These core spiritual issues are missed by secular solution-focused family therapy. Secular family therapy focuses almost exclusively on the human relationship—fixing the problems *between* family members. Biblical family counseling addresses those interpersonal issues, but instead of focusing first on social disharmony, it focuses on spiritual doubt, despair, and distance. It is soul-u-tion focused, because *social problems in the home always point to spiritual struggles in the heart.*

We do not ignore the family's primary pain—the pain of fractured family relationships. This is why chapters 5 and 6 equip us to climb in the family's casket of suffering. However, we also engage the family's secondary pain—the pain of spiritual doubt, despair, and distance. Put another way, we not only turn the family back to each other; we first turn the family back to Christ. Our ultimate role is to:

> *Help the family receive God's healing faith, hope, and love by bringing Christ's gospel of grace and peace into the center of their painful family narrative.*

Starting with the Gospel

Early in our counseling relationship, Eric, Becky, Kiara, and I read Ephesians 1:2: "Grace and peace to you from God our Father and the Lord Jesus Christ." Wanting to get to the good stuff in Ephesians, we tend to speed past Paul's greeting of "grace and peace." But not Martin Luther, who called these two words "the highest wisdom of Christians."[1]

> These two words, *grace and peace*, comprehend in them whatever belongs to Christianity. Grace releases sin, and peace makes the conscience quiet. The two fiends that torment us are sin and conscience. But Christ has vanquished these two monsters, and trodden them underfoot, both in this world, and in that which is to come. Moreover, these two words, *grace and peace*, contain in them the whole sum of Christianity. Grace contains the remission of sins; peace a quiet and joyful conscience.[2]

Luther understands what biblical family counselors must realize. Before we counsel family members to love like the Father, we first counsel them to grasp the Father's love. Paul builds his gospel imperatives (commands) in Ephesians 6:1–4 on the gospel indicatives (our identity in Christ, what Christ has done for us, who we are in Christ, our relationship to Christ) of Ephesians 1–3. The Spirit empowers family members to love one another on the basis of grasping that they are already loved by God (Eph. 3:17–19; 4:32–5:2).

Grace is the gospel gift of justification. It is our reminder that because of Christ, the Father says to us, "Not guilty! Forgiven!" *Peace* is the gospel gift of reconciliation. It is our reminder that because of Christ, the Father says to us, "Welcome home, son! Welcome home, daughter!" What is our identity in Christ? We are forgiven sons and daughters welcomed home by Abba Father.

Satan seeks to crop Christ's grace and peace out of our picture. He whispers to Eric, "You can't lovingly lead your family. God doesn't even want you in *his* family. All you are is an angry, impatient little boy." The serpent hisses to Becky, "Give up hope. You're just a depressed, pessimistic hopeless baby." The devil shouts at Kiara, "Curse God and die! You're a rebel. A prodigal. Your parents don't love you and God won't take you back."

In 2 Corinthians 2:5–11, Paul warns us not to be ignorant of Satan's scheme to overwhelm us with sorrow over sin by blinding us to the grace and peace we have with God through Christ. As counselors, if we are naïvely ignorant of this deeper battle going on in the souls of Eric, Becky, and Kiara, then our counsel will fall on deaf ears. Until they can together grasp the height, depth, breadth, and width of the Father's love in Christ (Eph. 3:14–21), any attempts at love will be flesh-oriented ("I'll love you if you'll love me") and flesh-empowered ("I'll try harder in my strength to love you better").

Loving from the Overflow of Christ's Love

God's Word paints a very different picture of family love. Rather than being flesh-oriented, it is other-centered. "Do nothing out of selfish ambition or vain conceit. Rather, in humility value others above yourselves, not looking to your own interests but each of you to the interests of the others" (Phil. 2:3–4). If you have counseled families, then you have experienced how Philippians 2:3–4 falls on deaf ears *if* the family members are trying to love in their own strength out of empty souls. "How can you ask me to love my dad when he treats me like that? I'm on empty. I get nothing from him!"

This is why Paul precedes Philippians 2:3–4 with truth about the source of our capacity to love others.

> If you have any encouragement from being united with Christ, if any comfort from his love, if any common sharing in the Spirit, if any tenderness and compassion, then make my joy complete by being like-minded, having the same love, being one in spirit and of one mind. (2:1–2)

We love others out of the overflow of Christ's love for us. Philippians 2:1–4 is a classic family counseling text for trialogues about our source of other-centered love.

- Kiara, I hear you. Dad's admitted that he's been guilty of exasperating you. God's working on Dad. But as Christians, our fuel for loving family members is not their love for us. It's Christ's love for us. So let's talk about Christ's love filling us and flowing out of us.

  » Dad has not always been your source of encouragement, comfort, and love. But Christ always is. Think about Philippians 2:1—you're united with Christ, you receive from Christ encouragement, comfort, and love. Think about that—*one with Christ*! You want to be understood? Christ understands you. You want to be encouraged? Christ is *the* Encourager. You want someone to comfort and love you—*the* Someone gives you that. In fact, the Comforter is *in* you!

  » How could you grasp and apply Christ's encouragement, comfort, and love? What difference could it make in your responses to Dad if you truly believed and received Christ's love for you?

  » You not only have Christ's love, you have fellowship with the Spirit and you have the Father's tenderness and compassion. The whole Trinity is shepherding you! So when Dad is being the opposite of tender and compassionate, how could the Trinity's tenderness and compassion fill you and fuel you . . .?

Applying the Gospel Where Family Life Hurts

It is helpful at this point in family counseling to recall the principal pain of parents and of children. Remember from chapters 4 and 6 what the Bible teaches about the God-designed longings of every parent to receive *honoring love* (Eph. 6:1–3). Parents are not to demand honor; they are not to make being honored an idol of their hearts. At the same time, parents are not to stoically deny the pain and emptiness of *dishonoring distance*.

God designed children to receive *holy love* from their parents (Eph. 6:4). Children are God-wired to long for parental involvement that beautifully combines truth and grace, justice and mercy, discipline and devotion—holy love. Parents are to give their children a finite sampler of the Father's infinite holy love. Children will experience deep pain and emptiness when, instead of receiving parental holy love, they receive parental *harsh detachment*.

In sustaining, we climb in the casket with parents hurting from dishonoring distance. We climb in the casket of pain children endure from harsh detachment. We join parents and children as they embrace their suffering.

In healing, we journey with parents and children as they embrace Christ in their suffering. They experience resurrection hope not only to survive family suffering but to thrive in Christ even while undergoing family suffering.

Since we want parents to be their children's shepherds, we could picture the family counseling process like this:

- We help parents embrace their parental suffering of dishonoring distance (sustaining).
- We help parents embrace Christ in their parental suffering (healing).
- We help parents embrace their children in their suffering of harsh detachment (sustaining).
- We help parents repent of and confess their harsh detachment (reconciling; see chaps. 10–11).
- We help parents help their children to embrace Christ in their suffering (healing).
- We help the family put off their old ways of relating and put on biblical, Christlike ways of relating (guiding; see chaps. 12–13).

What might this look like? The order and setting of family counseling will certainly vary. However, a general format might look like this:

- *Meet first with the parents.* This places them in the shepherding/leadership role from the outset.
- *Meet next with the entire family.* This connects the whole family and allows you to sense their family story and their family pain (suffering and sin).
- *Meet with the parents for healing of the parents' suffering.* As the parents go, so goes the family.
- *Meet with the entire family for healing of the children's suffering.* It is not wrong to meet with the children individually. At times, depending on the situation and the age of the children, this may be quite appropriate. However, if our goal is to empower the family by empowering the parents, then we'll want to assist the parents to bring healing to their children, as opposed to our being the "outside healing expert" who rescues the children.

Parents are the head of the family and Christ is the Head of the parents. When the parents are rightly connected to the Head, then the family can become rightly connected to each other. We strive to equip Psalm 23 parents—parents with the healing capacities of a shepherd. *We are equipping parents to be their kids' counselors.*

Sample Parental Spiritual Conversation Trialogues

What might it sound like to engage in healing spiritual conversations with hurting parents?

- Eric and Becky, what would it be like for you to take the parental ache in your soul to Christ right now?
- Tell me about how you've asked God for strength to endure your parental pain.
- What would it be like to worship God in the middle of the dishonor you're feeling from Kiara's rebelliousness?
- Eric, Becky, tell me about how you've been drawing nearer to God in the midst of Kiara's rebelliousness.
- In the middle of this mess, what are you most deeply longing for from God?
- When Kiara leaves you so empty, how does it help when you cling to Christ, when you hunger and thirst for him?
- You sense how distant Kiara is from you now. Where do you sense Christ is right now?
- In Kiara's disrespectful moments, you've heard plenty about how she sees you. And none of it is positive or encouraging. According to God's Word, how does Christ see you right now? What biblical passages could we explore to answer this question?

Sample Interactions for Parental Scriptural Exploration Trialogues

Recall that spiritual conversations explore and apply relevant biblical *principles*. Scriptural explorations examine and apply relevant biblical *passages*. In biblical family healing, the scriptural exploration process follows this basic methodology:

- Together explore a relevant biblical passage about loss or parental pain. The parable of the prodigal son or any of David's psalms of betrayal would be helpful. Or explore any biblical passage that combines earthly hurt and heavenly hope. Then explore the implications and applications.

  » How is this biblical narrative different from your family situation? How is it the same? How are the pain and suffering different? How are they the same? How is the process of hoping in God different? How is it the same?

» Are there any characters in this story who remind you of people in your life? Are there any themes in this story that remind you of your family situation?

» How do you react to this biblical story? How have you responded differently than the biblical character? How have you responded similarly?

» Where do you see gospel hope and resurrection power in this biblical narrative?

» What would it be like to apply that hope and power to your family story?

» What in this biblical narrative would you like to add to your story? How do you think you could do that through Christ's strength?

» If you were to write your own story, somewhat like this biblical story, what would the theme be? How might your story turn out? What role would God play? What role would you play in your story? Who else might be in your story? What would your relationship to God be like? How would God work your story out for good? How would God give you strength in your story? How would God comfort you?

» We've talked before about penning a psalm of lament. Based on this psalm, what would your psalm of resurrection hope sound like?

Romans 8 as a Sample Family Scriptural Exploration Trialogue

Since Kiara's parents are experiencing the shame of Kiara's dishonoring distance, gospel shalom—gospel grace and peace—will be Christ's vital curative medicine. *Grace is Christ's prescription for our disgrace.*

• Becky and Eric, Romans 8:1 says that "there is therefore now no condemnation for those who are in Christ Jesus." What does this mean for you when Kiara is condemning you?

• Romans 8:14–16 tells us that in Christ we are God's loved, accepted, and respected adult sons and daughters. What difference does this make in how you experience yourself right now as a person? As a parent? As a child of God?

• Romans 8:15 explains that we can cry out to God, "Abba, Daddy, Father!" What would it be like for you to cry out to Abba in the midst of Kiara's disrespect?

• Before Paul turns us to God's promises in Romans 8:28–39, he invites us to turn our problems and pain over to God—to groan to God.

What parental groanings are you taking to the Father's throne of grace?

- God promises in Romans 8:28 to work everything together for good for those who love him. What good work is the Father's good heart working out in your heart?

- Romans 8:29 promises us that God is conforming us to the image of Christ. How is he working out his promise in your life through your family situation?

- Romans 8:31–34 teaches that "if God is for us, who can be against us?" Who can condemn us if God accepts us in Christ? What impact does this truth have on you?

- Romans 8:37 insists that you are more than a conqueror! I know that you don't *feel* like that right this moment as a parent. However, that's how Christ views you. How would things be different if you viewed yourself as more than a conqueror in Christ?

- Romans 8:38–39 tells us that nothing will ever separate us from God's love in Christ. What do these words mean to you as you experience such painful rejection from Kiara?

Parents Shepherding Their Children

First you work with parents to help them experience Christ's gospel hope. Then you help parents "own" their own stuff, repent to God, and confess their parental sins to their children. As this process is occurring, you coach parents to counsel and disciple their kids.

The first healing Kiara will experience is when Mom and Dad confess to her their parental sin. Their humble repentance is one of the greatest healing gifts Kiara will ever receive. Of course, words without action mean little. So Becky and Eric will need biblical counseling that guides them to put off their old ways of harsh detachment and put on Christ's new way of parental holy love. Those changes will be Kiara's second healing gift.

Just as counselors want to point kids not to the counselor but to the parents, so parents want to point their kids not to themselves but to the ultimate Parent—to God the Father of Holy Love. Having begun to see examples of parental holy love from their parents, kids are much more prepared to receive the Father's holy love.

So now, in a session with just Kiara's parents, we coach them through spiritual conversations and scriptural explorations they can have with Kiara. They can then interact with Kiara about these either outside of counseling or with you in counseling. Here are some samplers. (These assume that Becky and Eric have already asked God and Kiara for forgiveness for their failure to provide Kiara with parental holy love.)

- Kiara, again, we're so sorry for how we've failed you and sinned against you by _____. Thank you for forgiving us. What are some ways we can begin showing you the shepherding holy love that Pastor Bob has been talking about?
- Kiara, as much as we'll try in Christ's strength to love you well, we'll still fail you. We'll be imperfect. How could you turn to Christ for his holy love and shepherding care during those times when we let you down?
- Kiara, even when we're empowered by Christ to love you well, our love is still so small in comparison to the Father's infinite love and holiness. How could we help you to develop the heart habit of turning to the Father daily for his shepherding love?
- Isaiah 40:10–11 is the passage that Pastor Bob was talking to us about. In these two verses we see a beautiful blending of God's holiness and love as Isaiah portrays God as our Shepherd-King. Could the three of us read these verses together and discuss how they apply to our lives?

Maturing as a Biblical Family Counselor
Applying Our Identity in Christ

1. In your life, where have you experienced Christ's grace and peace? Where have you heard the Father say, "Not guilty! Forgiven!" (the grace of justification in Christ)? Where have you heard the Father say, "Welcome home, son/daughter!" (the peace of reconciliation in Christ)?

2. Review the scriptural explorations on page 156 about Philippians 2:1–4.

   a. In your life, how are you experiencing encouragement from your union with Christ, comfort from Christ's love, fellowship with the Spirit, and the Father's tenderness and compassion?

b. When significant people in your life are not loving you well, how can you tap into the truths of Philippians 2:1 in order to love them well out of the overflow of the Trinity's love?

3. Review the sample parental spiritual conversation trialogues on page 158. Then write out half a dozen of your own sample trialogues.

4. Review the sample family scriptural exploration trialogue from Romans 8 on pages 159–60. Select a different passage and then write out half a dozen of your own family scriptural explorations.

CHAPTER

NINE

From Surviving to Thriving

Healing in Family Counseling, Part 2

Introduction: The Kellemen Family MVP Statement

Shirley and I moved from Indiana to Seattle in 2018 to be near our adult children and grandchildren. During our three-day cross-country drive, we spent a good deal of time reminiscing about our marriage and family life together. At one point, Shirley remarked, "Can you believe it's been twenty years since the four of us [me, Shirley, and our two children, Josh and Marie] worked together on our Kellemen Family MVP Statement?!"

Some background: for years I've consulted with churches and parachurch organizations and helped them collaboratively develop a ministry mission, vision, and passion statement—an MVP statement.

I describe mission as the *universal*, God-given, biblically defined reason that a church or parachurch organization exists. I lead ministry leaders through an in-depth biblical study of their ministry, culminating in a jointly created one- to two-sentence mission statement.

I define vision as the *unique* way God has designed a specific church or ministry—their one-of-a-kind fingerprint or DNA—that helps them identify their future dream for fulfilling their distinctive calling. This, too, results in a one- or two-sentence vision statement.

I define passion as a pithy, concise, succinct summary phrase or image that captures the essence of a group's identity and purpose—a tag line.

Back in 1998, twenty years before our cross-country move, the Kellemen family spent six months collaboratively crafting our Kellemen Family MVP Statement. Josh had just become a teenager, Marie had just turned double digits, and I won't tell you what age Shirley and I had just turned! Life has a way of beating down and attacking a thirteen-year-old, a ten-year-old, and their parents. So we thought it would be helpful if the four of us spent our family devotional/worship time examining Scripture to discern the universal mission of every Christian family. We scoured scores of verses together, evening after evening. Here is what we crafted for our Kellemen Family Mission:

> The Kellemen family exists to love Christ most with our most
> by treasuring and keeping God's principal principles:
> enjoying and exalting God,
> loving each other,
> and loving our neighbor as we love our self.

You can imagine some of the primary passages we drew these words from—words that God's Spirit reminded us of frequently during the next decade while we all still lived under one roof.

We then thought long and hard about how God had fearfully and wonderfully made each of us individually and how he had designed the four of us together as a family. Out of those discussions, we collectively penned our Kellemen Family Vision:

> It is our Kellemen family dream
> to boldly go where God shows (explorers)
> with our backpacks filled with God's guidebook
> (the Bible) as our compass,
> God's food (prayer) as our energy source,
> and our hands gripping God's rope of hope (perseverance)
> as we scale God's mountain of life and love.

You can surmise that we are a family that loves sci-fi, including *Star Trek*. Again, this family vision held us together through some wonderful times and through some challenging times.

Finally, we started pondering our pithy passion statement—what phrase would capture *us*? Unable to frame just one, we settled on two Kellemen Passion Statements:

> Christ's love makes our house a home.
> Christ's grace makes our home a safe place.

Those two singsong phrases have been an anchor in many storms.

Knowing our calling is vital for families and for family counselors. Our mission as family counselors is reflected in the first question of the Westminster Shorter Catechism: "What is the chief end of man?" The answer: "Man's chief end is to glorify God, and to enjoy him forever."

When a distressed, depressed, and discouraged family enters our counseling office, it is unlikely to be very helpful if we open by quoting the Shorter Catechism. However, this ultimate purpose for life—and for family life—must be at the center of our minds as Christian family counselors. You read in chapter 8:

Family counseling is a heroic adventure narrative set in a love story.

This is true because:

The Christian family is on a heroic adventure narrative (to exalt Christ) set in a love story (to enjoy Christ).

Rather than starting by quoting church history, we begin by *framing* family healing narratives: cropping Christ into the family portrait (chap. 8). This is what Shirley, Josh, Marie, and I were doing in 1998—proactively cropping Christ into the center of our family portrait—before the onslaught of the teen years, and the college years, and the young adult years . . .

Next, as family counselors, we *apply* our identity in Christ: co-authoring our family love story (chap. 8). When Becky, Eric, and Kiara are condemned by Satan, and at times by each other, we turn them back to who they are *in* Christ (saints) and who they are *to* Christ (sons and daughters). They enjoy Christ and bathe in his grace as they share that grace with each other—Christ's grace makes our home a safe place; Christ's love makes our house a home.

Now, in chapter 9, we help them *integrate* their victory through Christ: co-authoring their family adventure narrative. We also help them through *training* in teamwork on the family quest and through collaboratively *honing* homework that works.

Maturing as a Biblical Family Counselor
The Kellemen Family MVP Statement

1. *A family mission statement.* Mission involves examining Scripture to identify the *universal*, God-given, biblically defined purpose of every Christian family.

   a. What scriptural passages would you explore to develop the *universal*, God-given, biblically defined purpose of your family or your counselee's family?

b. How might you word your preliminary family mission statement? What is your one- or two-sentence summary of the biblical reason for your family's existence?

2. *A family vision statement.* Vision involves pondering the *unique* way God has fearfully and wonderfully designed each individual family member and the family collectively—the one-of-a-kind family fingerprint or DNA leading to a distinctive future family dream.

   a. How would you word your preliminary family vision statement? What is your one- or two-sentence summary of your ongoing, future vision or dream for God's unique calling on your family?

   b. How would it help a troubled family (or any family) if they were to spend time together collaboratively identifying their unique family DNA and their distinctive family dream?

3. *A family passion statement.* Passion involves identifying a pithy, concise, succinct summary phrase or image that captures the essence of a family's identity and purpose.

   a. How would you word your preliminary family passion statement? What tag line begins to crisply capture your family's identity and purpose?

   b. How would it help a troubled family (or any family) if they were to spend time together collaboratively capturing their family tag line or summarizing image?

4. "The Christian family is on a heroic adventure narrative (to exalt Christ) set in a love story (to enjoy Christ)." How could that summary of the Christian family impact your focus as a Christian family counselor?

Integrating in Our Victory through Christ:
Co-authoring Our Family Adventure Narrative

We heal the family's soul by hearing and healing the family's story. Over 75 percent of the Bible is narrative. God designed us in his storytelling image. We are meaning makers who not only tell stories, we *interpret* our family story. In the context of taking every thought captive to Christ, Paul reveals to the Corinthians that they are looking only on the surface of things (2 Cor. 10:7). They are interpreting life with their physical eyeballs only, instead of with spiritual eyes. They are focused on the temporal earthly story instead of looking at life with 20/20 scriptural, eternal vision.

Throughout his letter, Paul counsels the Corinthians to live by faith and not merely by sight (2 Cor. 5:7). They must fix their eyes not simply on what is seen, outward, and temporal but on what is unseen, inward, and eternal (2 Cor. 4:16–18).

We become the stories we tell ourselves. Eric, Becky, and Kiara interpret themselves and each other by outward appearance, from an external, temporal perspective. They have allowed Christ's resurrection power and eternal hope to be cropped out of their family portrait. As counselors, our calling is to enlighten them to Christ's perspective (2 Cor. 10:3), empower them to tap into his divine power to demolish strongholds (2 Cor. 10:4), and equip them to take every thought captive to Christ (2 Cor. 10:5).

Unearth the Earthly Family Story

We heal their family story by helping them to hear Christ's story and integrate his eternal story into their earthly story. Think about what this requires: they must first unearth their earthly story. They have each told their side of the story so often that it is ingrained in them. They do not recognize it as their *interpretation* of the facts.

We start by exploring the history of their family story. Family problems are not born full-grown. They develop through the family members' repeated failures to take every thought captive.

Take a Family Biopsy

As each family member shares their personal description of their family story, we help them condense it. As a soul physician, we take a *biopsy* of the problem *as they define it and experience it*. The stories of hurting families are all over the place! They tell incident after incident, with no one putting the pieces of the family puzzle together. We direct the family to explore one small area in depth.

- Becky, Eric, and Kiara, I hear a number of different threads that you're weaving as you tell your family story. I wonder if we could agree to focus on one area? [They agree to focus on Kiara's sense that she's been neglected ever since the turmoil started at church.]
- Kiara, tell us again what this has been like for you. [Kiara shares her story.]
- Becky, what did you hear Kiara saying just now? [Becky shares.]
- Eric, what did you hear Kiara saying? [Eric shares.]
- Now I'd like the three of you to talk about this. Let's not bring in any other topics, any other history. Only what the three of you have shared during the past few minutes.

Examine the Family Biopsy

As they interact, you listen, observe, think, watch. Be curious.

- What are their family values? What are their unstated relational rules? How do they relate? What interactional patterns do you notice? What is the function of their interactions: to get closer, to cover up, to keep a comfortable distance?
- What is the *theme* of their family story?
- What roles do they each assume?
- What is their family image of God? How do they see each other? How do they see themselves?
- Where are they failing to love with honoring love and holy love? Where are they sharing honoring love and holy love?
- When are they failing to turn to Christ for the thirsts of their soul? When are they turning to Christ?

Forge a Common Perception of the Family Problem

Now we help the family forge a common perception of the problem. At this point, we are not so much pursuing the biblical interpretation of their family problem. We are assessing how *they* perceive and interpret their family problem. We can pursue this in two main ways.

First, after they interact, ask each family member to write down a one-*paragraph* summary of the problem. Then ask them to write a one-*sentence* summary of the problem. Have them share their summaries. Then have them work together to develop a joint paragraph or sentence. They can use a whiteboard, a legal pad, an iPad, whatever.

Second, after they interact, share your picture of how you perceive them to be defining the issue. Use their family language. Be sure to check in by asking each family member, "How does this fit for how you see your family struggle?" Then work with them to make it fit even better for each of them individually and all of them together.

Once you collaboratively forge a common perception of the problem, *stick with it*. Use this as a running theme. Because families develop a habituated style of viewing life, the theme will likely be reflective of their typical pattern of interpreting life with physical eyes only.

Now the monster they are facing has a name. The problem has a label. It could be anything that the family perceives to be the core theme to their dominant problem-saturated story. They might be relatively accurate, biblically perceptive interpretations:

- We've acted as if Kiara was the Invisible Woman.
- We've each handled this on our own, rather than together in Christ. Christ is invisible in our story!
- We've lost that lovin' feelin' and we're each lonely, isolated, and frustrated with each other. We're all invisible—we're the Invisible Family.

On the other hand, the biopsy you took might be a cancerous, faulty, incomplete interpretation lacking spiritual insight:

- Kiara is the problem; she's way too sensitive!
- We've scarred Kiara for life! She'll never feel like a real person again.
- We're enemies. All we ever do is fight. We'll never fix this. We don't have the resources to make this right.

A lot of us habitually rush in to teach/tell God's eternal story—before we have even heard the family's version of their earthly story. By unearthing their earthly story, we have created a working alliance as we have joined with each person individually and the family jointly as they have described their problem. Then we helped them forge a common perception of the problem, a shared theme that they all own.

Biblically Diagnose the Family's Problem

Before we can assist the family to co-author a new, Christ-saturated interpretation of their family story, they may have to "un-author" or put off the old family story. We want to help them biblically diagnose the interpretation the family has given to their struggles.

If they say the problem is Kiara's oversensitiveness, then we explore this. How are we defining "oversensitive"? In what ways is she oversensitive? How are we understanding emotions—biblically or unbiblically? Are family members allowed to hurt? Is it possible that Becky and Eric are being insensitive?

How so? Are Kiara's expectations unrealistic or realistic? Are her parents' responses responsible or irresponsible?

Prescribe Biblical Truth to Treat the Family Problem

We help the family align their core view of their family with God's core view of families.

Perhaps during the course of our explorations, Becky and Eric come to see that Kiara has become their scapegoat. Rather than facing the truth that they have been insensitive to Kiara, they have made her out to be immature, overly emotional, and hypersensitive.

Biblically explore together what is motivating them to make Kiara a scapegoat. Why now? What does this say about how they view themselves? About how they view God? About how they view Kiara? About how they view family life? What would happen if they faced how they have failed their daughter?

Unveil the Eternal Story

To this point we have helped Eric, Becky, and Kiara more accurately identify the true battle they are facing as a family. And we have helped them—especially Mom and Dad—to begin to put off their old way of thinking. But we have yet to identify the resources this family has available to win this battle. They have been enlightened to biblical truth; now we seek to empower and equip them to apply that truth.

Integrate Their Victory in Christ into Their Family Story: Christ Equips Them on Their Family Adventure Narrative

Now is the time to integrate Christ's larger story into the family's smaller story. Start by applauding their spiritual humility through Christ.

- Wow! Becky and Eric, not many parents are able to identify and confess their sin to their children. And you've done it knowing that Kiara is not without her faults, without specks or motes of sin in her eye, in her relationship to you. That's amazing!
- Kiara, you've been honest to acknowledge that you have your own sinful role to play in this. What's it like to hear your parents take the mote out of their eye and ask your forgiveness? What does this say about their maturity—not about their perfection, because they are not perfect, but about their willingness to grow in Christ?

Continue by exploring their victory in Christ.

- Becky and Eric, how have you been able to tap into Christ's truth and grace to do this?

- When I think of this depth of parental humility, I think of the passage I've been referencing—Matthew 7 and taking the log or speck out of our own eye first. Could we explore this together—the four of us? As we do, Eric and Becky, I'd like to hear about how the Spirit has been softening your heart in such a remarkable way.

- I'd also like the four of us to think about how Mom and Dad's humble repentance drives a dagger into the heart of Satan's lie. Remember one of the themes you all came up with for your family problem: "We'll never make it." Kind of like Eeyore. But you're making it. You're changing. How is Christ making that happen . . .?

Integrate Christ's Victory into Their Family Story: Christ Empowers Them to Hope on Their Family Adventure Narrative

Family healing, hope, and victory begin when family members and the family unit start seeing who they are in Christ—*their identity in Christ*. As vital as this is, they also must see *the identity of Christ*. Ponder how Scripture communicates this:

- "We are more than conquerors [our identity in Christ] through him who loved us [the identity of Christ]" (Rom. 8:37).

- "I can do all things [our identity in Christ] through him who gives me strength [the identity of Christ]" (Phil. 4:13).

So we trialogue further, deeper, more richly with Kiara, Becky, and Eric.

- Let's think some more about the old Eeyore motto "We'll never make it." In one way it's true, right? In yourselves, you're not gonna make it. But *through Christ* you can do all things. Who is this Christ who gives you strength? Who is he to each of you?

- Your family crest now says, "Through Christ who loves us so, we are more than conquerors!" Who is this Christ who loves you so? What is his love like to each of you, for each of you?

- In 2 Corinthians 4:7–12, Paul says we have the treasure of the glory of Christ in us—in jars of clay. Our weakness shows that our victory comes from the all-surpassing power of God and not from us. What will it look like for each of you to depend totally on Christ for your family victory? How could you give all the glory to Christ for your family victory?

Maturing as a Biblical Family Counselor
Integrating in Our Victory through Christ

1. Ponder a recent time of relationship friction in your life.

    a. In what ways were you perhaps looking at this situation with eyeballs only—from a surface, temporal, earthly perspective? How did that perspective impact how you responded relationally?

    b. In what ways were you able to look at the situation by cropping Christ into the picture—with an eternal, heavenly, 20/20 spiritual vision? How did that perspective impact the way you responded relationally?

2. Think about a family situation or problem—it could be from your counseling ministry, your family growing up, your family now, or a made-up role-play scenario. Review each of the following sections from this chapter and write out a summary using that family situation.

    a. Take a family biopsy.

    b. Examine the family biopsy.

    c. Forge a common perception of the family problem.

    d. Biblically diagnose the family problem.

    e. Prescribe biblical truth to treat the family problem.

3. Think about a relational situation, issue, struggle, problem, or conflict in your life.

   a. How could you integrate your victory in Christ into your story?

   b. How could you integrate Christ's victory into your story?

Training in Teamwork on the Family Quest: Journeying Together

Picture the process and progress thus far. The family that had been hurting each other now hurts *with* each other (sustaining). The family that had been cropping Christ out of their picture and looking at life with only physical eyes now looks at their family life with Christ-focused, gospel-centered lenses (healing). This is *family progressive sanctification.*

So we build on this. They had been working against each other. Now we encourage and equip them to work together—teamwork on the family quest. They are moving from living in their own strength, which leads to despair, to a renewed mindset that says, "Through Christ, it's possible for us to hope in God together."

Hoping Together

Hope in God is their new mindset. Hoping *together* and working together is their new asset. Out of their mutual hope they birth mutual ministry to each other—they work together to co-create spiritual growth in each other and relational growth between each other. They do this *through Christ* as they learn to tap into Christ's grace resources that he has fearfully and wonderfully implanted into the family jointly and into each family member individually.

Identify Their Unique Ways of Co-creating

We want to help family members begin to see each other with grace eyes. This requires that *we* first see them not primarily through the lens of their problems but through the lens of Christ's family-specific work in them. So we ask ourselves:

- What are the unique strengths and special gifts of this family?
- Who are these people? What makes them tick? What makes them unique?
- How does this family work together compared to other families? How do they dance?
- What is special and different about their relationship to each other?
- How would I summarize this family's unique vision, calling, DNA, or dream from God?
- How would I capture this family's unique passion from God?

Share What You See in a Captivating and Motivating Way

As you gain a sense of their God-gifted uniqueness, fan that gift into flame by sharing what you see.

- Wow! Eric, Becky, and Kiara, have the three of you noticed how well you play off each other? I have a fun picture in my mind. Remember you talked about going to the Harlem Globetrotters game? They pass the ball from player to player. They dribble around others. They make perfect assists so they can dunk the ball. That's what you guys remind me of today. So in sync. How have you learned to play together so well?
- As the three of you relate, a picture keeps running through my mind. In *Star Trek: The Next Generation*, which you told me you guys all used to watch, Wesley Crusher was able to be a young adult at times and then at other times he was able to still be a kid. You seem to have worked out a similar relationship where, as parents, you allow Kiara to take on some real responsibilities, but you also allow her to kick back and be a kid. How long have you been able to work things out so well like this?

Encourage the Family to Identify God's Handiwork at Work in Them

As with all family counseling, while it is beneficial for the counselor to identify God-given family strengths, it is even more vital for the family to develop the ability to identify God's handiwork in themselves. Help the family to personalize Ephesians 2:10: "For we are God's handiwork, created in Christ Jesus to do good works, which God prepared in advance for us to do." This can begin with an exploration of their overall family history of mutual ministry.

- What positive impact have you had on each other during your family life?
- What would life be like without each other?
- Who have the three of you impacted together?

It can continue with a specific exploration of how they have worked together in the past and how they are now currently working together through Christ's strength to address their family struggles.

- Tell me about some times when you're already defeating some of these problems.
- As a family, how have you tapped into Christ's resurrection power to overcome this family temptation?
- Have you ever struggled with anything like this before as a family? How did you overcome it then?
- What could you take from that past victory and use now?

Based on their past and current growth in grace as a family, generate ongoing victory-in-Christ stories.

- What do you think your victory this past week says about the issue we've been discussing this morning?
- If you applied what you learned from that time with Kiara, what would you do to work through this issue now . . .?
- Kiara, Eric, and Becky, in light of that time of joint victory as a family, what will you do differently this week . . . ?

It is also helpful and hope-giving for the family to recognize that they are not in this alone. They have Christ *and* they have the body of Christ.

- Who else is on your side and in your corner as you guys all work to overcome these struggles?
- Who else is hurting with you guys as you struggle through all of this?

Provoke Joint Action

On the basis of their newfound insight into Christ's work within them, provoke joint action. Do this first by helping them to see their connection and then to *do more of the same*.

- Over the next week, I'd like you each to write down what happens in your relationship that you want to continue to have happen. [This is a general instruction to do more of the same.]
- During this week, I'd like the three of you to keep passing the ball to each other. I want you to see who can get the most assists. Keep track of all the times you are a team player.

- Before our next meeting, I'd like each of you to write down times when Kiara is like Wesley Crusher: times when she is a young adult and times when she is a kid. Also, jot down what you are doing differently during those times that helps you to work this out so well.

When the family returns, *expect the best.*

- So, tell me what is different or better.
- What's your report today? Tell me how you were able to apply what you learned last week.
- What was happening this past week that each of you wants to continue doing?

When they report success, *keep the ball rolling.*

- That's great! How did you do that?
- I'm impressed by your teamwork. How will you keep that going and growing in Christ?

When they report no change, respond with *further exploration.*

- Hmm. How have you been able to continue to cope with this as a family?
- I'm sorry to hear that it feels like the same old, same old. How have you managed to stay on top of things as a family through all of this?
- How did each of you keep matters from getting worse?
- No? Not even a little? Was there one time when you were able to experience a bit more victory together than previously?
- Are there actions or attitudes or words that you would do differently if you had the week to do over again?
- What do you think kept you from drawing on God's power to do this together as a family?

Garner Gender Resources

God made us male and female and has given each father and each mother unique gender strengths. Biblical family counselors draw these out and stir them up.

- Eric, I know your heart. You're a protector. Nobody messes with those you love. You love your daughter. I want to see you protect her right now. Protect Kiara from your own fear, from your distance.

Right this second, how could you draw on the way God has designed you as a dad to offer Kiara your strong involvement and loving shepherding?

- Becky, I've seen you support so many people in our church. Many times you've been my biggest fan. I'd like you to express your support and love for Kiara right now. She feels neglected. What could you do or say right this second, through how Christ has wired you as a mom, that would offer Kiara your supportive, caring, tender involvement?

Maturing as a Biblical Family Counselor
Training in Teamwork on the Family Quest

1. A family sits before you and is deeply struggling, sharing problem after problem.

    a. How difficult is it for you to see signs of Christ's hope and grace in a struggling family like this?

    b. What could you do to grow in your ability to see families with grace-eyes and to see signs of hope in the midst of despair? This does *not* mean pretending all is well. It means cropping Christ into your picture of the family.

2. "For we are God's handiwork, created in Christ Jesus to do good works, which God prepared in advance for us to do" (Eph. 2:10). How could these words:
    a. Shape the way you see and counsel troubled families?

    b. Shape the way discouraged family members see themselves and each other?

---

3. Think about your own family (either growing up or now). Use several of the trialogues under the heading "Encourage the Family to Identify God's Handiwork at Work in Them" to grow in Christ's hope-filled perspective of your family.

4. Picture a family—one you have counseled in the past, are counseling now, or know well. How could you use the trialogues under the heading "Provoke Joint Action" to minister to and counsel this family?

Honing Homework That Works: Keeping the Change Going

"Homework" is not necessarily my favorite word, but it is a common term in biblical counseling circles. "Growth projects" perhaps better communicates the essence—actions the family takes between sessions that help them put into practice the principles and passages discussed during a session. Homework is vital in sustaining, healing, reconciling, and guiding. So these principles fit throughout the biblical family counseling journey.

- *Cast a vision for 24/7 gospel application.* From the onset of counseling, communicate that there is no magic counseling hour that cures all human ills. Instead, the counseling hour prepares the family for the other 167 hours in their week. Communicate the following: "Here's what we've focused on today. What will it look like for all of you to apply these biblical truths in love with each other this week?"
- *Collaboratively create Scripture-focused, family-unique, situation-specific homework.* On the basis of what you focused on in the session, discuss with the family members what would be the best homework assignment during the week:

  » Of all the passages we explored today, which ones will be most important for you to study and apply this week? How will you each go about doing that?
  » Out of all the biblical principles we discussed today, which stands out as most important that you want to focus on and apply this week?

- *Families learn what they can expect to hear at the end of each session*. After a few sessions, I no longer need to ask. Throughout our meeting they have been thinking about what homework assignment they will give themselves—they are co-coaching each other in their family discipleship.
- *How and when to use specific passages for specific situations*. We all have our go-to passages for various issues. Often *during* the session I will direct families toward those verses or ask the family members what passages they see as relevant to a particular issue. These passages become fair game for homework. However, I want to avoid a canned, one-size-fits-all approach. Keeping homework assignments collaborative strikes a good balance here.
- *How to use your own time in the Word*. I avoid trying to apply to every family the passage that has impacted me that day or week. My life situation may require different biblical wisdom than their life situation. However, when God works in my heart, I want to be open to the possibility that this passage may have some specific application to this family.
- *How to use extrabiblical resources*. Collaboratively decide with the family on which pertinent Christian booklets, books, videos, discussion guides, or workbooks to use. Resources that have questions for parents or parents and children to work on together are especially beneficial. I typically do not cover this homework in detail during sessions, as if counseling is a class and they are being graded. Instead, I ask a couple basic accountability questions: "How is the study going? What are a couple of main points you've been gleaning and applying?"
- *Keep families connected to the local church*. We want families to understand that family counseling is a subset of the ongoing one-another discipleship ministry of the local church. Require family members to be in Sunday morning worship and part of a small group, children's ministry, or youth group. If the church has specific redemption or recovery ministries that fit a family's specific issues, at least the parents should be regularly participating. The parents should have an advocate or spiritual friend who is building into their life and family and who knows specifically about their family counseling—ideally even being a part of the sessions.
- *How to follow up*. Follow-up and accountability are vital. So I typically start with, "Last week the four of us agreed that you would focus on _____ throughout the week. Let's talk about how that's going . . ." Notice I said I *typically* start with that. There are times when it is obvious that the family has had a horrible week and they are in distress. The problem of the moment may trump homework follow-up.

Maturing as a Biblical Family Counselor
Honing Homework That Works

1. What has been your experience—homework given out by the counselor or homework collaboratively created by the counselor and counselees? What are the pros and cons of each approach?

2. You read several principles of honing homework that works.

   a. Which one, if any, surprises you? How?

   b. Which one, if any, do you disagree with? Why? What would you do differently?

   c. What principles would you add?

3. Between meetings, how do you keep family members connected to:

   a. the Word of God?

   b. the people of God (their local church)?

4. What are some best practices for following up on homework and keeping family members accountable?

TEN

Care-Fronting Family Sin

Reconciling in Family Counseling, Part 1

Introduction: Compassionate Concern for Heart Change

Families come to us not only with suffering stories but also with sinning and separating family stories. Trapped within destructive stories of their own making, they experience the inevitable consequence of sin: *turmoil.*

Twice in Isaiah we read that there is no peace—no shalom, wholeness, or rest—for the wicked (48:22; 57:21). The context is instructive. God—the Divine Counselor—simultaneously confronts and comforts his sinning people. In the space of a handful of verses, the Divine Counselor sustains, heals, reconciles, and guides his people.

> For this is what the high and exalted One says—
>   he who lives forever, whose name is holy:
> "I live in a high and holy place,
>   *but also* with him who is contrite and lowly in spirit,
> to *revive* the spirit of the lowly
>   and to *revive* the heart of the contrite.
> I will not accuse them forever,
>   nor will I always be angry,
> for then they would faint away because of me—
>   the very people I have created.
> I was enraged by their sinful greed;
>   I *punished* them, and hid my face in anger,
>   yet they kept on in their willful ways.
> I have seen their ways, but I will *heal* them;
>   I will *guide* them and restore *comfort* to Israel's mourners,
>   creating praise on their lips.

Peace, peace, to those far and near,"
   says the LORD. "And I will *heal* them."
But the wicked are like the tossing sea,
   which cannot rest,
   whose waves cast up mire and mud.
"There is no peace," says my God, "for the wicked." (Isa. 57:15–21)

The high and lofty One is the gracious and forgiving One. The all-holy God who confronts sin is "the LORD, the LORD, the compassionate and gracious God, slow to anger, abounding in love and faithfulness, maintaining love to thousands, and forgiving wickedness, rebellion and sin" (Exod. 34:6–7).

When I teach about confronting sin, I often tell counselors-in-training that if they *enjoy* confronting sin, they probably should *not* confront sin. We ought to be like Paul in 2 Corinthians 7:8–10, who is clearly conflicted over having to confront the Corinthians. He knows it is right and best, but it troubles his soul to trouble the souls of troubling people.

Paul further depicts our attitude as we confront people. "Brothers and sisters, if someone is caught in a sin, you who live by the Spirit should restore that person gently. But watch yourselves, or you also may be tempted" (Gal. 6:1). This is why I often describe confronting as "care-fronting": *humbly and lovingly exposing sin out of concern and with a desire for heart change.*

Our attitude as family counselors needs to be infiltrated by the truth of Romans 5:20 that where sin abounds, grace superabounds. We encourage families so that they are not hardened by the deceitfulness of sin (Heb. 3:12–13), exposing the truth that *it's horrible to sin.* We always also magnify the infinitely greater reality that in Christ *it's wonderful to be forgiven.* Because we want family members to take ownership for reconciling with each other, we seek to help them realize that *it's horrible to sin against Christ and each other, but through Christ it's wonderful to be forgiven and to forgive.*

Struggling against family besetting sins, families come to us in turmoil and in need of shalom, of family REST:

R Recognizing Destructive Family Relationships: Identifying Family Heart Sin (chap. 10)

E Enlightening Family Members to Destructive Family Relationships: Calling Sinners Home (chap. 10)

S Soothing the Family's Soul in Their Savior: Repenting to and Receiving Forgiveness from God (chap. 11)

T Trust-Making: Exhibiting Fruits of Repentance and Granting Forgiveness to Each Other (chap. 11)

Maturing as a Biblical Family Counselor
Compassionate Concern for Heart Change

1. Reread Isaiah 57:15–21.
   a. Can you identify aspects of the Divine Counselor's sustaining, healing, reconciling, and guiding in these verses?

   b. As biblical family counselors, what can we learn from God in Exodus 34:6–7; Isaiah 57:15–21; and Romans 5:20 about our attitude and actions in confronting (care-fronting) families in sin and turmoil?

2. What can we learn about confronting (care-fronting) family sin from 2 Corinthians 7:8–10; Galatians 6:1; and Hebrews 3:12–13?

3. "I often tell counselors-in-training that if they *enjoy* confronting sin, they probably should *not* confront sin." What do you think about my advice?

4. Care-fronting is *humbly and lovingly exposing sin out of concern and with a desire for heart change*. How might this definition of care-fronting impact the way you confront family sin?

5. "It's horrible to sin against Christ and each other, but through Christ it's wonderful to be forgiven and to forgive." How could this summary statement of reconciling family counseling impact your ministry to families struggling with besetting sin?

Recognizing Destructive Family Relationships:
Identifying Family Heart Sin

Recall from James 4:1–4 that in the midst of relational conflict, family members are poor judges of their role and responsibility in their fights and quarrels. So family members, especially parents, need our assistance to see the mote blinding their spiritual and relational eyesight.

As counselors, we need assistance too. In the cacophony of accusations and allegations, in the back-and-forth "he said, she said" of family conflict, where do we start? Where do we head? What do we look for? What do the behavioral signs and symptoms reveal about parental heart sin? About heart sins of children? How are we to make sense of all of this family messiness?

Seeing Life's Ultimate Purpose from God's Eternal Perspective

Biblical counselors start big by seeing life from God's perspective. What is God's purpose in our family suffering, struggles, and sin? Deuteronomy 8:2–3 paints this big picture.

> Remember how the LORD your God led you all the way in the wilderness these forty years, to humble you and to test you *in order to know what was in your heart*, whether or not you would keep his commands. He humbled you, causing you to hunger and then feeding you with manna, which neither you nor your ancestors had known, to teach you that man does not live on bread alone but on every word that comes from the mouth of the LORD.

Life is about either admitting our insufficiency or parading our self-sufficiency. Do we live, exist, and survive on bread alone—that we assume we can produce by our own hands? Or do we live by every word that comes from the mouth of God—that he graciously provides?

Even when God miraculously supplied the Israelites' needs, they still had a heart choice. Would they trust God or themselves? When they entered the promised land and built fine houses and their goods increased, would they remember God, or would their hearts become proud and forget the God who brought them out of the land of slavery (Deut. 8:12–15)?

External events, including family relational conflict, expose the posture of our heart. Are we remembering our absolute dependence on God and what he chooses to provide, or are we trusting in our own finite resources?

> He gave you manna to eat in the wilderness, something your ancestors had never known, to humble and test you so that in the end it might go well with you. You may say to yourself, "My power and the strength of my hands have produced this wealth for me." But remember the LORD your God, for *it is he who gives you the ability to produce* wealth. (Deut. 8:16–18)

In family counseling, are we simply offering people communication skills and conflict-resolution principles? Or are we first addressing their hearts? Teaching communication skills to a hard heart can potentially create a more self-sufficient sinner. Teaching conflict-resolution principles to a hard heart can potentially create a more efficient manipulator.

When you ponder your reconciling focus in family counseling, compare and contrast these two big picture purposes:

All secular models of family therapy reduce life to a set of principles and procedures designed to help families to better manage life without God.

All truly Christian models of family counseling expand life to God's eternal perspective designed to encourage family members to realize that they cannot live by bread alone.

Thinking in Biblical Categories

But how do we know what specific areas of family sin to explore and expose? This is where our chapters on a theology of family relationships become so foundational. As the family interacts in front of us, we seek to perceive discrepancies between God's design and the family's relationship.

The Mitchell family came to see me surrounded by chaos and swamped in turmoil. Rex (dad), Tamika (mom), Jake (fourteen-year-old son), and Jessica (twelve-year-old daughter) all tossed angry, frustrated words at each other like grenades. Everyone pointed fingers of blame at everyone else.

They all completed the Family Counseling Goals and Focus Form—each saying different words yet communicating a similar message: "We are verbally hurtful toward each other. And we can't seem to stop. It's getting worse and worse."

Rex and Tamika acknowledged a sinful impatience with and an increasing harshness toward their children, driven in their minds by consistent sinful disrespect from Jake and Jessica. Jake and Jessica admitted to growing increasingly disrespectful toward and angry with their parents, driven in their minds by "how mean and angry they always seem to be."

With parents like Rex and Tamika, we are considering two categories of parental sin.

- *Parental spiritual sin against God*: failing to entrust themselves to God's holy love and turning to idols of the heart
- *Parental social sin against their children*: failing to love their children with holy love and turning to consumer parenting

With children like Jake and Jessica, we are pondering two categories of family sin.

- *Children's spiritual sin against God*: heart foolishness
- *Children's social sin against parents*: dishonoring foolishness

Parental Spiritual Sin against God

In sustaining and healing, we seek to sense the pain of unmet parental longings. "What is it like for Tamika and Rex to experience this type of *dishonoring distance* (sustaining)? How can we help them in their *parental thirst* to find healing in God (healing)?" Most of us, when we face unquenched thirsts, need not only healing but also reconciling. As we saw in James 4:1–4 (and in chapter 4 of this book), relational sin includes mishandling the unmet desires of our souls.

Sinning parents become guilty of the sin spoken of in Jeremiah 2:13: "My people have committed two sins: They have forsaken me, the spring of living water, and have dug their own cisterns, broken cisterns that cannot hold water." Rather than humbly and submissively turning to God, seeking his holy love for comfort and strength to keep offering holy love to their children, they try to make life work apart from God. They seek to dig their own broken cisterns by demanding that their children meet their needs.

Parents become spiritual adulterers (Jer. 2:20–25; James 4:4) guilty of the false worship of making their children the idol of their heart. They long for their children's honoring love more than they long for God's holy love.

Our biblical theology of spiritual adultery pictures it for us:

- *Parental Paradise*: Created for honoring love from children and holy love from God
- *Parental Desert*: Receive dishonoring distance from children
- *Parental Thirst*: Experience emptiness, hurt, and grief
- *Parental Cistern*: Choose the creature (broken cisterns) over the Creator (God, the Spring of Living Water); choose manipulation and retaliation over worship and ministry

At some point in most parental counseling, we will transition from sustaining and healing to reconciling and guiding. The transition occurs when we have tapped into parental thirst (sustaining), and rather than turning to Christ for his healing hope (healing), parents like Rex and Tamika turn to their children in sinful, self-centered demandingness (reconciling).

Using these biblical images of cistern digging and spiritual adultery, we can prayerfully ponder questions like these as we listen to parents interact with their children.

- How are Rex and Tamika handling the unmet parental longings of their soul?
- Who do Tamika and Rex worship—God or their children? Are they turning to God, the Spring of Living Water, or to false idols of the heart and broken cisterns to quench their unmet thirsts?
- Do Rex and Tamika *long* for their children's honoring love, or do they *demand* their children's honoring love?
- Do Tamika and Rex ask God submissively and humbly, praying for the desires of their heart, or do they take matters into their own hands, trying to make life work without God, trying to live by bread alone?
- Do Rex and Tamika ask with a worship/ministry mindset, or do they ask amiss, living as consumers who believe that they must have honoring love from their children in order to survive?

It is essential that we first address these heart sins against God. Picture what happens if we start by care-fronting Rex and Tamika about their failure to offer Jake and Jessica holy love. First, without turning to God for his holy love, Rex and Tamika will be on empty. Our counsel will fall on thirsty souls. They will try—and fail—to work up holy love from the flesh. Our counsel will be the counsel of frustration. We are asking them to do in the flesh what can only occur through the Spirit.

Second, without repenting of worshiping the creature (their children) instead of the Creator, our counsel will fall on cold hearts. They will seek to offer holy love to their children as a quid pro quo—as an exchange, a bargain fueled by the flesh. "We'll offer you holy love, but you had better start offering us honoring love!"

Humbled, repentant parents filled by God, the Spring of Living Water, are spiritually prepared and equipped parents. Having addressed the sin in their hearts, now they are ready to deal with the sin in their home.

Parental Social Sin against Their Children

Recall from our study of James 4:1–4 what parents end up doing when they refuse to drink from the Spring of Living Water. They dig broken cisterns by trying to manipulate their children: "We'll be loving to you *so that* you'll start loving us." Or they dig broken cisterns by retaliating against their children: "You've left us empty; we'll leave you empty too. You've hurt us; we'll hurt you."

From our family theology chapters, we uncover three primary categories of parental social sin:

- Failure to follow God's design for our home
- Failure to parent like God parents us
- Failure to love maturely

Failure to Follow God's Design for Our Home

Our focus initially is less on exposing sin to parents and more on grasping the nature of their parental sin. We can use the Five Marks of GRACE-Focused Family Living to prayerfully ponder potential areas of parental sin against their children.

- Do Rex and Tamika demonstrate a *dedication* to depend upon God deeply and know him intimately?
- Do they demonstrate a commitment to turn to God and his Word as their source of *discernment* and wisdom?
- Do they demonstrate *devotion* to their children by loving them with grace-love?
- Do they demonstrate concern for their children by *disciplining* them with holy love?
- Do they demonstrate a pastoral heart for their children by *discipling* them with biblical love and truth?

Failure to Parent Like God Parents Us

We can use our biblical parenting model—the four styles of parenting—to discern a second category of parental sin awareness.

- Is the mood in the Mitchell home like that of *pharisaical* parenting, with tons of rules and little relationship, where the parents are harsh dictators who frighten and control their children?
- Is the mood in the Mitchell home like that of *neglectful* parenting, with few rules and little relationship, where the parents flee their children and are distant and aloof from their children?
- Is the mood in the Mitchell home like that of *permissive/possessive* parenting, with few rules and lots of relationship, where the parents fear their children, spoiling, pampering, rescuing, and hovering over their children?
- Is the mood in the Mitchell home like that of *godly* parenting, with rich relationships and age-appropriate rules, where the parents fellowship with their children, giving them grace-love and holy love?

Failure to Love Maturely

Family counselors can also assess how they experience the parents. This is especially possible and practical when we relate richly to them and when we observe them relating directly to their children. The following questions are profitable for our reflection.

- How do I feel as I relate to Tamika? To Rex? Do I feel invited in? Pushed away? Respected? Cared about? Discounted? Mistrusted? Discouraged? Intimidated? Do I detect similar styles of relating from Rex and Tamika to Jake and Jessica?

- As I observe Tamika and Rex relating to Jake and Jessica, what do I sense? Sarcasm? Emotional withdrawal? A critical spirit? The cold shoulder? Aloofness? Faultfinding? Arrogance? A judgmental spirit? Harshness? Warmth? Trust? Mutuality? Respect? Concern? Teamwork? Intimacy?

Children's Spiritual Sin against God: Heart Foolishness

As I have noted, biblical family counseling focuses primarily on counseling parents so that they can shepherd their children—becoming their children's best biblical counselors. However, depending on the age and maturity of the children, and typically with the parents present, it is certainly appropriate to counsel and care-front children.

As we prayerfully ponder sin in children, we look for signs of heart foolishness. Proverbs 22:15 tells us that "folly is bound up in the heart of a child, but the rod of discipline will drive it far away." Just as self-sufficiency is a core parental sin (Jer. 2:13; James 4:1–4), self-trust is a core sin of children from birth onward. "Those who trust in themselves are fools" (Prov. 28:26).

The foolish heart of a child is willful and self-sufficient: "I can get what I want on my own, without God!" (Ps. 10:4, 6, 11, 13; 14:1; Prov. 28:26). The foolish heart of a child is selfish and self-centered: "I want what I want and I want it now!" (Gen. 6:5; 8:21; Ps. 51:5). The foolish heart of a child is stubborn and self-sovereign: "I can get what I want without cost!" (Luke 12:16–21).

The Bible identifies overlapping *stages* of foolishness in the heart.

- *Initial Foolishness*: "Surely I was sinful at birth, sinful from the time my mother conceived me" (Ps. 51:5).

- *Developing Foolishness*: "Every inclination of the human heart is evil from childhood" (Gen. 8:21).

- *Practiced Foolishness*: "Even small children are known by their actions" (Prov. 20:11).

- *Disappointed Foolishness*: "They hated knowledge and did not choose to fear the LORD. Since they would not accept my advice and spurned my rebuke, *they will eat the fruit of their ways and be filled with the fruit of their schemes*. For the waywardness of the simple will kill them, and the complacency of fools will destroy them" (Prov. 1:29–32).

The Bible also identifies *styles* of heart foolishness.

- *Sluggard*: the irresponsible and lazy fool (Prov. 6:6–11; 12:24, 27; 13:4; 15:19; 22:13; 24:30–31)
- *Mocker*: the controlling and angry fool (Prov. 1:4, 22, 32; 7:7; 9:4, 6, 16–17; 14:15; 22:3)
- *Wicked*: the retaliating and abusive fool (Prov. 3:34; 9:7–8, 12; 14:9; 15:12; 22:10; 24:9; 29:8, 10)
- *Simple*: the withdrawing and naïve fool (Prov. 2:12–14, 22; 4:14–17; 11:18; 12:5; 18:3; 21:29; 26:24–26)

On the basis of these biblical principles of childhood foolishness, as we are counseling a child, we can be prayerfully pondering probes such as:

- Where do I see signs of Jake trusting in himself instead of in Christ?
- Where do I detect symptoms of Jessica communicating, "I can get what I want without God"?
- Where do I hear Jake saying by his actions, "I want what I want and I want it now, and I won't wait on God for it"?
- Where is Jessica communicating, "I can get what I want without cost because God is not going to hold me accountable"?
- Where am I seeing symptoms of initial, developing, practiced, or disappointed heart foolishness in Jake or Jessica as they trust in and cling to anyone or anything but Christ?
- Where am I seeing emotional, behavioral, rational, and relational signs of the sluggard (irresponsible fool), mocker (controlling fool), wicked (abusive fool), or simple (naïve fool) in Jessica or Jake?

Children's Social Sin against Parents: Dishonoring Foolishness

As you have Rex, Tamika, Jake, and Jessica interact in front of you, watch for actions, attitudes, words, and demeanors that communicate the core sin of children against parents: the lack of honoring love and the presence of dishonoring distance.

- Where do I see relational evidence of Jessica showing disrespect for her parents?
- Where do I see relational evidence of Jake withholding love from his parents?
- Where do I see signs of Jake manipulating his parents?
- Where do I see signs of Jessica retaliating against and hurting her parents?

Maturing as a Biblical Family Counselor
Recognizing Destructive Family Relationships

1. How could the two contrasting summaries of the purpose of family counseling impact your practice of family counseling?

   All secular models of family therapy reduce life to a set of principles and procedures designed to help families to better manage life without God.

   All truly Christian models of family counseling expand life to God's eternal perspective designed to encourage family members to realize that they cannot live by bread alone.

2. How could the five questions from pages 186–87 under the heading "Parental Spiritual Sin against God" shape your family counseling understanding of parental sin?

3. How could the five questions from page 188 under the heading "Failure to Follow God's Design for Our Home" shape your family counseling understanding of parental sin?

4. How could the four questions from page 188 under "Failure to Parent Like God Parents Us" shape your family counseling understanding of parental sin?

5. How could the two sets of questions from page 189 under the heading "Failure to Love Maturely" shape your family counseling understanding of parental sin?

6. How could the six questions on page 190 under "Children's Spiritual Sin against God" shape your family counseling understanding of children's sin?

7. How could the four questions from page 190 under the heading "Children's Social Sin against Parents" shape your family counseling understanding of children's sin?

Enlightening Family Members to Destructive Family Relationships: Calling Sinners Home

You have become aware of areas of heart sin in the lives of each member of the Mitchell family. Now God calls you to fulfill James 5:19–20: "My brothers and sisters, if one of you should wander from the truth and someone should *bring that person back*, remember this: Whoever turns a sinner from the error of their way will save them from death and cover over a multitude of sins."

"Bring that person back"—what a joyful portrait of the purpose of family care-fronting. It reminds us of Luke 15 and the prodigal son who came to his senses and came back home. Care-fronting in family counseling desires to see family members return home to God the Father in repentance and return home to their family members in reconciliation.

Call Sinners Home

Family members like Jessica, Jake, Tamika, and Rex return home through the ministry of God's Spirit, God's Word, and God's people.

Leave the Repentance to God: God's Spirit

In biblical counseling, we do not want the counselee engaging in a power struggle with us over their need to confess and repent. Instead, we point them to God and his Word. Then, if there is any power struggle, it is with the all-powerful Triune God.

The Lord's servant must not be quarrelsome but must be kind to everyone, able to teach, not resentful. Opponents must be gently instructed, in the hope that *God will grant them repentance* leading them to a knowledge of the truth, and that they will come to their senses and escape from the trap of the devil, who has taken them captive to do his will. (2 Tim. 2:24–26)

Our role: godly character and gentle teaching.

God's role: grant repentance and lead to a knowledge of the truth.

The family members' role: repent and come to their senses.

The result: Rex, Tamika, Jake, and Jessica escape from the devil's snare and the devil's enslavement.

Biblical counselors never usurp the Holy Spirit's job of changing hearts. Christ sent his Spirit—the Divine Counselor—to convict the world of guilt in regard to sin and righteousness and judgment (John 16:7–11). Leave the repentance to God.

Share Gospel Truth: God's Word

God's Spirit works through God's Word to bring sinners to their senses. Biblical counselors speak gospel truth in love (Eph. 4:15–16). We care-front via our words about God's Word because only God's Word has the power to reveal family heart sin.

For the word of God is alive and active. Sharper than any double-edged sword, it penetrates even to dividing soul and spirit, joints and marrow; it judges the thoughts and attitudes of the heart. Nothing in all creation is hidden from God's sight. Everything is uncovered and laid bare before the eyes of him to whom we must give account. (Heb. 4:12–13)

We can care-front confidently in the power of God's Word. "All Scripture is God-breathed and is useful for teaching, rebuking, correcting and training in righteousness, so that the servant of God may be thoroughly equipped for every good work" (2 Tim. 3:16–17).

Care-Front as Family Members: God's People

We care-front (lovingly and humbly speak truth in love to one another out of concern for heart change) as family members, as brothers and sisters. Two verses we have already looked at bear repeating: "See to it, brothers and sisters, that none of you has a sinful, unbelieving heart that turns away from the living God. But encourage one another daily, as long as it is called 'Today,' so that none of you may be hardened by sin's deceitfulness" (Heb. 3:12–13). Sin blinds; brothers and sisters enlighten.

We care-front in humility, realizing that we are all subject to temptation. "Brothers and sisters, if someone is caught in a sin, you who live by the Spirit should restore that person gently. But watch yourselves, or you also may be tempted" (Gal. 6:1).

Care-Fronting Principles to Remember

Before we explore how to enlighten family members to their heart sin, it will help if we recall several family counseling principles.

Listen Well, Comfort First, Care-Front Next

We must lovingly listen well to the Mitchell family's earthly story of family sin before we share God's eternal story of family confrontation. "To answer before listening—that is folly and shame" (Prov. 18:13). As a general rule:

> Families should feel our support and understanding be-
> fore they experience our challenge and confronting.

Any number of factors, events, specific situations, or family experiences can alter this basic plan of comfort first, care-front next. But in general, the more the family members know you have heard them and cared about them, the greater the impact your words of care-fronting will have on them. So a possible sequence in family counseling might look like this:

- Empathy for children—for their failure to receive holy love
- Empathy for parents—for their failure to receive honoring love
- Enlightenment of parents—for their failure to give holy love
- Enlightenment of children—for their failure to give honoring love

Offend and Affirm

Previously we learned that when we empathize with the parents, we often offend the children, and when we empathize with the children, we often offend the parents. Likewise, when we care-front either the parents or the children, they may become offended and the other family members may feel affirmed.

Perhaps Jessica blurts out, "Yes! Finally. Someone is confronting my parents. You tell them, Pastor!" So we remind each family member, "I'm not wanting to take anyone's side. I'm on God's side. I'm on your family's side. I'll do the best I can to fairly encourage each of you and to fairly confront each of you—as necessary . . ."

Expose Heart Sin by Looking for Relational Patterns

Earlier in this chapter you read a host of questions to be asking yourself about parental and child heart sins against God and against family members.

During sessions and between sessions, be asking God for wisdom. "Father, help me to see the relational patterns, themes, and connections between the various signs, symptoms, attitudes, and actions so that I can sense the internal heart sin behind those external behavioral sins."

Catch Them Red-Handed

When our family counseling is soul-to-soul, like Paul in 1 Thessalonians 2:8, rather than at arm's length, aloof, academic, and mechanical, then the immediacy and intensity in the room allow for connecting intimately. We then use the *relationships in the room* as fodder for catching family members red-handed: *exposing where they are sinning against each other right now in the room.*

Often, care-fronting loses its power if we try to confront sin that happened in the home a week ago or a month ago. We run into too much "he said, she said." We expend time and energy trying to decipher what really happened. Rather than being a historical detective, be a current witness.

Once again we *keep the relationship in the room.* "Rex, Tamika, Jake, and Jessica, we could spin our wheels all day trying to figure out who did what, when, and why with what happened last week. Maybe instead of telling me your side of the past story, let's have the four of you work this through right now. I'll slide my chair back a bit, and the four of you tell each other how you're feeling right now about what happened last week . . ."

In sustaining, you observed the family dance and the family dirge. Now, in reconciling, you observe the family dance and the *family depravity.* How are they sinning against each other even as they talk about their past sin against each other? Now there is no histrionics, no "he said, she said." You have just watched what they each have said and how they relate—in the moment.

Now you explore with the Mitchell family this current interaction that unfolded in front of you.

- Tamika, Rex, Jessica, and Jake, is this how things usually turn out at home when you try to talk things through?
- Guys, what I just witnessed, is this your typical pattern? Is this what usually occurs when you try to work things out?

Then invite them to interact about what is happening right now as they relate.

- Jake, Jessica, Tamika, and Rex, could we discuss what's happening between the four of you now as you relate?
- What's going on inside right now? What are you feeling?
- How are you guys experiencing your relationship right now?

To continue to empower the family to interact intimately, help them explore the impact they are having on each other right now.

- Tamika and Rex, just now as Jessica was giving you feedback, what was going on inside? Were you patiently listening and really hearing? Were you waiting for her to stop talking so you could tell her your side? Were you seething with frustration? Were you grief-stricken by the pain you had caused her? What best reflects your heart as you listened?

- Rex and Tamika, do some self-counsel right now. Step back and assess how you responded just now when Jessica shared her hurts. Is there anything you wish you had done or said differently in the last fifteen minutes?

- Jessica, as Mom and Dad responded to what you were sharing just now, how did you feel? Invited in? Pushed away? Respected? Discounted? Cared about? Mistrusted? Discouraged? Encouraged?

Trialogue Using Gospel Conversations

Throughout the process of care-fronting, we trialogue.

Care-Fronting Scriptural Explorations

Recall that in scriptural exploration trialogues, we explore together relevant biblical passages.

- Tamika and Rex, what Scriptures could we look at that might clarify God's view on how you are responding to Jessica right now?

- Jessica, as you step back and reflect on how you just interacted with Mom and Dad, what do you think God's Word says concerning your current way of relating to them? About your attitude toward them? Could we look at Ephesians 4:25–32 together to explore that?

- Rex and Tamika, what passages have you found helpful in gaining God's perspective on this way of relating to Jessica? Maybe we could explore Philippians 2:1–11 together.

Care-Fronting Spiritual Conversations

In spiritual conversation trialogues, we examine together relevant biblical principles. We can relate them to the family interaction that just occurred in our office.

- Rex, as you think about the conversation with Jessica over the past ten minutes, in what ways did your words give life? In what ways did they discourage?

- Rex, have you asked for feedback about your words from Jessica or Jake? Could you ask Jessica right now how your words over the past ten minutes have impacted her?

- Jessica, as Dad's words hurt you right now, did you want to lash out? Did you want to stuff your feelings and try to ignore them? Were you praying for Dad? What was going on inside?

- So, Tamika, as you and Jessica were in conflict just a moment ago, do you think your responses tended to heighten the battle, flee the argument, or seek a solution?

We can also use spiritual conversations to discuss overall relational heart patterns in families. We can interact about these during our meetings, or we can use these as homework assignments for family members to prayerfully ponder.

- Rex, in light of your interactions today, I'd like you to jot down a couple of things to reflect on. Where do you as a parent fail to be a strong shepherd? Also, describe times when your shepherding strength has meant the most to Jessica.

- Tamika, could you jot these questions down for me? Think about them this week, and then we could talk about them next week when we meet. How does what you described as "people-pleasing" hinder your family relationships? When were some sweet times that you didn't people-please or people-bash but shared your heart humbly in love?

- Tamika and Rex, could the two of you prayerfully ponder and discuss this over the next week? As you approach your kids, even in their rebelliousness, do you acknowledge your own brokenness? Do you have a forgiving heart toward Jessica and Jake?

- Jake, could you jot these questions down for me? Think about them this week, and then we can talk about them next week. Where do you, as a son, fail to be respectful? Describe times when your honor has meant the most to your folks.

- Jessica, in light of today's interaction, I'd like you to put a couple of things in your iPad to think about this week. Are you forgiving in your relationship with your parents? When do you find yourself withholding forgiveness?

Softening Stubbornness

Loving and firm biblical care-fronting does not guarantee that hearts will soften. Family sin runs deep. So counselors need to practice the art of softening stubbornness.

- "Rex, what do you think a *perfect way of relating* to Jake might have been in those two situations?" This helps Rex contrast how he related and how he could have related.
- "Tamika, *how would you have felt* if the shoe had been on the other foot?" Empathy for the person we have sinned against can help to soften hard-hearted stubbornness.
- Explore with Tamika and Rex *other possible relationships* where others have felt the way their children felt (threatened, intimidated, boundaries overstepped, etc.). You are seeking to *identify relational patterns* so they cannot flippantly say, "Oh, even if this were true, it's just an isolated incident caused by Jessica's rebellious attitude."
- With *loving firmness explain what you sense.* Provide specific feedback of the pattern of relating that you are witnessing.
- *Share your battles, scars, defeats, and victories.* "Rex, I know for me it's hard to recognize and admit when I've given in to my impatience." Share. Then ask, "Do you ever find yourself being resistant to seeing how your impatience impacts your kids?"
- *Predict.* "Jake, I'm no prophet, but I will make a prediction about what's likely to happen if you don't take a serious look at this." The greatest power in this may come far down the line. When your prediction comes true, Jake may be at your door again seeking your wisdom.

Maturing as a Biblical Family Counselor
Enlightening Family Members to Destructive Family Relationships

1. Reread 2 Timothy 2:24–26 and the section titled "Leave the Repentance to God: God's Spirit." How can it help you to remember that your role is to share truth in love; God's role is to lead family members to repentance?

2. Review this general rule: families should feel our support and understanding before they experience our challenge and confronting.

   a. In what types of family counseling situations might you need to break this rule?

   b. In situations where it is appropriate to follow this guideline, how could you apply it? How might it be helpful to the counseling process and counseling relationship to apply it?

3. You read about catching family members red-handed, sinning against each other right in the room.

   a. How different or novel is this approach to family counseling for you? How comfortable do you think you would be with engaging in this process?

   b. How do you think this process could empower your family care-fronting? What skills would you need to develop to implement this?

4. Review the care-fronting trialogues on pages 196–97. Think of a current family counseling scenario you are involved in, or develop a role-play family counseling situation. Write out your own paraphrased versions of those trialogues, applying them specifically to your scenario.

5. You read six principles for softening family stubbornness. Which of those six seem most useful or powerful for you as a family counselor? Why?

ELEVEN

Forgiveness from the Father and from the Family

Reconciling in Family Counseling, Part 2

Introduction: The Richness of Biblical Reconciliation

Ponder the richness packed into our synopsis of family reconciling:

> *It's horrible to sin against Christ and each other, but through Christ it's wonderful to be forgiven and to forgive.*

It is rarely an easy process and almost never a quick progression for family members to recognize and repent of their sin—to God and each other. We spent all of chapter 10 focused on helping the Mitchell family move toward recognizing the horrors of their heart sin. We used the first two letters in our REST acronym to learn this family counseling process:

R Recognizing Destructive Family Relationships: Identifying Family Heart Sin

E Enlightening Family Members to Destructive Family Relationships: Calling Sinners Home

In my counseling with them, after several weeks, Rex, Tamika, Jake, and Jessica were each coming to a place of "owning their own stuff."

However, there had been so much pain and anger for so long that they each struggled to truly believe that God could forgive them. They needed to apply the gospel to themselves as Christians. They needed help understanding that

1 John 1:8–2:2 applies not only to unbelievers coming to Christ for salvation but also to believers continually returning home to the Father for forgiveness and reconciliation. They needed to know that God is faithful and just to forgive them of their sins and to purify them from all unrighteousness because they have an Advocate who speaks to the Father in their defense—Jesus Christ, the Righteous One.

Rex, Tamika, Jake, and Jessica also had major struggles forgiving each other. And they found it even more difficult and incredibly challenging to trust each other again. They needed to learn how to apply the gospel of Christ's grace to one another. They needed help applying the reality of 2 Corinthians 2:5–11, which says we need to comfort each other, forgive each other, and reaffirm our love for each other, and that if we fail to do this, then family members can become overwhelmed with excessive sorrow and become snared in Satan's condemning trap.

The Mitchell family was struggling to live out the reality that *through Christ it's wonderful to be forgiven and to forgive*. So here in chapter 11 we learn how to help folks like the Mitchells apply the biblical truths of the second two letters in our REST acronym:

S Soothing the Family's Soul in Their Savior: Repenting to and Receiving Forgiveness from God

T Trust-Making: Exhibiting Fruits of Repentance and Granting Forgiveness to Each Other

---

Maturing as a Biblical Family Counselor
The Richness of Biblical Reconciliation

1. Consider our summary of biblical reconciling in family counseling: *It's horrible to sin against Christ and each other, but through Christ it's wonderful to be forgiven and to forgive.*

   a. In your life and relationships, which aspect of this statement seems to be most difficult? Why? How do you address it?

b. In family counseling, which aspect of this statement seems most difficult to help family members with? Why do you think that is? What have you found helpful in addressing each area with family members?

2. We often apply 1 John 1:8–2:2 as a gospel passage for witnessing to unbelievers. Yet the context focuses on brothers and sisters in Christ.

   a. How can you apply to your life the truth of a faithful and just Father who forgives and cleanses you because of your Advocate—Jesus Christ, the Righteous One?

   b. How can you apply to your family counseling the truth of a faithful and just Father who forgives and cleanses family members because of their Advocate?

3. Read 2 Corinthians 2:5–11 about our responsibility to a repentant Christian who has sinned against us. We are to forgive them, comfort them, and reaffirm our love for them.

   a. This is a high and holy, difficult and challenging calling. How has Christ empowered you to relate like this to repentant Christians who have hurt you?

   b. How could you help family members work through this process of forgiving, comforting, and reaffirming?

4. In 2 Corinthians 2:5–11, Paul indicates that when we do not forgive a believing brother or sister who has repented of sin against us, that person can become overwhelmed with excessive sorrow and be caught in Satan's condemning scheme.

    a. Have you ever experienced this in your life—being overwhelmed with excessive sorrow and being condemned by Satan? If so, how have you dealt with this in Christ?

    b. How could you help family members understand the impact of unforgiveness on each other? How could you help them to grant forgiveness to a repentant family member?

Soothing the Family's Soul in Their Savior: Repenting to and Receiving Forgiveness from God

In chapter 4 we introduced the Puritan concept of *loading the conscience with guilt*. The family member hardened and blinded by sin needs the loving exposure of their heart sin and their relational sin. In chapter 10 we learned how to help family members recognize that *it's horrible to sin against Christ and each other*.

In chapter 4 we also highlighted the Puritan idea of *lightening the conscience with grace*. The repentant family member with a tender conscience needs to magnify grace. Here in chapter 11 we learn how to help family members apply the truth that *through Christ it's wonderful to be forgiven and to forgive*.

Take Words with You: Relational Return

In 1 John 1:8–2:2, John teaches us that if we, as believers, claim to be without sin, we deceive ourselves. Instead, we are to confess our sins. The book of Hosea portrays repentance as relational by using the image of a wayward wife returning to her faithful husband: "Return, Israel, to the LORD your God" (14:1). Luke 15 uses another family image for relational return—that of a father and son, as the son comes to his senses and returns to his father's house in remorse and repentance.

Hosea 14:2 specifically commands us, "Take words with you and return to the LORD. Say to him: 'Forgive all our sins and receive us graciously, that we may offer the fruit of our lips.'"

In Hosea 14:3, Hosea emphasizes confession of heart idolatry and spiritual adultery. Our relational return continues as we confess that "Assyria cannot save us; we will not mount warhorses. We will never again say 'Our gods' to what our own hands have made, for in you the fatherless find compassion."

So we trialogue with the Mitchell family.

- Rex, Hosea 14:1–13 commands us to take specific words of confession to our heavenly Father, repenting of our heart sins against him and of our relational sins against our family members. What specific words of repentance is God's Spirit prompting in you?
- Tamika, let's explore Luke 15. The prodigal son comes to his senses and returns to his father in repentance. How is God's Spirit returning you to your senses and returning you home to God? As you face your heavenly Father, what words of confession do you want to share with him?
- Jake, 1 John 1:8–9 says we deceive ourselves if we claim to be without sin. Instead, we are to confess our sins to our faithful, just, and forgiving Father. What specific sins against God and against your parents is God's Spirit revealing in your heart?
- Jessica, we saw in James 4:1–4 and Jeremiah 2:13 that ultimately we can't blame our family members for our sinful responses. We sin—we fight and we quarrel—when we turn to anyone but God, our Spring of Living Water. What is God's Word prompting you to own in how you have sinned against God and your parents?

Pen Psalms of Homecoming

Hosea 14, Luke 15, and 1 John 1–2, along with Psalms 32 and 51 (and scores of other passages) beautifully and powerfully blend confession and forgiveness. Recall the words we already read from Hosea: "Forgive all our sins and receive us graciously . . . for in you the fatherless find compassion" (14:2–3). And the Father responds with words of homecoming: "I will heal their waywardness and love them freely, for my anger has turned away from them" (14:4).

John encourages us with the reminder that because of our Encourager and Advocate, Jesus Christ, the Righteous One, God is faithful and just to forgive us our sins. And Luke amazingly pictures the sinned-against father shamelessly rushing to his repentant son, throwing his arms around him, kissing him, receiving him back into the family with the family ring, sandals, and robe, and welcoming him home with a boisterous party.

While we sometimes think of Psalms 32 and 51 only or primarily as psalms of confession, we would do well to remind ourselves that they are psalms of homecoming that combine confession with the joy of restored fellowship. David launches his confession of sin with this reminder of the forgiveness of his sin: "Blessed [joyous] is the one whose transgressions are forgiven, whose sins are covered" (Ps. 32:1). Having confessed his sin against God, David longs for restoration to God. "Restore to me the joy of your salvation and grant me a willing spirit, to sustain me" (Ps. 51:12).

So we again trialogue with the Mitchells . . .

- Jessica, what would it be like for you to pen a psalm of homecoming—like Psalm 32 or Psalm 51—where you confess your sin *and* you confess your confidence in God's gracious forgiveness because of Christ?

  » I'm wondering what words and images you will use to describe how God has totally wiped your slate clean . . .

- Jake, between now and next week, could you read Psalms 32 and 51 and pen your own psalm of homecoming—including your specific words of confession and your specific words of confidence in Christ's forgiveness of you?

  » I'll be curious and excited to see what words you use to express your gratitude to God for his forgiveness . . .

- Tamika, I can see the guilt and even the sense of shame you are experiencing as you see now the ways you've sinned against God and your kids. In Luke 15, God presents himself as a Father who longs for his prodigal child, rushes out to meet him, embraces him, and celebrates with him.

  » How is this image of God similar to your image of God? How is it dissimilar?
  » What do you suppose accounts for the difference?
  » What difference would it make in your life if you saw God as a Father willing to forgive you and longing to reconcile and celebrate with you?

- Rex, as you confess your sins, please be sure to keep the rest of 1 John 1:8–2:2 in mind. When you hear that God is faithful and just to forgive your sins, what does this promise mean to you?

» God doesn't forgive you based on anything *you* have done or earned. God forgives you because Christ is your Advocate, your Defense Attorney, your Defender, your Encourager. Because *Jesus* is the Righteous One, God sees you through *his* righteousness. How do those truths impact you as you see and confess your sins . . .?

Calm the Conscience: Dispense Christ's Grace

In chapter 4 we used the image of the biblical family counselor as a *dispenser of grace*. Grace is God's medicine of choice to heal our sin; grace is Christ's prescription for our disgrace. Calming the conscience by dispensing grace is necessary because Satan is skilled at the old bait and switch. First he tempts us with the bait: "Sin! Sin! What pleasure you'll enjoy if only you'll allow yourself what you deserve!" Then he switches tactics, snaring us with the trap, taunting us and condemning us: "And you call yourself a Christian? You sinned *like that* against God. He'll never forgive you. And if he ever did, he'd never want you back. And certainly you're useless to him now!"

So we engage in grace trialogues with the Mitchell family . . .

- Mitchell family, I can tell you're all hurting—feeling godly sorrow along with feeling Satan's worldly shame. Let's spend some time focused on Romans 8:1–39, taking turns reading it . . .

  » What do we all think of how Paul starts and ends—no condemnation in Christ and no separation from Christ. How can these truths encourage the four of you . . . ?

  » Let's focus on Paul's list of over a dozen things that could never separate us from the love of God in Christ . . .

  » I love the biblical truth that if God is for us, who can be against us? Who can overcome us? Who can condemn us successfully? What do these truths mean for the Mitchell family . . . ?

  » Another phrase we read and that I love is where Paul says that since God did not spare his own Son to save us, he will graciously give us all things now that we are his sons and daughters. How can you guys apply this beautiful truth together?

- Where do you guys think you were recruited into this idea that God is angry with you and rejects you when you sin?

  » Where was this idea modeled for you?

  » Does it square with Scripture?

  » Is it perhaps coming from the evil one—the accuser of God's people in Revelation 12:10?

- Here's a list of Scriptures to turn to in order to understand the love, grace, and forgiveness of Christ: Luke 15; Romans 5–6; 8; Galatians 5; Ephesians 1:15–23; 3:14–21; Colossians 1:21–23; Hebrews 2:14–18; 4:14–16; 7; 9; 10:19–25; 1 John 1:9. I want you each to pick one of these passages, and during the week I want the four of you to spend at least ten minutes talking about each of those four passages . . .

- Mitchell family, the Bible talks so much about God's grace, forgiveness, and acceptance on the basis of Christ's death for us . . .

  » When are you most aware of and impacted by God's grace?
  » What does God seem to do to bring you to an awareness of his forgiveness? How do you tend to be cooperating with God as he brings you to these points of awareness?
  » How are you allowing each other to help you enjoy, magnify, and appreciate Christ's grace?
  » As a family, what are some ways you could use family devotional times—worship together, listening to Christian music, praying together, or Bible study—to help each of you appreciate Christ's grace . . . ?

- Rex, throughout his Word God tells us that we have peace with him because of Christ.

  » When do you experience this peace to the greatest extent? What are you doing and thinking differently when you experience God's peace through Christ?
  » Tell me about your past experiences of the peace of God. What is it like for you?

- Tamika, instead of seeing God as an angry Judge, how will you be seeing him now?
- Jessica, when you begin to feel overwhelmed with guilt and thoughts that God no longer loves you or can no longer forgive you, what do you do? What have you done before to fight these thoughts?

  » How might it help if at these times of doubt about the grace of God, you imagine hearing Christ say, "Father, forgive Jessica"?

- Jake, I know you are a history buff. Martin Luther used to say that when we feel like God is angry with us, we should shout at the devil, laugh in his face, and remind him that Christ died for our sins and that God can never again be angry at his children. What do you think about this advice? How would you say it differently?

Satan loves chaos and turmoil. He hates shalom and adores shame. Christ offers peace and rest because he is our peace with God (Eph. 4:15) and he is the Restful One (Matt. 11:28–30). As dispensers of Christ's grace, we come alongside repentant family members when they are enduring Satan's judgment. We help them soothe their soul in their Savior. In sustaining, they turn to him as the Man of Sorrows who is acquainted with their grief. In reconciling, they turn to Christ as their Advocate, the Righteous One who walks them boldly into the Father's presence.

Maturing as a Biblical Family Counselor
Soothing the Family's Soul in Their Savior

1. On pages 204–5 you read several passages and trialogues that encouraged family members to *take words with you* and that promote *relational return*.

   a. What additional passages do you take family members to in order to teach them the biblical truth of repentance and confession of sin to God?

   b. Craft four trialogues that you would use to encourage Rex, Tamika, Jake, and Jessica to take words with them and return to their forgiving Father.

2. On pages 206–7 you read several trialogues related to *penning psalms of homecoming*. Craft four trialogues you could use to encourage the Mitchell family to repent *and* to receive the Father's forgiveness through Christ's grace.

3. On pages 207–9 you read many grace trialogues related to *calming the conscience by dispensing Christ's grace*. Craft five trialogues you could use to encourage the Mitchell family together and each family member individually to soothe their soul in their Savior.

4. Satan delights to discourage and condemn us as biblical counselors.

   a. When have you faced Satan's condemnation?

   b. Who has been a dispenser of Christ's grace in your life?

   c. What passages do you meditate on to soothe your soul in your Savior?

Trust-Making: Exhibiting Fruits of Repentance and Granting Forgiveness to Each Other

In Christian circles, we are familiar with the concept of peacemaking. In biblical counseling and reconciling with family members, I tweak this slightly and use the term *trust-making*. Family members have sinned against, hurt, and harmed each other, and trust has been broken. Trust is reestablished as family members engage in

- confessing sin to each other
- exhibiting fruits of repentance
- granting forgiveness to each other

The Mitchell Family's Home Renovation Project

The Mitchell family serves as a case study in how to address these three points. As we slowly worked through the process of reconciliation, I wrote three passages on the whiteboard: 1 Corinthians 5:1–5; 2 Corinthians 2:5–11; and 2 Corinthians 7:8–13. I asked Rex to read the first one, Tamika and Jessica to read the second one, and Jake to read the third one.

We discussed how Paul had to confront the Corinthian believers in 1 Corinthians 5:1–5 because they were not confronting a brother who was involved in sexual immorality. We then interacted about the holiness and justice of God and how he calls on each of us to confess our sins and repent.

Then we discussed 2 Corinthians 2:5–11, and I noted that many commentators believe this passage relates back to 1 Corinthians 5. The Corinthians confronted this sinning brother and he repented, yet the Corinthians got stuck on confrontation. Paul informs them that unless they comfort, forgive, and reaffirm their love for this repentant man, they would end up joining Satan's team and scheme—to condemn and overwhelm their brother with excessive sorrow. Then we explored God's love and grace as I wrote on the whiteboard in large letters:

HOLY LOVE

We read together several passages that combined ideas and images about God's holiness and his love, his justice and his grace, including the following words from Isaiah 40:10–11:

> See, the Sovereign LORD comes with power,
>   and he rules with a mighty arm.
> See, his reward is with him,
>   and his recompense accompanies him.
> He tends his flock like a shepherd:
>   He gathers the lambs in his arms
> and carries them close to his heart;
>   he gently leads those that have young.

I explained how these verses depict God in his affectionate sovereignty. "He is holy and transcendent—infinitely above us. He is loving and immanent—intimately close to us. He is our sovereign Shepherd of Holy Love. He models holy justice to confront sin and loving grace to forgive sin—a model the Mitchell family could follow."

As we began to talk about forgiving each other, it was Jake whose honesty and candor spoke for the entire Mitchell family. "Yes, but—and I know I'm not *supposed to* 'yes but' things—how do any of us know that all this confession isn't just for your sake, Pastor Bob? We'll all behave and be good and say the right things. But we've had a long time of being really hateful to each other. I may be able to say, 'I forgive you,' but I'm not sure I can say, 'I trust you, Mom and Dad.'"

"My boy has a point, Pastor Bob," Rex said as he, Tamika, and Jessica all nodded in agreement.

"Yep. I agree," I responded. "While we've come a long way in this process of God rebuilding the Mitchell home, we've got a ways to go yet, don't we? So let's look at the third passage that I wrote and Jake read: 2 Corinthians 7:8–13."

I explained that several commentators believe this passage also ties in to 1 Corinthians 5:1–5 and 2 Corinthians 2:5–11. Because God is a God of holy love, of justice and grace, he insists that we confess our sin *and* that he is faithful and just to forgive us our sins. But he also insists that we put off our old ways of relating and put on new ways—showing the fruits of repentance, which is what Paul focuses on in 2 Corinthians 7:11. In this one verse, Paul highlights seven fruits of repentance.

"We're going to talk about these evidences of true change—in each of your lives. Would the four of you agree to keep working with me as we work through these three passages together—1 Corinthians 5:1–5; 2 Corinthians 2:5–11; and 2 Corinthians 7:8–13? If so, we'll work through confessing your sins to one another, receiving God's grace, showing fruits of repentance, and comforting, forgiving, and reaffirming your love for one another. How does that sound for a Mitchell family home renovation project?"

Confessing Sin to One Another

Picture where the Mitchell family is in the process. They have sensed their sin, confessed their sin to God, and received God's forgiveness. Now they need to confess their sin to one another (Matt. 18; James 5:16). I first began to address this next stage in their family journey during a session with just Rex and Tamika present.

- Rex and Tamika, I'm amazed at your brokenness. Your repentance before God is beautiful. Could we go one step further? You've also sinned against your son and daughter. James 5:16 urges us to confess our sins to one another.
  » If Jake and Jessica were here, what specific confession would you want to make to them? What would it sound like?
  » How hard would that be? Are there any things—attitudes or actions or past history—that would make this hard? How could we address those now?

- People tend to say things like, "I apologize if you were offended by what I said." This really is saying, "You're too sensitive; too bad if you were offended. Get over it." It also fails to ask for forgiveness—it doesn't lead to reconciliation. It's peacefaking instead of peacemaking.
  - » How could you guys specifically seek your son's and daughter's forgiveness?
  - » They might be skeptical. "Talk is cheap" can be the mindset. How can your words begin to reflect that something is truly different now?

- Sometimes it's helpful to think through how conflict resolution and family reconciliation have gone in the past . . .
  - » When you're in a conflict with your children, do you tend to heighten the battle, flee the argument, or seek a solution? What factors prevent the latter?
  - » As you've approached your kids in the past about a conflict, have you acknowledged your fault and sin? If so, how have they responded?
  - » Would the two of you prefer to have this conversation with Jake and Jessica at home, without me? Or would it be helpful for us to start this process of confession and seeking forgiveness during our next joint family meeting? What are the pros and cons of each option . . . ?

The Mitchells decided to have me shepherd the confession process. First, I set the parameters. We reviewed 1 Corinthians 5; 2 Corinthians 2; and 2 Corinthians 7. We also discussed Matthew 7:1–5 about looking at the plank in our own eye first. And we explored Matthew 18:15–17 and how brothers and sisters in Christ deal with sins against one another.

I encouraged the parents to confess first—they are the shepherds in the home and they lead by humble example. Then I scooted back my chair and encouraged them to interact. I only stepped in as needed or requested. In sessions like this one, when things go well and there is mutual confession, we often weep together with tears of cleansing and joy.

Exhibiting Fruits of Repentance

When things are not going well, you will often hear comments like, "I've heard all of this before!" or "They will never truly change. I just can't trust them anymore!"

When this happened with the Mitchells, we returned to our discussion of 2 Corinthians 7:8–13. I shared a brief handout that outlines and explains "Paul's Seven Marks of Godly Sorrow and the Fruits of Repentance" (see fig. 11.1). After reading and discussing it, we trialogued.

- We all agree that talk is cheap. So let's talk about what's different this time. I'd like each of you to think about and share why you believe God is going to help you truly change this time . . . why it's not just talk but genuine heart change . . .
- Soon we're going to talk about how God empowers us to change. How he helps us to put off the old and put on the new. I'm going to work with you guys on this. But for right now, let's talk about what changes need to happen now—what heart changes and what relationship changes. And let's be specific.

  » I want each of you to think ahead six months from now. You've repented to God and confessed your sin to each other. Share with each other specifically how you want to be different six months from now—new ways of handling your emotions, new ways of responding to each other, new ways of thinking biblically, new ways of relating to each other.
  » Over the next six months, what commitments are you making about what you're going to be putting off—not doing anymore? What are you going to be putting on—what are you going to be doing differently?

- Let's look at Paul's list from 2 Corinthians 7, and let's make it specific, practical, and applicable to each of you . . .

  » Mitch, can we start with you? With the sin that you've confessed, how can you demonstrate the fruit or evidence of repentance in any of those seven areas Paul highlights?
  » Family, as you think about Dad's repentance and change, what specific ways do you think he could demonstrate any of Paul's seven areas . . . ?
  » Now let's go to each of the rest of you—Tamika, then Jake, and then Jessica—and let's walk through the same process we just walked through with Dad . . .

Figure 11.1

Paul's Seven Marks of Godly Sorrow and the Fruits of Repentance

1. **Earnest Care/Earnestness.** Not a carelessness or a winking at sin, but an earnest desire to bear the fruits of repentance by eagerly putting off the old relational patterns and putting on new ways of relating to God and others.
2. **Eagerness to Clear Myself.** A desire to demonstrate my transformed heart. Making no excuses, offering a clear admission of guilt, and receiving correction that leads to a change in attitudes and actions.
3. **Indignation.** Indignation with myself rather than with those who accused me. Mourning my sin, owning my sin, and feeling indignant over the consequences of my sin.
4. **Alarm/Fear.** Fear of God, of consequences, and of falling back into sin and thereby disgracing God's grace and damaging those I love.
5. **Longing.** Desire for restoration and reconciliation with God and others. Desire for renewed relationships of trust and affection—doing what is needed to accomplish relational renewal.
6. **Zeal/Concern.** Passion for doing, thinking, and living rightly for God's glory and the good of those I love.
7. **Avenging/Readiness to See Justice Done.** Readiness to right the wrong by making restitution, upholding holiness, and putting my house in order.

Granting Forgiveness to Each Other

Granting forgiveness often becomes something of an emotional and relational tug-of-war between applying 2 Corinthians 2 and 2 Corinthians 7. "I will grant forgiveness *if and when* I see a long history of evidence of true change!"

I urge family members to work on both simultaneously. "You work on your process of true change. It's going to take time. There will be ups and downs. This will be true for each of you. While you're all working with Christ's power to put off the old and put on the new, also be working on forgiving, comforting, and reaffirming your love for one another. If you wait until Dad changes 100 percent before you ever forgive him, then you'll never forgive . . ."

At this point, we start specifically applying 2 Corinthians 2:5–11 to their family. I explain what the Scriptures say will happen if the family members refuse to move toward forgiveness. "You're going to discourage each other! In fact, you're going to prevent the very thing you want. Mom and Dad, you want Jake and Jessica to change, but if you keep harping on how you'll never trust them again, then they'll be so discouraged that they'll never change.

Paul says that they will be overwhelmed by excessive sorrow. He's picturing someone drowning in guilt and condemnation. It's like drowning in quicksand, sorrow upon sorrow, completely swallowed up and engulfed in despair, discouragement, and remorse. I know that's not what you want for your kids. Let's talk about what you do want for your kids . . ."

After interacting and trialoguing, I continue. "What does Paul say you need to do instead? He says to forgive. The word means to be gracious toward, to speak generously to. It means to not hold the person's sin against their account. It means to realize that their sin, like your sin, has been paid in full on the cross. It means to do what God does in Christ and say, 'Your sins are forgiven.' Let's talk about what this would look like for each of you. About how Christ can help you forgive just as you've been forgiven . . ."

We interact again. Then we return to the text. "Paul also says to comfort one another. 'Comfort' means to encourage, to console, to come alongside and help, to defend as an advocate. Satan whispers his condemnation into your children, saying, 'You are losers! Give up!' But you whisper and shout your encouragement: 'You are victors in Christ!' Let's talk about what that would look like and feel like for each of you . . ."

Again we interact, then we return to the Scriptures. "Then Paul says to reaffirm your love. The phrase means to demonstrate your love conclusively. Specifically, it means to have a change of heart toward your children who have had a change of heart. Instead of moving away from them, retreating, and being aloof, move toward them, be intimately involved with them. What do you all think of this? How could you all tap into Christ's resurrection power to reconcile like this?"

After further interaction, we conclude with a warning and an encouragement. "If you don't live out this passage, then you'll be joining Satan's scheme. He tries to outwit us and take advantage of us. He's the accuser of God's people. He wants to cheat the Mitchell family out of the joy of Christ's grace. He wants you to live by works and in fear of condemnation. Instead, give each other grace, dispense grace. What would it be like for the Mitchell family to fight together against Satan instead of fighting against each other?"

One Caveat: What about Trusting an Abusive Family Member?

Whenever I teach or counsel on this, someone raises the question about trusting an abuser or a con artist who talks the talk but doesn't walk the walk. It's a fair question. And it's the reason that 2 Corinthians 7 and the holiness and justice of God are so vital to this reconciliation process.

First, no one in the family is being asked to entrust themselves to another human being. We entrust ourselves to God. Second, no one is being asked to naïvely trust mere words. We are insisting upon consistent heart change and relationship change over time based on 2 Corinthians 2:7–13, and we are monitoring that process and progress. Third, if at any point we become aware of or perceive abusive behavior, we immediately confront the abuser—individually, through church discipline, and with the proper outside authorities. Family members are protected, supported, cared for, and comforted in counseling (apart from the abuser) and by the body of Christ as they face the trauma of family abuse.

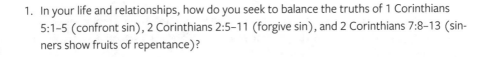

Maturing as a Biblical Family Counselor
Trust-Making

1. In your life and relationships, how do you seek to balance the truths of 1 Corinthians 5:1–5 (confront sin), 2 Corinthians 2:5–11 (forgive sin), and 2 Corinthians 7:8–13 (sinners show fruits of repentance)?

2. Reread the vignette titled "The Mitchell Family's Home Renovation Project." With families like the Mitchells, how would you walk through, talk through, and trialogue through 1 Corinthians 5:1–5 (confront sin), 2 Corinthians 2:5–11 (forgive sin), and 2 Corinthians 7:8–13 (sinners show fruits of repentance)?

3. Review pages 212–13 on confessing sin to each other. Craft several trialogues you could use to help family members biblically think through confession of sin.

4. Review pages 213–15 on exhibiting fruits of repentance. Craft several trialogues you could use to help family members biblically think through demonstrating evidence of repentance.

5. Review pages 215–16 on granting forgiveness to each other. Craft several trialogues you could use to help family members biblically think through forgiving each other, comforting each other, and reaffirming their love for each other.

6. What biblical family counseling safeguards do you put in place to address the concern about forgiving and trusting an abusive family member?

CHAPTER

TWELVE

Family Wisdom and Strength from Christ

Guiding in Family Counseling, Part 1

Introduction: A New Want-To, Can-Do, What-To, and How-To

In the spaghetti relationships of family counseling, we have experienced plenty of ups and downs and our fair share of two steps forward, one step backward in our journey with families. Yet we have seen God do his progressive sanctification work. Families have not only been sustained, healed, and reconciled; they have learned how to sustain, heal, and reconcile *each other*.

- Family sustaining: Like Christ, we care about each other's hurts.
- Family healing: Through Christ, it's possible for us to hope in God together.
- Family reconciling: It's horrible to sin against Christ and each other, but through Christ it's wonderful to be forgiven and to forgive.

For many counselors, getting to these points of progress is so remarkable that they think, "We're done. What more is there to do or accomplish with this family? They're caring about each other; they're hoping in God together; they're confessing their sins, forgiving each other, and reconciling. Wow! Thank you, Lord. Next family . . ."

To a certain extent, I agree. This is amazing progressive sanctification. However, our family counseling ministry has more spaghetti to cook! And for me, this final course on our four-course family counseling meal is the most fun, rewarding, and exciting. Family counseling, which is a subset of family discipleship, now emphasizes equipping and empowering the family. The family is now in a great place to learn to put off the old ways of relating to one another and to put on the new ways of relating in Christ. We are prepared to help the family communicate by their actions:

- Family Guiding: It's supernatural to love each other like Christ, through Christ, for Christ.

Thankfully, we do not engage in this process in our own power. Instead, we join the family in cooperating with the work God has already done in them. Christian families have:

- A new *want-to*: gospel indicatives and regeneration—a new heart, a new creation in Christ (Rom. 6:1–8; 2 Cor. 5:17)
- A new *can-do*: gospel indicatives and redemption—a new power, more than conquerors (Rom. 6:1–18; 8:28–39)

Gutzon Borglum, the sculptor behind the four presidential faces on Mount Rushmore, was once asked how he had carved out the faces from all that rubble of rock. He responded, "I didn't carve those faces out. They were already in there. I just needed to chisel away anything and everything that hid those faces."[1]

Christian, the face of Jesus is already in you. Biblical counselor, for the Christian families that you counsel, the face of Jesus is already in them. Our calling is not to put Christ into family members. Our calling is to equip and empower family members to put off the rubble that hides the face of Jesus and to put on the new person they already are in Christ (Rom. 6:1–18; Eph. 4:17–24; Col. 3:1–11).

Theologians and counselors describe this progressive sanctification process using the terms "gospel indicatives" and "gospel imperatives." Gospel indicatives relate to what Christ has already done for us—our salvation, including our regeneration and redemption. Gospel indicatives relate to who we are in Christ.

Gospel imperatives relate to our calling to live out the person we already are. We put off what is already dead, what has been crucified with Christ; we put on what is already alive, what has been resurrected with Christ (Rom. 6:1–18).

In the gospel indicative of regeneration, believing family members have a new heart. They are new creations in Christ (2 Cor. 5:17). Their new heart includes a new want-to—a new affection and desire to live and love like Christ (Rom. 6:1–6; Col. 3:1–3; Titus 2:11–13).

In the gospel indicative of redemption, believing family members have a new can-do, a new power to experience increasing victory over sin. They have been redeemed—bought out of their slavery to sin.

For we know that our old self was crucified with him so that the body ruled by sin might be done away with, that we should no longer be slaves to sin—because anyone who has died has been set free from sin. Now if we died with Christ, we believe that we will also live with him. For we know that since Christ was raised from the dead, he cannot die again; death no longer has mastery over him. . . . In the same way, count yourselves dead to sin but alive to God in Christ Jesus. (Rom. 6:6–9, 11)

When I shared the Borglum illustration with our men's ministry, one of our elders could barely contain himself. "Men, men! Do you understand what Pastor Bob is saying? In discipling, I used to put so much pressure on myself. I thought *I* had to work up goodness and strength and power in the people I was mentoring. But it's already in there! Christ is in them. Christians have the desire and the power to live for Jesus. I don't put it in them; I just stir up and fan into flame the gift of God that is already in them!"

This is equally true for us as biblical family counselors. Our role in guiding family discipleship is to help family members live out:

- A new *what-to*: gospel imperatives and biblical enlightenment—wisdom to know what is best (Phil. 1:9–11)
- A new *how-to*: gospel imperatives and biblical empowering and equipping—putting off the old and putting on the new (Rom. 6:1–18; Eph. 4:17–24; Col. 3:1–11)

Family members like Rex, Tamika, Jake, and Jessica have confessed, repented, forgiven, and reconciled. They have a new start. They also have a lot of new decisions to make. What does it look like to put off their old angry, chaotic, disrespectful, self-centered ways? Not just generically but specifically—what is God calling each of them to do? How is he calling each of them to love? This is where the biblical counselor's prayer becomes the biblical family's prayer.

And this is my prayer: that your love may abound more and more in knowledge and depth of insight, so that you may be able to discern what is best and may be pure and blameless for the day of Christ, filled with the fruit of righteousness that comes through Jesus Christ—to the glory and praise of God. (Phil. 1:9–11)

Our calling is to help families discern their family calling. Their family love must abound more and more in biblical knowledge and depth of insight (family wisdom) so they can discern what is best and live increasingly pure and blameless family lives—all to the glory and praise of God. We explore God's Word with them, helping them discern their new what-to—what to do and how to live loving family lives to the glory of God.

We also help them apply God's Word, helping them discover their new how-to—how to live out, in Christ's resurrection power, the new persons they already are. It is one thing to know the truth; it is another to apply truth in real life. We help family members like Rex, Tamika, Jake, and Jessica put off and put on in affection, attitude, and action what is already put off and put on in Christ.

In biblical family guiding, we help families that have previously been experiencing chaos, turmoil, conflict, and shame to experience shalom—peace in their souls and peace in their relationships. Family guiding leads toward family PEACE:

P Putting On Christ's Wisdom Perspective: Enlightening Families through God's Word (chap. 12)

E Empowering Families to Live in Light of Their Victory in Christ: Strengthening Families through Christ's Resurrection Power (chap. 12)

A Activating Application: Engaging Families in the Present Moment (chap. 13)

C Coaching Families: Equipping Families for Christ-Centered Living (chap. 13)

E Emboldening Families: Sending Families Out with Confidence in Christ (chap. 13)

Maturing as a Biblical Family Counselor
A New Want-To, Can-Do, What-To, and How-To

1. By now, you have gained more than a cursory understanding of family sustaining, healing, reconciling, and guiding.

   - Family sustaining: Like Christ, we care about each other's hurts.
   - Family healing: Through Christ, it's possible for us to hope in God together.
   - Family reconciling: It's horrible to sin against Christ and each other, but through Christ it's wonderful to be forgiven and to forgive.
   - Family guiding: It's supernatural to love each other like Christ, through Christ, for Christ.

   a. Of these four aspects of family counseling, which ones seem to come most naturally for you? Which ones do you enjoy the most and thrive at when you engage in them?

b. Of these, which ones seem to take the most work for you? How will you be growing in developing those areas of family counseling that might not come as naturally for you?

2. How could Borglum's quote, when related to our new identity in Christ, impact your family counseling ministry?

3. How will the two gospel indicatives impact your biblical family counseling ministry?

- A new *want-to*: gospel indicatives and regeneration—a new heart, a new creation in Christ (Rom. 6:1–8; 2 Cor. 5:17)
- A new *can-do*: gospel indicatives and redemption—a new power, more than conquerors (Rom. 6:1–18; 8:28–39)

4. How will the two gospel imperatives impact your biblical family counseling ministry?

- A new *what-to*: gospel imperatives and biblical enlightenment—wisdom to know what is best (Phil. 1:9–11)
- A new *how-to*: gospel imperatives and biblical empowering and equipping—putting off the old and putting on the new (Rom. 6:1–18; Eph. 4:17–24; Col. 3:1–11)

Putting On Christ's Wisdom Perspective: Enlightening Families through God's Word

In biblical healing, we focused on cropping Christ's *hope* back into the family picture. In biblical guiding, we focus on cropping Christ's *Word/wisdom* back into their picture. This is their new what-to—biblical discernment for family living. In guiding, we also seek to crop Christ's *victory* back into their family portrait. This is their new how-to—tapping into Christ's resurrection power to put off the old and put on the new.

Modeling Trust in the Sufficiency and Relevancy of Scripture for Family Living

Biblical counselors consistently highlight the sufficiency of Scripture for biblical counseling.[2] God's Word, rightly understood and wisely applied, provides the authoritative wisdom that we need to grow more like Christ and to glorify God.

I like to add the word "relevance" to this discussion. The Bible provides the discernment we need for life in our broken world. Gospel-centered family counseling turns to the riches of God's Word for insights on navigating the real and raw issues that today's families face.

Most families are desperate by the time they come to us. They have been looking for any and every source of insight for family living.

The situation was not much different in Paul's day. The Colossian saints had access to multiple sources of supposed wisdom for life. They could turn to the pre-Gnostics who taught that Christians need the Bible *plus* the secret knowledge of the world's elite thinkers. They could turn to the philosopher-psychologists of the day who taught that Christians needed the Bible *plus* the world's wisdom for living. They could turn to the Judaizers of the day who taught that Christians need Christ *plus* the works of the law.[3]

Putting On Trust in the Wisest Person Who Ever Lived—Jesus

In addressing their struggles, Paul directed the Colossians to one source. "To them God has chosen to make known among the Gentiles the glorious riches of this mystery, which is *Christ in you,* the hope of glory" (Col. 1:27).

In his nouthetic counseling ministry for sin and sanctification, Paul turned to the wisest person who ever lived. "[Christ] is the one we proclaim, *admonishing* [the Greek word *noutheteo,* which focuses on biblical reconciling] and *teaching* [the Greek word *didasko,* which focuses on biblical guiding or discipleship] everyone with all wisdom, so that we may present everyone fully mature in Christ" (Col. 1:28).

In his parakaletic counseling ministry for suffering and sanctification, Paul turned to the wisest person who ever lived. "My goal is that they may be *encouraged* [the Greek word *parakaleo,* which focuses on biblical sustaining and healing] in heart and united in love, so that they may have the full riches of complete understanding, in order that they may know the mystery of God, namely *Christ,* in whom are hidden all the treasures of wisdom and knowledge" (Col. 2:2–3).

Before counselees can put on trust in Christ's wisdom, counselors must truly believe that God's Word is richly relevant. Biblical counselors must believe that Jesus is the wisest person who ever lived—the One in whom are hidden *all* the treasures of wisdom and knowledge.

Putting Off Worldly Wisdom

Having established the one true source of wisdom for living, Paul clearly explains why he has built this foundation. "I tell you this so that no one may deceive you by fine-sounding arguments" (Col. 2:4). "See to it that no one takes you captive through hollow and deceptive philosophy, which depends on human tradition and the elemental spiritual forces of this world rather than on Christ" (2:8). Paul is adamant. "Beware! Be on guard! Do not be deceived! Do not be taken hostage! People separated from the life of God cannot teach you how to live life for God!"

Of course, this does not mean that we build our approach to biblical family counseling in ignorance of legitimate descriptive research. But Paul is not talking here about descriptive research. He is talking about theories and theologies of people, problems, and solutions. He is talking about prescriptive theories of how to live the good life out of a good heart for the good of others and the glory of God.[4] And Paul is clear: we have two choices. We can learn wisdom from the wisest person who ever lived—the Creator. Or we can seek wisdom from the world—the creature.

Distraught families will follow our lead. They need to experience sustaining, healing, reconciling, and guiding that is based in the counselor's confidence that God's Word is richly relevant for family relationships.

Instilling Wisdom through Instruction

In addition to modeling trust in the sufficiency and relevance of the Word, we help family members—especially parents—put on Christ's wisdom perspective through trialogues, through interactive teaching, and through training in righteousness.

Instilling Wisdom through Trialogues

Trialogues are a vital way to equip families to turn to and trust in the wisdom of God's Word for family life. The Mitchell family is working through the forgiveness and reconciliation process—related specifically to Rex and Tamika's parental impatience and harshness and to Jake and Jessica's disrespect and anger. Recall that this includes demonstrating the fruits of repentance—Christ-empowered growth and change over time.

Families like the Mitchells often have little experience in even knowing what healthy relationships look like. They have experienced almost constant chaotic conflict. Their repentant and softened hearts are hungry for practical wisdom from Scripture. So you trialogue. You explore God's Word with them, teaching them to "fish the Scriptures."

- Rex, Tamika, Jake, and Jessica, I appreciate how honest you guys have been about not knowing what it might look like to love each other. Rex, I think you used the word "clueless." What do you say we read together Ephesians 4:25–32 . . . ?

- I like to think of verse 25 as *speak truthful words with love* [I write this phrase on the whiteboard]. Let's be honest—you guys haven't always been honest with each other, right?

  » What do you think some of the reasons are that you all have gotten into a habit of not being up-front? When are you most tempted to tell a lie instead of the truth?

  » Let's talk about a specific situation when one of you was not a truth teller. And let's look at what it would mean to put off that old way and to put on the new way . . .

- I like to think of verses 26–28 as *speak controlled words with patience* [I write on the whiteboard again]. Sometimes you guys don't tell each other the truth. Other times you tell the truth—but you don't do it in love. You've done it in anger, right?

  » One point I don't want us to miss—Paul says you can be angry and *not* sin. You don't have to stuff your anger. And you don't have to throw your anger at each other like spears. You can do something constructive with your anger. First, that would mean taking your anger to God. Have any of you done that—vented and lamented to God? What has it been like? How has it helped?

  » Again, let's talk about a specific time that one of you lost it. Jake volunteered last time with truthfulness. Who wants to work through this anger with me now . . . ?

- I label verses 29–30 *speak encouraging words with wisdom* [writing on whiteboard]. Paul is honest—real and raw. He talks first about unwholesome words. That literally means putrid, poisonous, and rotten. Sounds like Paul has been listening in on some of the past conversations in the Mitchell home, huh?

  » Let's talk about putting off that old poisonous communication and about putting on helpful communication that encourages and builds each other up. That would be refreshing and remarkably different, wouldn't it . . . ?

  » Jake and Rex volunteered the first two times. That means Tamika or Jessica—which one of you wants to talk about a specific recent time when you lost it with your words and how we can apply these verses next time . . . ?

- Finally, I describe verses 31–32 as *speak grace words with humility* [I write that on the whiteboard]. Again, notice how relevant Paul is— he starts by talking about bitterness, rage, anger, brawling, slander, malice. Like we said, he's been listening in on some of your past conversations . . .

  » Tamika, it looks like it may be your turn. Can you share with us a recent time when you didn't do so well with grace words? Then let's talk about what it might look like to apply these verses to the next situation . . .

Instilling Wisdom through Interactive Teaching

My emphasis on trialogues rather than monologues does not mean that there is never a time for teaching in biblical counseling. In the previous vignette with the Mitchell family on Ephesians 4:25–32, I would take time during each discussion point to teach, instruct, and explain the meaning of the passage and the application of those truths to their family relationships. I find that my teaching and trialoguing merge because I will teach a point and immediately move into a conversational trialogue with the family.

During family counseling, I will often teach about principles of family life, such as the five Ds of parental dedication, discernment, devotion, discipline, and discipleship. I will teach about God's calling on children to offer their parents honoring love. Parents will hear me teach about their calling to offer their children holy love. I will teach about the four styles of parenting, about four stages and styles of foolishness, and much more.

I also seek to instill wisdom by exposing the family to solid biblical teaching outside of counseling. They may be required to attend a small group, a Sunday school class, or a seminar on parenting or family life. They may be assigned to read a book or watch a video on parenting or family life.

Since our primary goal is to empower parents to equip their children, we want to encourage parents to take the lead in family instruction. Rex and Tamika can take the discussion we started on Ephesians 4:25–32 and explore and apply that passage with Jake and Jessica during family worship or devotional time. For some parents, leading family devotions will require coaching, resourcing, and encouraging from their counselor.

Instilling Wisdom through Training in Righteousness

Now you send them home to apply your teaching and trialoguing (recall the principles about family counseling homework from chapter 9). Co-create the homework assignment, making it specific to their particular situation and unique family personality.

When they return, debrief. "So . . . who wants to go first? Who wants to tell me how it went as you each sought to apply Ephesians 4:25–32?"

If it went well, cheer them on. Explore how they were able to tap into Christ's resurrection power to change and grow.

If it went poorly, listen and explore. What made it hard? What old patterns rose to the surface? How could they have put off the old?

If it did go poorly, now you have a perfect opportunity and a teachable moment for our next biblical family counseling competency. They have experienced the reality that knowing what the Bible says to do and knowing how to do what it says can be two very separate matters.

Maturing as a Biblical Family Counselor
Putting On Christ's Wisdom Perspective

1. Regarding the sufficiency and relevance of Scripture for biblical counseling and family living:

   a. How would you define the sufficiency of Scripture for biblical counseling?

   b. How would you define the relevance of Scripture for family living?

   c. As a biblical family counselor, what are specific ways you can demonstrate your confidence in the Bible's sufficiency and relevance?

   d. What role do you believe descriptive research plays in a biblical family counselor's ministry? What examples would you give where you might use descriptive research?

e. What role, if any, do you think secular family theory/therapy might play in your counseling? How might a study of Colossians 1–2 impact your thinking on this?

2. On pages 226–27 you read scriptural exploration trialogues from Ephesians 4:25–32.

   a. How might you word any of those trialogues differently? What might you add or subtract?

   b. Select another passage relevant to issues that families bring to counseling. Develop a series of trialogues that you might use to help a family think through the application of that passage for their family—discerning the "what to do."

3. What are some of the go-to passages that you explore with families? How can you merge your teaching and your trialoguing?

4. In training in righteousness, you co-create family-specific homework. We discussed the reality that sometimes homework does not work—if "work" means they effortlessly applied the truth. We also discussed the value/usefulness of those times—they become teachable moments for learning how to tap into Christ's resurrection power. How could you use failed homework as a means for further progressive sanctification work?

Empowering Families to Live in Light of Their Victory in Christ: Strengthening Families through Christ's Resurrection Power

First we help family members put on a *new what-to*—wisdom from God's Word to discern biblical principles for family relationships. Determining how God calls us to relate is vital; however, moving from knowledge to relational change is often a difficult transition for family members. This is why our statement on guiding highlights the word *supernatural*: "It's *supernatural* to love each other like Christ, through Christ, for Christ." To address this, our second guiding marriage counseling competency focuses on empowering families to live in light of their victory in Christ—a *new how-to*.

"De-Power" Family Members

Without wisdom, our tendency is to turn to anyone but the Creator of life for wisdom for living. With the application of wisdom, our tendency is to try to change in our own power. As we saw with Manoah and his wife in Judges 13, this is why God did not send them a how-to manual. Instead, he called them to God-dependence.

This is why Paul, as we have seen, builds bookends of God-dependence around his teaching on family life. And it is why we take parents and children to Ephesians 5:18 and Ephesians 6:10–18 whenever we talk about applying truth to family life.

- Rex, Tamika, Jake, and Jessica, what do you make of the fact that before Paul ever talks about how to love family members, he talks about being filled with the Spirit?
- Let's talk about what the Bible means by being filled with the Spirit. Let's apply that specifically to the homework assignments you each found difficult to do this past week.
- Paul also concludes his section on family life with a focus on our inability and Christ's ability. Let's read Ephesians 6:10–18 together . . .
- When you were in the midst of messing up this week, what might have happened if you had stopped and read and prayed Ephesians 6:10? "Father, I'm weak in myself. I can't do this godly anger thing. Help me to be strong in you and in your mighty power."
- Let's read and think about Ephesians 6:18 in a family context. Mom, Dad, Jake, and Jessica, pray in the Spirit on all occasions when you are trying to love each other. With all kinds of prayers and requests, pray for each other. With your calling to apply Ephesians 4:25–32 in

mind, be alert and always keep praying for yourself and each other. What would it be like to pray this . . . ?

- I'd like to take about fifteen minutes and walk through each piece of the armor of God, looking at it as family armor. Then, let's discuss what it would be like for each of you to put on that family armor . . .

Part of this de-powering process may include exploring whether each family member has truly surrendered their life to Christ and is truly born again—forgiven, cleansed, and made new. Initial intake sheets will often have a space for family members to share their testimony of salvation in Christ alone. In sessions, I will ask family members to share their salvation story. This is an opportunity to talk about their eternal need for Christ for salvation and their daily need for Christ for sanctification. Paul's point in Romans 6:1–18 is not only that Christ saves us from eternal separation from God but also that through Christ's death and resurrection we can put off the old sinful patterns and put on new Christlike ways of relating.

Empower Family Members through Christ's Resurrection Power

Once family members begin to grasp their *inability* to change themselves, the soil of their souls becomes fertile ground for learning how Christ changes lives. So we explore, teach, and trialogue about gospel indicatives. We apply passages like Romans 6:1–8; 2 Corinthians 5:17; and Colossians 3:1–11 about their new want-to and their being new creations in Christ.

- Rex, it can be discouraging to think that we're stuck in the same old condition. But 2 Corinthians 5:17 says you are a new creature in Christ. You have a new heart that wants to obey Christ and love your family. It could be helpful, then, for you to share with Tamika, Jake, and Jessica the new desires you have to love them, disciple them, be with them, care for them, and shepherd them . . .

We also trialogue and teach about their new can-do—their new power in Christ to experience victory over sin.

- Tamika, let's take a look at Philippians 3:1–10 . . . Did you notice how in the first few verses Paul talked about the futility of trying to change in his own power? It was worthless. But then later, especially in 3:10, Paul talks about the source of his power to change. "I want to know Christ and the power of his resurrection." What would it look like for you to tap into Christ's resurrection power . . . ?
- Jessica and Jake, I know you both feel discouraged. Really beaten down. It's like Frodo in *The Lord of the Rings* and the scene at the

end of the second movie that we talked about last week. Frodo is about ready to give up and give in. Sam tackles him to keep him from surrendering to that evil flying creature. Then Frodo says, "I can't do this. I can't go on." In his own power, he could *not* go on. He needed strength from above. Let's take a look at Ephesians 1:19–20 to see Christ's resurrection power at work in *you*. Paul prays that their eyes would be open to see God the Father's "incomparably great power for us who believe. That power is the same as the mighty strength he exerted when he raised Christ from the dead and seated him at his right hand in the heavenly realms." Did you get that? The same power that raised Christ from the dead is in you, Jessica, and in you, Jake! It's changed you. It's unchained you! It's empowered you—even to love Mom and Dad.

Maturing as a Biblical Family Counselor
Empowering Families to Live in Light of Their Victory in Christ

1. In our flesh, we each have a tendency to depend on our own wisdom and strength in addressing family relationship struggles.

   a. Where have you seen this play itself out in your life and family relationships? How do you tap into Christ's resurrection power and eternal wisdom to break free from these tendencies?

   b. How have you seen this play itself out in families you have counseled or ministered to? How do you seek to help them tap into Christ's resurrection power and eternal wisdom to break free from these tendencies?

2. Select a passage you could use to help de-power family members—to help them see that they cannot change on their own. Craft several trialogues you could use from that passage.

3. Select a passage you could use to empower family members—to help them tap into Christ's resurrection power. Craft several trialogues you could use from that passage.

CHAPTER

THIRTEEN

Family Progressive Sanctification
Guiding in Family Counseling, Part 2

Introduction: Loving Each Other Like Christ, through Christ, for Christ

The Mitchell family—Rex, Tamika, Jake, and Jessica—seem to feed on fighting. Feeling powerless to bond in healthy ways, they strive to connect through chaos and conflict. Without recognizing it, they act as if drama and trauma are their only possible points of contact. Take those away and they would be left with nothing—no relationship, no connection, no involvement.

Satan had snared them in his twisted trap: pursue God-given, legitimate desires for connection in God-dishonoring, illegitimate ways. The devil's age-old strategy is at work in this modern family. Forsake God, your Spring of Living Water, and dig broken cisterns that can hold no water (Jer. 2:13). Bend your desire for connection into a self-centered demand filled with self-sufficiency and self-protection (James 4:1–4).

How do we help the Mitchells escape the serpent's snare? Our mission is *not* to help them kill the desire for connection. Desire is God's idea. In the beginning, God created us to desire him—to walk with him and fellowship with him in the cool of the day. God also designed us to desire one another—it is not good for us to be alone.

Our calling is to help the Mitchells put off pursuing legitimate desires in illegitimate, demanding, self-centered ways. Our calling is to help them put on pursuing relational connection—holy love and honoring love—in legitimate, other-centered, Christ-honoring ways.

Instead of letting them continue feeding on fighting, we help them drink from God, the Spring of Living Water, and then fill each other from the overflow of Christ's love. Instead of connecting through chaos and conflict, we help them join together in loving like Christ. Instead of drama and trauma being their points of contact, mutual sacrificial love becomes their basis for involvement.

As we learned in chapter 8, we disciple the Mitchell family to apply Philippians 2:1–4. Since they are filled with encouragement from their relationship with Christ, since they are filled with fellowship from their relationship with the Spirit, since they are filled with tenderness and compassion from their relationship with the Father, they can love each other out of the overflow of the Trinity's love. They can move toward being like-minded, sharing the same love, being one in spirit and of one mind. They can stop interacting out of selfish ambition and vain conceit; instead, in humility they can value each other above themselves, not looking simply to their own interests, but each of them looking to the interests of the others. In their relationships with each other, they can have the mindset of Christ. Rex, Tamika, Jake, and Jessica need discipling and coaching to live out the guiding truth that *it's supernatural to love each other like Christ, through Christ, for Christ.*

Maturing as a Biblical Family Counselor
Loving Each Other Like Christ, through Christ, for Christ

1. Have you ever experienced or witnessed family life (yours or someone else's) where family members seem to feed on fighting, connect through chaos and conflict, and relate through drama and trauma?

   a. If so, what was the experience like? Through Christ's power, was it ever changed?

   b. How would you counsel a family that connects in these ways?

2. Satan wants us to pursue God-given, legitimate desires for connection in illegitimate ways that dishonor God. He tempts us to bend our desire for connection into a self-centered demand filled with self-sufficiency and self-protection.

   a. Have you ever experienced this temptation in your family relationships? If so, how have you fought against this lie and put on the truth?

   b. How would you counsel families caught in this serpentine snare?

3. Have you ever had someone, in an attempt to help you address desires you struggled with, counsel you to kill your desires? If so, how did this impact you?

4. Our mission is *not* to help the family members kill the desire for connection. Our calling is to help them put off pursuing legitimate desires in illegitimate, demanding, self-centered ways. Our calling is to help them put on pursuing relational connection—holy love and honoring love—in legitimate, other-centered, Christ-honoring ways. In what specific ways could that summary impact how you counsel families?

5. Read and reflect on Philippians 2:1–4.
   a. How could the truths of those verses impact your family relationships?

   b. How could you use those truths in biblical family counseling?

Even as biblical counselors who proclaim progressive sanctification, we can become frustrated with the slow, halting pace of family change. We think, "They saw their sin, repented, and confessed. They were forgiven by God and each other. They have Christ's wisdom. We helped them tap into Christ's resurrection power. In Christ they have the new want-to and can-do, and through counseling they have the new what-to and how-to. Why are they so slow to change?"

Sometimes our impatience may be because we do not truly believe our own theology—sanctification is a progressive process, not a quick fix. If that is the case, then we need to repent of our bad theology or of not believing our own theology.

At other times our impatience may be because our counselees have become *our* broken cistern that can hold no water. We want, need, and demand that the family members change *so they can make us look good.* If this is the case, then we need to repent of our self-centered, manipulative cistern-digging. And we may also want to pursue some counseling of our own—nothing at all wrong with a counselor receiving counseling.

Assuming that our theology is right and our heart is right, a family counselor can respond to the halting pace of family change by being an ACE:

A Activating Application

C Coaching Families

E Emboldening Families

Relating Maturely in the Present Moment

Whether with sustaining, healing, or reconciling, I have encouraged us to focus on what is happening between the family members in the room—dealing with the present moment. I have the same recommendation for guiding.

The Mitchell family returns to my office and they timidly share, "Pastor Bob, we didn't do too well this past week applying all the stuff we talked about last week." One way to respond is to explore with them what they did last week that did not work (see chap. 12). Another response is to have them readdress that issue right now in front of you. Not as a reenactment of the past interaction—as if it is a role-play of a past historical event—but as a fresh opportunity to engage this issue right now with you present as their family coach.

In reconciling, we are doing this in part to catch them red-handed—to humbly, lovingly, and graciously expose their sin so they can be freed from the deception and blindness of sin. In guiding, we have them relate in front of us so we can coach them to apply eternal truth to their daily relationships—activating application.

They *have* repented and *are* repenting of their heart sins and self-centered ways of relating (James 4:1–4). They are increasingly grasping the truth of gospel-empowered relating (Phil. 2:1–5). Now we want to help the Mitchells take the truth that is in their minds and apply it actively in their relationships. We coach Rex, Tamika, Jake, and Jessica to shift from their old pattern of consuming each other to their new pattern of ministering to each other. We help them experience movement away from James 4:1–4 living to Philippians 2:1–5 living. We equip them to identify and put off their old self-centered way of relating and to put on, in the power of Christ, their new other-centered way of relating.

Parents-to-Children Active Application

Rex and Tamika's old pattern was filled with anger over being disrespected (not receiving honoring love). Their anger was fueled by the fact that they had made Jake and Jessica their cistern—their idol, their object of self-worship and self-affirmation. Tamika and Rex were consumers, takers, and demanders: "Make us look good! Make us feel good!" Now they are repenters—repentant and repenting. Now, instead of being cistern-diggers, they are God-drinkers—drinking from the Spring of Living Water. Being filled with the Trinity's encouragement, fellowship, tenderness, and compassion (Phil. 2:1), Rex and Tamika can offer their children holy love from the overflow of the Trinity's holy love.

- Rex and Tamika, it sounds like this week when you didn't see Jake and Jessica changing, when you didn't see them being respectful, that you guys reverted back to the old ways. We've seen that part of this is because your goal, your idol, has been that your kids *must* fill you. Do you think that was going on again at all this week . . . ?

After some interaction, awareness, and acknowledgment, you direct Rex and Tamika back to Jake and Jessica.

- I really appreciate, Tamika and Rex, your humility in confessing that you blew it—in your hearts and then in your response to your kids. What do you want to say to God now, and what do you want to say to your kids now . . . ?

Possibly this prompt encourages Tamika and Rex to stop and pray, asking God for forgiveness and asking him to help them live out Philippians 2:2–5 in the power of Philippians 2:1. Perhaps this has also inspired them to ask their kids to forgive them for responding to their disrespect with disrespect of their own. That could be a whole session!

But we are not done coaching Mom and Dad yet. This has been the "love" part of parental holy love. What about the "holy" part?

- Tamika and Rex, *and* Jake and Jessica, we've just talked through part of godly parenting. Mom and Dad have been humble and loving just now. But there's that second part we've talked a lot about—parental holiness and discipline and discipleship. Jake and Jessica were disrespectful. Mom and Dad, right now, with me here, I'd like you to address that with your kids—in loving firmness. I'll help if you need it, stepping in if necessary . . .

Again, this could be an entire session—especially with a family like the Mitchells that has such a long history of chaotic conflict. Who knows where the conversation and interaction goes next. Wherever it goes, you are there to coach Mom and Dad to apply gospel-energized holy love.

Children-to-Parents Active Application

We do not stop with the parents—especially when counseling children the ages of Jake (14) and Jessica (12).

- So, Jessica and Jake, your turn. You knew I wasn't going to put this all on Mom and Dad and let you guys off the hook [*said smiling and teasingly*]. Let's start by hearing what you think was going on in your hearts when you responded to Mom and Dad . . .

Ideally, this could lead to a gospel conversation where they acknowledge their sinful response and recognize and repent over their heart sin.

- I'm amazed, Jessica and Jake, at your insight and honesty, humility and repentance. Thank you. Now that you have taken care of this with God, let's see you take care of this with Mom and Dad. What do you want to say to them about how you related to them last week? Like with Mom and Dad, I'll step in and help, referee, and coach when you want and need me to . . .

We activate application by coaching Rex, Tamika, Jake, and Jessica to relate to God and each other right there with us. Several concepts and competencies are at work simultaneously in these discipling trialogues.

- *Drawing out Christlike attitudes*. The Mitchell family has already verbalized their new central values—to relate like Christ relates. We now draw out those values actively in the present moment.

- *Strengthening relationships and connections*. We become counselor-coach as we equip Rex, Tamika, Jake, and Jessica to interact out of their new, godly style of relating. Since "out of the abundance of the heart the mouth speaks" (Matt. 12:34 ESV), this new style will reveal itself in their interactions, especially their intense interactions.

- *Highlighting and changing patterns of thinking*. Through the power of God's Word, we have been dismantling (taking every thought captive) the old thinking patterns (mindsets). Now we highlight the new, Christlike thinking patterns by reminding the family of them and calling on the family to apply these new mindsets and heart patterns.

- *Cementing commitment*. The family has said, "We want to be different." Activating application helps the family to live out their new commitments. We lovingly but firmly say, "Do what you said. Just do it!" In the safety of our coaching and refereeing, they can practice what the gospel preaches.

Maturing as a Biblical Family Counselor
Activating Application

1. Time to counsel the counselor. Do you ever find yourself needing and demanding your counselees to change so you look good and feel good about yourself? If so, how can you address this heart issue, which will surely come out in your counseling relationships?

2. In reconciling, we have families relate in front of us so we can catch them red-handed, lovingly expose their sin, and free them from sin's deceitfulness. In guiding, we have families relate in front of us so we can coach them to apply eternal truth to their daily relationships.

   a. Which of these two counselor competencies do you think comes more naturally for you? Why?

b. How could you further develop the competency that does not come as naturally for you?

3. Create your own family counseling scenario—ideally from a family you are currently counseling. Craft a series of coaching trialogues where you would disciple the parents to interact with their children about a specific issue.

4. Create your own family counseling scenario—ideally from a family you are currently counseling. Craft a series of coaching trialogues where you would disciple the children to interact with their parents about a specific issue.

Coaching Families: Equipping Families for Christ-Centered Living

Let's track where we are in the guiding process. The repentant and forgiven Mitchell family knows where to go to discern the what-to. They are equipped to go to the Bible for family discernment. They also know where to go for the how-to. They are empowered by turning to Christ's resurrection power. And now you have discipled them in the controlled environment of the counseling room as they interact together.

But they still have to get out there into the everyday world of messy family relationships. And ultimately the family is not just about the family. The healthy growing family has locks and hinges—locks to know when to focus on the family, and hinges to know when and how to focus the family on impacting the world for Christ. So we want to coach and equip families to live out the gospel in their homes, their neighborhoods, their schools, their places of work, their churches, and their extended family.

The Goals of Family Coaching

Coaches emphasize specific goals, measurable objectives, and tangible targets. Here are biblical family coaching goals stated in the language of this training manual.

- Equipping parents to offer their children holy love.
- Equipping children to offer their parents honoring love.
- Equipping parents to put off pharisaical parenting, possessive/permissive parenting, or neglectful parenting and to put on godly parenting.
- Equipping children to put off foolishness and to put on age- and stage-appropriate wisdom.
- Equipping parents to put on the five Ds of dedication, discernment, devotion, discipline, and discipleship.
- Equipping family members to apply Christ's eternal gospel story to their daily family relationships.
- Equipping family members to turn to the Trinity as their Spring of Living Water and, out of the overflow of the Trinity's encouragement, fellowship, tenderness, and compassion, to relate to one another like Christ, through Christ, and for Christ.
- Equipping families to apply the truth that *it's supernatural to love each other like Christ, through Christ, for Christ.*
- Equipping families to apply the truth that *our family can supernaturally minister together to love others like Christ, through Christ, for Christ.*

This last bullet point is vital. Biblical family counseling is not just about the nuclear family. It is about family members seeing themselves as the family of God sent on a mission together to impact the world like Christ, through Christ, and for Christ. Healthy things grow. Healthy families grow. Healthy biblical counseling grows families that catch God's vision to be ambassadors of reconciliation. Family members in counseling are not simply consumers of our services. They graduate and become givers of service and ministry to others.

Think about the Mitchell family. Though I have changed their names and various aspects of their situation to keep their identities confidential, they represent an actual family I have counseled. As their family life began to slowly, progressively change from chaotic conflict to Christ-centered connection, people took notice. They began asking, "What happened to you guys? You're different! You've changed." What an opportunity to share the reason for the change and hope within them.

The Perspective of the Family Coach

What is the mindset that every family counselor-coach needs to develop? We state it within our summary phrase that captures the essence of guiding, and within the additional phrase added in this section:

> *It's supernatural to love each other like Christ, through Christ,*
> *for Christ. Our family can supernaturally minister together*
> *to love others like Christ, through Christ, for Christ.*

Counselors believe, and we coach families to believe, that because of Christ, families are not their disabilities. They are not their struggles. They are not their past defeats. Because of Christ, every Christian family has the resources to share holy love and honoring love. In Christ, every Christian family is capable of love—for each other *and* for others outside their family. In Christ, every Christian family can live victoriously for the ultimate goal of glorifying Christ by being ambassadors for Christ.

Counselors who see themselves as coach-equippers realize that the coach's job is not to play the game but to prepare the players to play at their peak level. In particular, we coach parents to coach their children, we disciple parents to be their children's disciple-makers, and we equip parents to equip their children. Specifically, family coaches see themselves called to equip the family members, especially the parents, to:

- Fan into flame the gift of God within each other (2 Tim. 1:5–7).
- Encourage one another so that no family member is taken captive by the deceitfulness of sin (Heb. 3:11–15).
- Stir up love and good deeds among one another (Heb. 10:24–25).
- Equip one another to live out the Great Commandment (Matt. 22:35–40) and the Great Commission (Matt. 28:16–20) for the praise of God's glorious grace (Eph. 1:3–14).

Equipping Family Members to Live Out Their Unique Identity in Christ

Several chapters before Paul directly counsels Christian families in Ephesians 6, he counsels all Christians to understand who/whose we are in Christ. In

Ephesians 1:15–23, Paul keeps praying that the glorious Father would open the eyes of our hearts *so that* we would be enlightened to know the hope to which he has called us, the riches of his glorious inheritance as his saints, sons, and daughters.

When I ponder this passage in light of the larger biblical narrative of God's design for men and women, fathers and mothers, sons and daughters, I keep these four family identities in mind. I seek to enlighten fathers, mothers, sons, and daughters to see themselves in Christ as:

- *A Christian Father in Christ.* A king and shepherd-hero in a grand adventure of epic proportion. A noble knight. An adult son of God. A man of power, love, and wisdom who is an ambassador for Christ.
- *A Christian Mother in Christ.* A queen and shepherd-lover in a great love affair of eternal duration. A collaborative celebrator. An adult daughter of God. A woman of tenderness, love, and insight who is an ambassador for Christ.
- *A Christian Son in Christ.* A knight-in-the-making, a king-to-be, with a strong and tender set of shepherding parents who help him to see his gifts, control and enjoy his passions, and pursue his dreams. A boy maturing to be a godly man with increasing strength, passion, and discernment who is an ambassador for Christ.
- *A Christian Daughter in Christ.* A princess-in-the-making, a queen-to-be, with a strong and tender set of shepherding parents who help her to see the beauty of her soul, express and control her compassion, and connect with others with openness. A girl maturing to be a godly woman of increasing encouragement, compassion, and wisdom who is an ambassador for Christ.

I might hand these out and have questions for discussion/trialogue:

- Rex, Tamika, Jake, and Jessica, each of you take a look at each description. Then I want the four of you to discuss the following items . . .

  » What are some positive examples where you see each other already living out some of these areas in Christ?
  » How could you help each other grow more like each of these descriptions?
  » What characters in Scripture do you most identify with as you read the description that relates to your role in the family?

- Rex, Paul says in 2 Timothy 1:6–7 that every man has planted within him power, love, and wisdom. How does that compare to how you see yourself as a father?
- Tamika, in Proverbs 31, Solomon describes the ideal woman as a noble woman with energy from God to care for her family. How does this description compare to how you see yourself?
- Jake, the description of a godly son reminds me of Timothy in 1 and 2 Timothy. Let's look together at several passages in those two books and see areas that you can apply to your life . . .
- Jessica, Esther certainly reminds me of the description of the godly young woman. Let's look at passages in the book of Esther and explore aspects of her life that you can emulate . . .

Maturing as a Biblical Family Counselor
Coaching Families

1. On page 243 you read a list of goals for biblical family coaching.
   a. Which ones resonate the most for you? Why? How could you pursue those as a counselor?

   b. What two or three additional family coaching goals would you add to the list?

2. In this section we added this important piece to the ultimate goal of biblical family counseling: "Our family can supernaturally minister together to love others like Christ, through Christ, for Christ."

   a. How could that goal change or expand your focus as a family counselor?

   b. How would you word the ultimate, overarching biblical goal or outcome of family counseling? What passages would you use to develop that goal?

3. On page 245 you read descriptive images of a Christian father, mother, son, and daughter in Christ.

   a. How would you change, tweak, edit, or add to those descriptions?

   b. What biblical passages would you use to develop your own descriptions or images that capture the essence of a Christian father, mother, son, and daughter in Christ?

Emboldening Families: Sending Families Out with Confidence in Christ

I have two timelines in mind when I talk about sending families out with confidence in Christ. The first timeline is during each counseling session in which guiding is our primary focus. The second timeline is in our final "commencement" counseling session. (Some counselors call the final session the termination session, but for many reasons I prefer commencement.)

When I think of the word "emboldening" I like to break the word in two: em-bold. In other words, to put boldness into; to stir up courage and fan it into flame. Family life can become complicated and grueling, exhausting and discouraging. This can especially occur in the midst of guiding. You are all excited about the trust-making progress. They have connected well with you. They do not want to let you down. But they have messed up again. They need their courage and boldness fanned into flame.

Emboldening Families during Guiding Counseling Sessions

We never want to be that counselor who is all "happy-happy," a Mr. Positivity who looks at life through rose-colored glasses. If we have done our sustaining and reconciling work, then no one could accuse us of that. We also never want to be that counselor who is always "gloom-and-doom," a Mrs. Negativity who always sees the cup of life as half empty.

Biblical counselors are creation-fall-redemption-consummation realists. We understand God's original design for the family (creation). We recognize the fallen shape of the family (fall). We prescribe God's cure for the family (redemption). And we look forward to the future day when all sorrow and sin will be wiped away (consummation).

Biblical counselors are also death and resurrection realists. We understand the depths and horrors of sin that led to Christ's crucifixion. We also grasp the grandeur of grace and the power of Christ's resurrection to produce victory over sin—including family victory. As resurrection realists, we help discouraged families become en-couraged in Christ. We challenge them to move forward together through:

- Affirming victory
- Anticipating growth
- Applying the resurrection

Affirming Victory

You become the family's number one fan. Their biggest cheerleader. When they move forward in a positive way, you respond with:

- Wow, I'm truly amazed! I've seen such great growth in your family relationship in just the past three weeks. What do you attribute it to?
- Tamika and Rex, how have the two of you learned to overcome that old style?
- Jake, that's a very different response than previously. How did you manage to do that? How do you explain that?

Anticipating Growth

If we believe our own theology, then we know that God has given every believing family all that they need for life and godliness. This is why we created an expectant attitude from the very first session. Recall the section on infusing hope and the Ephesians 3:20 questions:

- Let's create an Ephesians 3:14–21 vision for your family. Think ahead three months. As God does exceedingly, abundantly above all that you could ask or imagine in your heart and in your family, what two or three amazing changes are you envisioning, praying for, and hoping for? What needs to happen in your heart and in your family relationship so that through Christ's strength these amazing changes start occurring?

We can ask this question in a number of different, anticipatory ways:

- How will you know that our family counseling has been successful?
- What will each of you be doing differently after successful counseling?

- How will each of you be relating differently after successful family counseling?

We can also anticipate growth at the conclusion of every session.

- As all of you leave here today and you're on track, what will you be doing differently? How will you be thinking differently? Relating differently?
- What will you each be doing instead of the old way of relating . . . ?
- Specifically, *how* will you be doing this?

Applying the Resurrection

Remember that where sin abounds, grace superabounds. Recall that Christian family members have died to sin with Christ and have been raised with Christ to victory over sin. With this resurrection perspective in mind, we explore how Christ is helping families to live victoriously.

- When is your family *already* experiencing some of the victory you long for? When is your family *already* doing some of what you want and what the Bible commands?
- When are you experiencing victory over this family problem? What is different in your relationships at these times? What are you each doing differently? How are you each thinking differently?
- How have you each been cooperating with Christ to overcome this struggle together?
- How will you guys keep this change going through Christ?

When the family is not currently experiencing victory, you can explore the past and imagine the future . . .

- Tell me about the time before all of this stuff started . . .
- In past times, have you ever overcome this, even once? What was different about those times/that time? How could you repeat that now? How do you think Christ was at work in your family then? How could you tap into his power again now?
- What would you like to see happen instead . . . ?
- How do you see Christ defeating this problem in the future?
- When you experience victory through Christ and this relational conflict is resolved, what will you each be doing differently?

When the family has had some times of victory, while you do not want to be a naysayer or a prophet of gloom, realism says that change is imperfect. So you may want to share:

- Are there times you can imagine when it may be tempting for all of you to go back to the old ways rather than continuing to grow?

    » What might those times be like for each of you?
    » How could you prepare for them?
    » How might you handle that temporary setback?

Emboldening the Family in Commencement Counseling Sessions: Equipping the Family to Live Out Their Unique Family Calling in Christ

In chapter 9 you read about the Kellemen Family MVP Statement. As a family coach, I want to equip every family to prayerfully ask and biblically answer the question, As a family, who is God calling us to be and what is God calling us to do?

In a final session with families, I will often walk them through the process of crafting their own family MVP statement as one way of answering the question about their family calling. Other times, rather than a full-blown MVP statement, I might spend time in a final session trialoguing about questions such as:

- What unique gifts has God given each of you individually and all of you together?
- As you think about your family's history, gifts, and unique makeup, what special purpose is God calling your family to pursue?
- How do you imagine your family uniquely living out God's vision for you?
- If there were one phrase you could use to summarize what's special about your family in Christ, what would it be?
- Tell me about the future you hope and pray for each other? For your family? How will you be moving toward becoming this sort of family in the next year?
- What dead things do you anticipate Christ resurrecting in your family? What will your family look like when God resurrects them?
- What movie have you watched that depicts the sort of theme your family wants to live out? What book have you read that pictures the sort of theme God is calling your family to live? What song conveys the message that your family wants to share?

- What Christian family impresses you? Why? What about them would you like to imitate? How might you start doing that?
- What passages could we explore that picture God's dream for your family?
- How can your family live out the attitudes of Ephesians 6:1–4?
- How can your family arm yourselves with God's spiritual family armor?
- Do you have a family verse? If so, how are you applying it? If not, what verse or passage captures your heart as a family?
- When you first started counseling with me, you answered the Ephesians 3:20 question. Let's answer it again now, going further into the future and tweaking the wording a bit. Think ahead one year. As God does exceedingly, abundantly above all that you could ask or imagine through your family, what two or three amazing ways do you envision God using your family to glorify Christ? What needs to happen in your family so that through Christ these amazing things happen?

Maturing as a Biblical Family Counselor
Emboldening Families

1. Who stirs up boldness in you, especially when you are discouraged? How do they do it?

2. Do you tend to be more of a Mr. Positivity or a Mrs. Negativity? How could you move toward becoming a counselor who is more of a resurrection realist?

3. On pages 248–50 you read several sampler trialogues for affirming victory, anticipating growth, and applying the resurrection.

   a. Craft several of your own affirming victory trialogues.

b. Craft several of your own anticipating growth trialogues.

c. Craft several of your own applying the resurrection trialogues.

4. On pages 250–51 you read several trialogues for equipping families to live out their unique family calling in Christ. Craft five trialogues of your own that will be useful for helping families tap into God's special calling for them.

Trialogue #1

Trialogue #2

Trialogue #3

Trialogue #4

Trialogue #5

Gospel-Centered Family Counseling Commencement

Family Counseling Prayer and Praise

In the introduction to this book, I started by discussing my incompetence without Christ. In Christ, we can all become competent biblical family counselors (Rom. 15:14). Just as with family life, counselor growth is a lifelong progressive sanctification process. Christ works in us as we work through his power.

To help us to keep growing, I am repeating our summary of the twenty-two gospel-centered family counseling relational competencies in figure C.1. Use figure C.1 to complete the Maturing as a Biblical Family Counselor exercises and questions.

My final words to you come from the same passage as my first words to families in family counseling.

The Biblical Family Counselor's Commencement Prayer and Praise

Now, biblical family counselor,
depend upon him alone and give glory to him alone
who is able to do immeasurably more than all we ask or imagine
through our family counseling and in the parents and children we counsel,
because our ministry of family counseling is according to his resurrection power
that is at work within us and within the families we counsel,
to him—the Divine Counselor, the Wonderful Counselor—be glory in the church
and in Christ Jesus throughout all generations, for ever and ever!
Amen.
(based on Eph. 3:20–21)

Figure C.1

Overview of Gospel-Centered Family Counseling

22 Biblical Family Counseling Relational Competencies

Infusing Hope

H Having Hope as a Family Counselor (chap. 5)

O Offering Hope to Hurting Families (chap. 5)

P Prompting Parents to Tap into God-Given Resources (chap. 5)

E Encouraging the Family to See Signs of Christ on the Move (chap. 5)

Parakaletic Biblical Family Counseling for Suffering Families

- **Sustaining**: Like Christ, we care about each other's hurts.

   L Looking at Families through the Lens of Suffering (chap. 6)

   O Observing, Openly Joining, and Orchestrating the Family Dance and the Family Dirge (chap. 6)

   V Venturing Together across the Family Chasm (chap. 7)

   E Equipping the Family to Comfort Each Other with Christ's Comfort (chap. 7)

- **Healing**: Through Christ, it's possible for us to hope in God together.

   F Framing Family Healing Narratives (chap. 8)

   A Applying Our Identity in Christ (chap. 8)

   I Integrating in Our Victory through Christ (chap. 9)

   T Training in Teamwork on the Family Quest (chap. 9)

   H Honing Homework That Works (chap. 9)

Nouthetic Biblical Family Counseling for Sinning Families

- **Reconciling**: It's horrible to sin against Christ and each other, but through Christ it's wonderful to be forgiven and to forgive.

   R Recognizing Destructive Family Relationships (chap. 10)

   E Enlightening Family Members to Destructive Family Relationships (chap. 10)

   S Soothing the Family's Soul in Their Savior (chap. 11)

   T Trust-Making (chap. 11)

- **Guiding**: It's supernatural to love each other like Christ, through Christ, for Christ.

   P Putting On Christ's Wisdom Perspective (chap. 12)

   E Empowering Families to Live in Light of Their Victory in Christ (chap. 12)

   A Activating Application (chap. 13)

   C Coaching Families (chap. 13)

   E Emboldening Families (chap. 13)

Maturing as a Biblical Family Counselor
Gospel-Centered Family Counseling Commencement

1. Review figure C.1.
   a. Which of these twenty-two relational competencies are you strongest in? Is that due more to natural giftedness and how God has wired you, or is it due more to discipline in developing that area?

   b. Which of these twenty-two relational competencies do you need to work on the most? How could you develop those areas? Why do you suppose those areas are not your strengths?

2. Reflecting back on your time reading through and working through this equipping manual:

   a. What truths will you take with you for your life and for your family?

   b. What truths will you take with you for your family counseling ministry?

3. If you have worked through this equipping manual in a small group lab:

   a. What has been most rewarding for you in the group process?

   b. What words of encouragement and affirmation would you like to share with members of your group?

4. As you commence . . .

    a. What will you do to keep the change going and growing in your life?

    b. What will you do to keep the change going and growing in your family counseling ministry?

Notes

Introduction

1. I also discuss these five marks of GRACE-focused family living and counseling in my book *Raising Kids in the Way of Grace* (Youngstown, OH: 10Publishing, 2018).

Chapter 2 Parenting Like Our Heavenly Father

1. J. I. Packer, *Knowing God* (Downers Grove, IL: InterVarsity, 1993), 201.

Chapter 4 Our Family Counseling GPS for Family Suffering, Sin, and Sanctification

1. Frank Lake, *Clinical Theology* (London: Darton, Longman, & Todd, 1966), 21, italics in original.
2. See Jay Adams, *Competent to Counsel, The Christian Counselor's Manual*, and *A Theology of Christian Counseling*.
3. For a comprehensive development of sustaining, healing, reconciling, and guiding, see Bob Kellemen, *Gospel Conversations* (Grand Rapids: Zondervan, 2015).

Chapter 5 Infusing HOPE in the Midst of Hurt

1. Rob and Stephanie Green address pre-parental preparation in *Tying Their Shoes* (Greensboro, NC: New Growth, 2019).

Chapter 8 Gospel Hope for Family Hurt

1. Martin Luther, *Commentary on Galatians*, trans. P. S. Watson (Grand Rapids: Revell, 1988), 18.
2. Luther, *Commentary on Galatians*, 30–31.

Chapter 12 Family Wisdom and Strength from Christ

1. Quoted in Bob Kellemen, *Gospel-Centered Counseling* (Grand Rapids: Zondervan, 2014), 205.
2. See Bob Kellemen and Jeff Forrey, eds., *Scripture and Counseling* (Grand Rapids: Zondervan, 2014), as one example of a book-length discussion of the sufficiency of Scripture for biblical counseling.
3. See chapters 1–2 of Kellemen, *Gospel-Centered Counseling*.
4. See chapters 1–2 of Kellemen, *Gospel-Centered Counseling*.

Resources for Family Life
and Family Counseling

I have designed this bibliography for the practical use of family counselors and parents. By organizing the bibliography into categories, counselors and parents can select resources appropriate for the specific family and their unique situation. Many of these resources are in booklet or discussion guide format or have workbooks associated with them—making them excellent for family counseling homework and small group use. Rather than alphabetical, this listing of resources is chronological/topical: broad gospel-centered principles of parenting, parental evangelism, parenting young children, parenting adolescents, parenting adult children, and so forth.

Preparing for Parenting

Green, Rob, and Stephanie Green. *Tying Their Shoes: A Christ-Centered Approach to Preparing for Parenting*. Greensboro, NC: New Growth, 2019.

Juliani, Barbara. *Preparing for Motherhood*. Greensboro, NC: New Growth, 2012.

Gospel-Centered Parenting

Farley, William P. *Gospel-Powered Parenting: How the Gospel Shapes and Transforms Parenting*. Phillipsburg, NJ: P&R, 2012.

Fitzpatrick, Elyse, and Jessica Thompson. *Give Them Grace*. Wheaton: Crossway, 2011.

Kellemen, Bob. *Raising Kids in the Way of Grace: 5 Practical Marks of Grace-Focused Parenting*. Youngstown, OH: 10Publishing, 2018.

Köstenberger, Andreas, with David Jones. *God, Marriage, and Family*. Wheaton: Crossway, 2010.

Lowe, Julie. *Child Proof: Parenting by Faith, Not Formula*. Greensboro, NC: New Growth, 2018.

Moore, Russell. *The Storm-Tossed Family: How the Cross Reshapes the Home.* Nashville: B&H, 2018.

Newheiser, Jim. *Parenting Is More Than a Formula.* Phillipsburg, NJ: P&R, 2015.

Tautges, Paul. *Raising Kids in a "You Can Do It!" World.* Youngstown, OH: 10Publishing, 2019.

Tripp, Paul. *Parenting: 14 Gospel Principles That Can Radically Change Your Family.* Wheaton: Crossway, 2016.

Parental Evangelism of Children

Klumpenhower, Jack. *Show Them Jesus: Teaching the Gospel to Kids.* Greensboro, NC: New Growth, 2014.

Machowski, Marty. *Leading Your Child to Christ: Biblical Direction for Sharing the Gospel.* Greensboro, NC: New Growth, 2012.

Family Worship and Devotions

Helm, David, ed. *Big Beliefs!: Small Devotionals Introducing Your Family to Big Truths.* Phillipsburg, NJ: P&R, 2016.

Helopoulos, Jason. *A Neglected Grace: Family Worship in the Christian Home.* Fearn, Ross-shire, UK: Christian Focus, 2014.

Kruger, Melissa. *5 Things to Pray for Your Kids.* Purcellville, VA: The Good Book Company, 2019.

Meade, Starr. *Comforting Hearts, Teaching Minds: Family Devotions Based on the Heidelberg Catechism.* Phillipsburg, NJ: P&R, 2013.

———. *Training Hearts, Teaching Minds: Family Devotions Based on the Shorter Catechism.* Phillipsburg, NJ: P&R, 2000.

Thompson, Jessica. *Exploring Grace Together: 40 Devotionals for the Family.* Wheaton: Crossway, 2014.

Whitney, Don. *Family Worship.* Wheaton: Crossway, 2016.

Parental Teaching of Young Children

DeYoung, Kevin. *The Biggest Story.* Wheaton: Crossway, 2015.

Lloyd-Jones, Sally. *The Jesus Storybook Bible.* Grand Rapids: Zondervan, 2007.

Machowski, Marty. *The Ology: Ancient Truths, Ever New.* Greensboro, NC: New Growth, 2015.

Powlison, David. *Jax's Tail Twitches: When You Are Angry.* Greensboro, NC: New Growth, 2018.

———. *Zoe's Hiding Place: When You Are Anxious.* Greensboro, NC: New Growth, 2018.

Welch, Ed. *Buster's Ears Trip Him Up: When You Fail.* Greensboro, NC: New Growth, 2018.

Parental Teaching and Discipleship

Carter, Joe. *The Life and Faith Field Guide for Parents*. Eugene, OR: Harvest House, 2019.

Fitzpatrick, Elyse, and Jessica Thompson. *Answering Your Kids' Toughest Questions*. Bloomington, MN: Bethany House, 2014.

Peace, Martha, and Stuart Scott. *The Faithful Parent*. Phillipsburg, NJ: P&R, 2010.

Priolo, Lou. *Teach Them Diligently*. Simpsonville, SC: Timeless Texts, 2000.

Tripp, Tedd, and Margy Tripp. *Instructing a Child's Heart*. Wapwallopen, PA: Shepherd Press, 2008.

Ware, Bruce. *Big Truths for Young Hearts*. Wheaton: Crossway, 2009.

Younts, John. *Everyday Talk: Talking Freely and Naturally About God with Your Children*. Wapwallopen, PA: Shepherd Press, 2005.

Parental Discipline

Crabtree, Sam. *Parenting with Loving Correction: Practical Help for Raising Young Children*. Wheaton: Crossway, 2019.

Emlet, Michael. *Angry Children: Understanding and Helping Your Child Regain Control*. Greensboro, NC: New Growth, 2008.

Hubbard, Ginger. *"Don't Make Me Count to Three!": A Mom's Look at Heart-Oriented Discipline*. Wapwallopen, PA: Shepherd Press, 2004.

Smith, William. *How Do I Stop Losing It with My Kids?* Greensboro, NC: New Growth, 2008.

Tautges, Paul, and Karen Tautges. *Help! My Toddler Rules the House*. Wapwallopen, PA: Shepherd Press, 2014.

Tripp, Tedd. *Shepherding a Child's Heart*. Wapwallopen, PA: Shepherd Press, 2005.

Family Communication and Conflict Resolution

Jones, Robert. *Pursuing Peace*. Wheaton: Crossway, 2012.

Mack, Wayne. *Your Family, God's Way: Developing and Sustaining Relationships in the Home*. Phillipsburg, NJ: P&R, 1991.

Sande, Ken, and Tom Raabe. *Peacemaking for Families*. Colorado Springs: Focus on the Family, 2002.

Smith, William. *Parenting with Words of Grace*. Wheaton: Crossway, 2019.

Parenting Adolescents: General

Coats, Dave, and Judi Coats. *Help! My Teen Is Rebellious*. Wapwallopen, PA: Shepherd Press, 2016.

Horne, Rick. *Get Outta My Face! How to Reach Angry, Unmotivated Teens with Biblical Counsel*. Wapwallopen, PA: Shepherd Press, 2009.

Miller, Keith, and Patricia Miller. *Quick Scripture Reference for Counseling Youth.* Grand Rapids: Baker Books, 2014.

Tripp, Paul. *Age of Opportunity: A Biblical Guide to Parenting Teens.* Phillipsburg, NJ: P&R, 2001.

———. *Peer Pressure.* Greensboro, NC: New Growth, 2008.

Parenting Adolescents: Sex, Sexuality, and Sexual Addiction

Challies, Tim. *Help! My Kids Are Viewing Pornography.* Wapwallopen, PA: Shepherd Press, 2017.

Huie, Eliza. *Raising Teens in a Hyper-Sexualized World.* Youngstown, OH: 10Publishing, 2017.

Mulvihill, Josh. *Preparing Children for Marriage: How to Teach God's Good Design for Marriage, Sex, Purity, and Dating.* Phillipsburg, NJ: P&R, 2017.

Thompson, Jessica, and Joel Fitzpatrick. *Mom, Dad . . . What's Sex?* Eugene, OR: Harvest House, 2018.

Tripp, Paul. *Teens & Sex: How Should We Teach Them?* Greensboro, NC: New Growth, 2002.

Parenting and Sexual Abuse Prevention and Healing

Holcomb, Justin, and Lindsey Holcomb. *God Made All of Me: A Book to Help Children Protect Their Bodies.* Greensboro, NC: New Growth, 2015.

Kellemen, Bob. *Sexual Abuse: Beauty for Ashes.* Phillipsburg, NJ: P&R, 2013.

Newheiser, Jim. *Help! Someone I Love Has Been Abused.* Wapwallopen, PA: Shepherd Press, 2010.

Reju, Deepak. *On Guard: Preventing and Responding to Child Abuse at Church.* Greensboro, NC: New Growth, 2014.

Parenting and Same-Sex Attraction

Black, Nicholas. *Your Gay Child Says, "I Do."* Greensboro, NC: New Growth, 2012.

Geiger, Tim. *Explaining LGBTQ+ Identity to Your Child.* Greensboro, NC: New Growth, 2018.

———. *Your Child Says, "I'm Gay."* Greensboro, NC: New Growth, 2017.

Marshall, Ben. *Help! My Teen Struggles with Same-Sex Attractions.* Wapwallopen, PA: Shepherd Press, 2014.

Fathers

Farmer, Andy. *A Father's Guide for Raising Girls.* Greensboro, NC: New Growth, 2015.

Green, Rob. *A Father's Guide for Raising Boys*. Greensboro, NC: New Growth, 2015.

Reju, Deepak. *Preparing for Fatherhood*. Greensboro, NC: New Growth, 2015.

Zollos, Steve. *Time for the Talk: Leading Your Son into True Manhood*. Wapwallopen, PA: Shepherd Press, 2011.

Mothers

Furman, Gloria. *Missional Motherhood*. Wheaton: Crossway, 2016.

——. *Treasuring Christ When Your Hands Are Full*. Wheaton: Crossway, 2014.

Kruger, Melissa. *Walking with God in the Season of Motherhood*. Colorado Springs: WaterBrook, 2015.

Payne, Brenda. *Motherhood: Hope for Discouraged Moms*. Phillipsburg, NJ: P&R, 2013.

Single Parenting

Jones, Robert. *Single Parents: Daily Grace for the Hardest Job*. Greensboro, NC: New Growth, 2008.

Trahan, Carol. *Help! I'm a Single Mom*. Wapwallopen, PA: Shepherd Press, 2017.

Blended Families

Baker, Jeff, and Amy Baker. *Keys to Successful Stepfamilies*. Lafayette, IN: Faith Resources, 2006.

Smith, Winston. *Help for Stepfamilies*. Greensboro, NC: New Growth, 2008.

Children and Divorce

Baker, Amy. *Children and Divorce: Helping When Life Interrupts*. Greensboro, NC: New Growth, 2012.

Parenting Children with Special Needs

Deuel, Dave. *Help! My Grandchild Has a Disability*. Wapwallopen, PA: Shepherd Press, 2019.

Emlet, Michael R. *Asperger Syndrome*. Greensboro, NC: New Growth, 2005.

Hendrickson, Laura. *Finding Your Child's Way on the Autism Spectrum*. Chicago: Moody, 2009.

Jamison, Rita. *Parenting Your ADHD Child*. Greensboro, NC: New Growth, 2011.

Viars, Steve. *Your Special Needs Child*. Greensboro, NC: New Growth, 2011.

Welch, Edward T. *A.D.D.: Wandering Minds and Wired Bodies*. Phillipsburg, NJ: P&R, 1999.

Wilson, Andrew, and Rachel Wilson. *The Life We Never Expected*. Wheaton: Crossway, 2016.

Parenting Adult Children

Fitzpatrick, Elyse, and Jim Newheiser. *You Never Stop Being a Parent*. Phillipsburg, NJ: P&R, 2010.

Parenting Prodigal Children

Fitzpatrick, Elyse, James Newheiser, and Laura Hendrickson. *When Good Kids Make Bad Choices*. Eugene, OR: Harvest House, 2005.

Jones, Robert. *Prodigal Children: Hope and Help for Parents*. Phillipsburg, NJ: P&R, 2018.

Miller, John, and Barbara Juliani. *Come Back, Barbara*. Phillipsburg, NJ: P&R, 1997.

Adoption

Borgman, Brian, and Dan Cruver. *After They Are Yours*. Hudson, OH: Cruciform, 2014.

Moore, Russell. *Adopted for Life*. Wheaton: Crossway, 2016.

Tripp, Paul. *Helping Your Adopted Child*. Greensboro, NC: New Growth, 2008.

Parenting and Anger

Emlet, Mike. *Angry Children: Understanding and Helping Your Child Regain Control*. Greensboro, NC: New Growth, 2008.

Lane, Tim. *Family Feuds: How to Respond*. Greensboro, NC: New Growth, 2008.

Priolo, Lou. *Keeping Your Cool: A Teen's Survival Guide*. Phillipsburg, NJ: P&R, 2014.

Parenting and Anxiety

Lowe, Julie. *Helping Your Anxious Child*. Greensboro, NC: New Growth, 2018.

Addictions and Families

Shaw, Mark. *Addiction-Proof Parenting: Biblical Prevention Strategies*. Bemidji, MN: Focus Publishing, 2010.

———. *Divine Intervention: Help for Families of Addicts*. Bemidji, MN: Focus Publishing, 2007.

Alzheimer's Disease and the Family

Mast, Ben. *Second Forgetting: Remembering the Power of the Gospel During Alzheimer's Disease*. Grand Rapids: Zondervan, 2014.

Smith, Robert. *Alzheimer's Disease: Help for Families in Crisis*. Greensboro, NC: New Growth, 2014.

Miscarriage

Green, Stephanie. *Miscarriage: You Are Not Alone*. Greensboro, NC: New Growth, 2014.

Infertility

Baker, Amy. *Infertility: Comfort for Your Empty Arms and Heavy Heart*. Greensboro, NC: New Growth, 2013.

Biblical Counseling Theology

Adams, Jay. *A Theology of Christian Counseling: More Than Redemption*. Grand Rapids: Zondervan, 1986.

Biblical Counseling Coalition. "BCC Confessional Statement." Updated July 2018. http://biblicalcounselingcoalition.org/about/confessional-statement/.

Kellemen, Bob. *Gospel-Centered Counseling: How Christ Changes Lives*. Grand Rapids: Zondervan, 2014.

Kellemen, Bob, and Jeff Forrey, eds. *Scripture and Counseling: God's Word for Life in a Broken World*. Grand Rapids: Zondervan, 2014.

Kellemen, Bob, and Steve Viars, eds. *Christ-Centered Biblical Counseling: Changing Lives with God's Changeless Truth*. 2nd ed. Eugene, OR: Harvest House, 2020.

Lake, Frank. *Clinical Theology: A Theological and Psychiatric Basis to Clinical Pastoral Care*. London: Darton, Longman, & Todd, 1966.

Lambert, Heath. *A Theology of Biblical Counseling: The Doctrinal Foundations of Counseling Ministry*. Grand Rapids: Zondervan, 2016.

Lelek, Jeremy. *Biblical Counseling Basics: Roots, Beliefs, and Future*. Greensboro, NC: New Growth, 2018.

Packer, J. I. *Knowing God*. Downers Grove, IL: InterVarsity, 1993.

Powlison, David. *Seeing with New Eyes: Counseling and the Human Condition through the Lens of Scripture*. Greensboro, NC: New Growth, 2003.

Equipping Biblical Counselors

Kellemen, Bob. *Equipping Counselors for Your Church: The 4E Ministry Training Strategy*. Phillipsburg, NJ: P&R, 2011.

———. *Gospel Conversations: How to Care Like Christ*. Grand Rapids: Zondervan, 2015.

Nicewander, Sue. *Building a Church Counseling Ministry Without Killing the Pastor*. Carlisle, PA: Day One, 2012.

Biblical Counseling Methodology and One-Another Ministry

Adams, Jay. *The Christian Counselor's Manual: The Practice of Nouthetic Counseling*. Grand Rapids: Zondervan, 1986.

———. *Competent to Counsel: Introduction to Nouthetic Counseling*. Grand Rapids: Zondervan, 1986.

Emlet, Michael R. *CrossTalk: Where Life and Scripture Meet*. Greensboro, NC: New Growth, 2009.

Holmes, Jonathan. *The Company We Keep: In Search of Biblical Friendship*. Minneapolis: Cruciform, 2014.

Kellemen, Bob. *Counseling Under the Cross: How Martin Luther Applied the Gospel to Daily Life*. Greensboro, NC: New Growth, 2017.

Kellemen, Robert, and Kevin Carson, eds. *Biblical Counseling and the Church: God's Care through God's People*. Grand Rapids: Zondervan, 2015.

Kruis, John. *Quick Scripture Reference for Counseling*. Grand Rapids: Baker Books, 2013.

Lane, Tim, and Paul Tripp. *How People Change*. Greensboro, NC: New Growth, 2008.

Powlison, David. *Speaking Truth in Love: Counsel in Community*. Greensboro, NC: New Growth, 2005.

Scott, Stuart, and Heath Lambert, eds. *Counseling the Hard Cases*. Nashville: B&H Academic, 2012.

Tripp, Paul. *Instruments in the Redeemer's Hands: People in Need of Change Helping People in Need of Change*. Phillipsburg, NJ: P&R, 2002.

Welch, Ed. *Caring for One Another: 8 Ways to Cultivate Meaningful Relationships*. Wheaton: Crossway, 2018.

———. *Side by Side: Walking with Others in Wisdom and Love*. Wheaton: Crossway, 2015.

Robert W. Kellemen, PhD, is vice president of strategic development, academic dean, and professor at Faith Bible Seminary in Lafayette, Indiana. The founder of RPM Ministries, he also served as the founding executive director of the Biblical Counseling Coalition and has pastored four churches. He is the author of twenty books, including *Gospel-Centered Counseling*.

Connect with Bob

JOIN THE
Gospel-Centered Biblical Counseling Community on Facebook

Find encouragement and support from fellow counselors and equippers passionate about the sufficiency of Scripture for all of life and ministry.

  BobKellemen

CHANGING LIVES with
CHRIST'S CHANGELESS TRUTH

RPMministries.org

Most Christians care deeply but struggle to speak the truth in love. RPM Ministries exists to equip pastors, lay people, educators, students, and biblical counselors to change lives with Christ's changeless truth.